TERENCE

The Eunuch, Phormio, The Brothers

TERENCE

THE EUNUCH, PHORMIO, THE BROTHERS

A Companion to the Penguin translation

John Barsby

Published by Bristol Classical Press
General Editor: John H. Betts

A CIP catalogue record for this book is available from the British Library

© John Barsby, 1991

First published in 1991 by
Bristol Classical Press
226 North Street
Bedminster
Bristol
BS3 1JD

ISBN 1-85399-125-2

Printed in Great Britain by
Billing and Sons Ltd, Worcester

Contents

Preface

This Companion is intended to introduce Terence to students reading his plays in the Penguin translation. Three plays have been chosen of very different types. *The Eunuch* is Terence's most boisterous play, with its audacious eunuch impersonation and the stock figures of the swaggering soldier and the flatterer; *Phormio* is essentially a comedy of intrigue, with an engaging trickster helping two sons to outwit their fathers in the cause of true love; and *The Brothers* has a more serious tone, dealing as it does with the theme of how fathers should bring up their sons.

The introduction sets Terence in his context in the Roman theatre, outlining the stock situations and characters of Roman comedy and explaining the forms and conventions of the theatre. It also considers the ethical background to Terence's plays and the ways in which he set about adapting the Greek plays on which his own are based. The commentaries follow the technique sometimes known as 'performance criticism', that is, they try to interpret the plays as they would have struck an audience watching a performance rather than with the hindsight of someone who already knows the ending. They also go behind the translation to bring out some important aspects of style and structure which the translation tends to disguise. Actual Latin words are identified where this seems helpful, and references are made to other comedies (including those of Menander and Plautus) to give the student a broader picture of Terence's work.

The commentaries are liberally provided with cross-references, in the belief that a serious study of an author and his work demands some re-turning of the pages. The annotation tends to be denser in the earlier parts of each play, where features are being met for the first time; there is also some repetition from play to play for the sake of those who are not reading all three plays in the order presented.

This book is indebted to the work of numerous Terentian scholars, especially (but not only) those whose names appear in the Select Bibliography. I should like to express my thanks in particular to Malcolm Willcock and Richard Hunter, who both read parts of the book in draft and made their usual penetrating comments.

John Barsby
Dunedin, N. Z.,
December 1990

References and Abbreviations

1. References by page number (**p. or pp.**) are always to page numbers of the Penguin translation.

2. References to the plays of Terence are given in dual form, line numbers of the Latin text and page numbers of the Penguin translation; thus *Phorm.* 729 (**p. 262**) means line 729 of *Phormio* which can be found on page 262 of the Penguin translation.

3. References to the plays of Menander, Plautus, and Terence are given by abbreviated form of the play's original Greek or Latin title and by line number of the original text (e.g. **Men.** *Dysk.* **265, Plaut.** *Amph.* **1006, Ter.** *Hec.* **123**). This seems the simplest procedure, granted that many titles do not have established English equivalents. A full list of abbreviated titles and their common English equivalents is given overleaf.

4. References to other Greek and Roman authors are given in full, using the most familiar form of the author's name and the title of the work.

5. Cross-references within this Companion take the following forms:
   Introd. §2: see section 2 of the Introduction,
   36 n.: see the note on line 36 of the play under discussion,
   Eun. **146 n.:** see the note on line 146 of *The Eunuch*,
   Eun. **81ff n. 5:** see note [5] on the scene beginning at *Eun.* 81.

6. References to the modern works named in the Select Bibliography are to the author's name and the page number of the work; thus **Sandbach 126** means see page 126 of Sandbach's *Comic Theatre* book as listed in the Bibliography. Different works by the same author are distinguished by addition of the date; thus **Arnott (1975) 55** is a reference to page 55 of his *Menander, Plautus, Terence.*

7. The following general abbreviations are used:
   CHCL: Cambridge History of Classical Literature
   OCD: Oxford Classical Dictionary

Checklist of Play Titles

Menander
Asp(is): The Shield
Dysk(olos): Old Cantankerous, The Bad-Tempered Man
Epitr(epontes): The Arbitration
Eun(ouchos): The Eunuch
Her(os): The Hero
Kol(ax): The Flatterer, The Toady
Perik(eiromene): The Rape of the Locks, The Shorn Girl
Perin(thia): The Girl from Perinthos
Phas(ma): The Spectre, The Phantom
Sam(ia): The Girl from Samos, The Samian Woman
Sik(yonios): The Man from Sicyon
Syn(aristosai): The Women at Breakfast
Thes(auros): The Treasure

Plautus
Amph(itryo)
As(inaria):The Comedy of Asses
Aul(ularia): The Pot of Gold
Bacch(ides): The Two Bacchises, The Bacchises
Capt(ivi): The Prisoners
Cas(ina)
Cist(ellaria): The Casket
Curc(ulio)
Epid(icus)
Men(aechmi): The Brothers Menaechmus, The Two Menaechmuses
Merc(ator): The Merchant
Mil(es Gloriosus): The Swaggering Soldier, The Braggart Warrior
Most(ellaria): The Ghost, The Haunted House
Pers(a): The Persian
Poen(ulus): The Little Carthaginian
Pseud(olus)
Rud(ens): The Rope
Trin(ummus): The Three-Bob Day
Truc(ulentus)

Terence
Ad(elphoe): The Brothers
Andr(ia): The Girl from Andros, The Lady of Andros
Eun(uchus): The Eunuch
Heaut(ontimorumenos): The Self-Tormentor
Hec(yra): The Mother-in-Law
Phorm(io)

Introduction

The Penguin translation has a good general introduction to Terence and brief introductions to the separate plays. These should be read before studying the plays, and nothing would be gained by repeating the information here. It seems more useful to bring together in this Introduction the discussions of more general points which would otherwise have been scattered through the commentaries. Cross-references are made from the commentaries as appropriate.

CHARACTERS, SITUATIONS, THEMES

Roman comedy is based on a fairly limited number of stock characters and situations, which it inherited from Greek New Comedy. The originality of the dramatist, and the interest of the play to the audience, therefore lay in the particular way in which these characters and situations were manipulated in the particular play. The audience came with a whole set of expectations about character and plot and treatment, and the dramatist could either fulfil those expectations, which itself would provide satisfaction of a kind, or, more interestingly, exploit them by providing variations or even reversals. This latter technique was already practised by the Greeks, and Terence was something of a master of the art. So we clearly need to know what the stock elements of comedy were, so that we can appreciate what Terence is doing.

The following paragraphs take the stock characters one by one, and outline not only their characteristics but also the typical situations in which they are involved and the attitudes which comedy takes towards them. Any such account involves a good deal of over-simplification, since there are only three comic dramatists (Menander on the Greek side, and Plautus and Terence on the Roman) whose works survive to us in more than fragments. But in general terms Plautus (who died in 184 B.C., eighteen years before Terence's first play) can be taken to represent the norms of Roman comedy and it is often the case that, where Terence is departing from these, he is returning to the approach of Menander.

§1. One of the major stock characters of Greek and Roman comedy is the 'young man' (Lat. *adulescens*). Most young men in comedy are cast in the role of lovers: some are hopelessly infatuated with mercenary courtesans, others fall in love with young slave-girls whom they are too poor to purchase from their owners, others are involved with poor citizen girls whom in many cases they have got pregnant at some nocturnal festival. If the girl is a citizen, we can be sure that the young man will eventually obtain his father's consent and that a marriage will follow (as with Sostratos in Men. *Dysk.* and Moschion in Men. *Sam.*). If she is an orphan or of apparently non-citizen parentage, there is a fair chance that she will turn out to be the long-lost daughter of one of the characters of the play (having been exposed in infancy or captured by pirates), and again a marriage will ensue (as with Glycerium in Ter. *Andr.*). If the girl is a young slave in the hands of a pimp, the *adulescens* may eventually with his slave's help scrape together enough money to buy her out (as does Calidorus in Plaut. *Pseud.*). If she is a hardened courtesan, the conclusion is not so clear cut, since an affair with a courtesan by definition cannot be permanent or have a happy ending. The common characteristic of young men is their weakness, which causes them to depend on the help of friends or slaves and makes them afraid to face up to their fathers; but this is offset by a basic decency which leads them to stand by their girl-friends and in the end to accept their fathers' admonitions. Young men are often called upon to help each other in their love affairs, and loyalty is another common characteristic. The portrayal of the *adulescens* in comedy is thus on the whole sympathetic, though a few are caricatured, especially those who are besotted by greedy courtesans (such as Clitipho in Ter. *Heaut.*). On the *adulescens* see Duckworth 237-42.

§2. The plays show a fairly consistent attitude to love, which must in the end reflect the attitude of society (whether Greek or Roman), though we have to make due allowance for humorous exaggeration and the conventions of the genre. There are two significant background aspects, one social, the other moral and philosophical. The most important social factor is the difficulty young people had (both at Athens and at Rome) in forming any kind of romantic attachment, when arranged marriages at a comparatively early age were the norm; this is why the affairs of young men in comedy tend to be with courtesans or with citizen girls who are not recognised as such or who have been met at nocturnal festivals. On the moral and philosophical side we have to reckon with the influence of Greek ethical philosophy (the Greek comic dramatist Menander was a pupil of the Peripatetic school founded by Aristotle, and Greek philosophers were beginning to teach at Rome in Terence's day) and for the possible tension between Greek ideals of moderation and the stricter traditional Roman view of morality. In fact the attitude to young men's amatory escapades in comedy is generally lenient. Some fathers may grumble at money spent on courtesans, but others reflect that they did the same themselves when they were young; and even rape is excused as the effect of youth, love, and wine, provided that the *adulescens* stands by the girl and undertakes to marry her. But it is notable that the focus is entirely on the young men; except for the dominant courtesan type, the girls concerned rarely appear on stage, and the plays do not take much interest in their point of view. On men and women in comedy see Hunter 83-95; on love and marriage Duckworth 279-85.

§3. A second stock character of comedy is the 'old man' (Lat. *senex*). The most common role of the old man is as father of the *adulescens*, though some are fathers of the girl-friends concerned. Fathers fall into two sub-types, the stern (*senex durus*) and the lenient (*senex lenis*). Plautus is particularly fond of the 'angry old man' (*senex iratus*), a version of the stern old man, who is oblivious of his son's debaucheries, is easily fooled by his slave, and is furious when he finds out the truth (e.g. Theopropides in *Most.*). In many plays the fathers are major characters from the beginning, and the plot centres on the attempts of the young men to outwit them or otherwise overcome their objections; in others (e.g. Ter. *Eun.* and Men. *Dysk.*) the father is introduced only near the end, and his character is not so fully drawn. Another category of old man is the 'lecherous old man' (*senex amator*), typically a married man who falls for a courtesan; he is usually absurdly lecherous, he is sometimes a rival for his son's girl, and he is generally found out by his wife. This is a type particularly developed by Plautus (e.g. Lysidamus in *Cas.* and Demipho in *Merc.*); it is not found in extant Menander, and the one example in Terence (Chremes in *Phorm.*) is treated much more realistically than his Plautine counterparts. A third category is the 'charming old man' (*senex lepidus*), often a bachelor (of which the prime examples are Megadorus in Plaut. *Aul.* and Periplectomenus in Plaut. *Mil.*). On the *senex* see Duckworth 242-9.

§4. Relations between fathers and sons are thus an important ingredient in comedy, and education (i.e. the upbringing of sons by their fathers) is a recurring theme. The theme was clearly one which interested Terence, since it is the central to both *Heauton* and *Adelphoe*, but the interest must be derived from Menander, who wrote the Greek originals of *Heauton* and *Adelphoe* and indeed of a third Roman play (Plaut. *Bacch.*) in which the theme is again prominent. The attitude of Menander may well have been influenced by the ethical theories of the Peripatetic (i.e. Aristotelian) school of philosophy, with its emphasis on humanity, reasonableness, and moderation; and it is possible to trace echoes of Aristotle's *Ethics* and of his views on education in Terence's plays. But the Roman playwright had to reckon with the fact that traditional Roman morality was much stricter than Greek, and that the traditional Roman father (*paterfamilias*) with his powers of life and death over his family was a more stern and august figure than his Athenian counterpart. It is often suggested that Terence actually altered the slant of Menander's *Adelphoi* so as to discredit the 'permissive' theories of the Greek *senex lenis*. Whether or not this is true, there is a tension here of which we need to be aware between Greek and Roman ethical assumptions. On fathers and sons in comedy see Hunter 95-109; on education Duckworth 285-7.

§5. Parallel to the *senex* but not nearly so prominent is the *matrona* ('married woman'). The commonest sub-type of the *matrona* is the 'dowried wife', who is generally represented in comedy as being domineering and unpleasant. There are complaints about dowried wives in the fragments of Menander (and a clear example of a hen-pecked husband in Men. *Sam.*), but the type is particularly developed by Plautus, who gives us some notable examples (such as the wife in his *Men.*). Dowried wives tend to be extravagant with their husbands' money, and do not earn much sympathy if their husbands are unfaithful (as is often the case), and bachelor characters are quick to explain why they have no wish to marry women of this sort. But not all *matronae* belong to this type; there is only one dowried wife in Terence (Nausistrata in *Phorm.*), and she is treated much more sympathetically. Another class is the long-suffering loyal wife: in Terence's *Heauton* Sostrata stands up to some unpleasant abuse from her husband with dignity, and in his *Hecyra* another Sostrata, equally maligned by her husband, sacrifices her own interests to restore her son's marriage. A third type, repre-sented by the Sostrata of Terence's *Adelphoe*, is the poor widow anxious for the fate of her daughter. In general marriage is not represented as a desirable state in comedy, not at least when the partners have reached middle age; what is interesting about Terence is that, where there is a conflict betweeen the *senex* and the *matrona*, the wife is generally in the right. On the *matrona* see Duckworth 255-8; on attitudes to marriage Duckworth 282-5.

§6. The attitude of the Roman audience to the portrayal of wives in comedy will again have been affected by the Roman social background. The status of women at Rome was in general higher than at Athens, and the Roman *matrona* held a position of greater dignity and respect in the household than the Athenian wife. A comedy that satirised the traditional *matrona* was likely to appeal to (or, from a different point of view, to offend) the same classes who enjoyed (or were offended by) the comic portrayal of the traditional *pater-familias*. The particular prominence of wealthy wives in Roman comedy seems to reflect the social conditions of the time. Wealth was flooding into Rome in the wake of Roman wars overseas, and families who shared in this wealth could afford larger dowries for their daughters; it is also significant that in the lifetime of Plautus and Terence the Romans passed laws designed to limit the opulence of women. On dowried wives at Athens and Rome see Hunter 90-92.

§7. The slave (Lat. *servus*) is the third major stock character of comedy, along with the *adulescens* and the *senex*. There are various sub-types of slaves, and they play a variety of roles: where they have a major part in the plot, it is usually in relation to the love affairs of their younger masters. Their attitude may be sympathetic or disapproving or even positively scornful, and their involvement may be anything from incidental advice or assistance to a total manipulation of the situation. The fullest development of the character is found in Plautus, where the ebullient 'tricky slave' (*servus callidus*) dominates the plot, carrying out a whole series of improbable but ingenious deceptions, treating his older master and his other adversaries with contempt, and uttering extravagant monologues of triumph or foreboding (e.g. Chrysalus in *Bacch.*, Tranio in *Most.*, and Pseudolus in *Pseud.*). The character tends to be more muted in Menander and Terence, but it is always a matter of interest how the role will be developed in any particular play: one possibility is that it may be inverted, so that the would-be 'tricky slave' becomes in the end the 'bungling slave'. In general the attitude to slaves is sympathetic. We can be sure that the tricky slave will not receive the punishment he deserves; indeed he may be able to manipulate the situation in such a way as to be granted his freedom. And not all slaves are 'tricky' or 'bungling'; there is also the slow but loyal type, who protect their masters' interests with greater or smaller success. On the *servus* see Duckworth 249-53.

§8. The relationship of the slave of comedy to the slave of real life is problematical. The Plautine tricky slave seems to be a clear case of the comic inversion of real-life roles. But less extreme examples of what looks like impudence on the part of the slave towards his younger master have to be seen against a social background (in Athens and increasingly by Terence's time in Rome) in which a slave was commonly attached to the son of the house to act as his tutor (Lat. *paedagogus*), where advising and reprimanding would be a part of his function. In general comedy presents a humane picture of master-slave relationships, in which slaves have considerable freedom of speech but are nonetheless kept conscious of their status; the moral enunciated by slaves in several plays of Plautus is that slaves who serve their masters loyally can expect to be treated reasonably well. And this may be a fair reflection of attitudes to household slaves in Greece and Rome, though slaves in the mines or on agricultural estates are a different story. See Duckworth 288-91.

§9. Of the minor characters of comedy one of the most interesting types is the *meretrix* (traditionally translated 'courtesan' for lack of a better English equivalent). Courtesans in comedy fall into two sub-types. On the one hand, there are the young girls who work for pimps or bawds; these are often innocent or inexperienced, and they may fall genuinely in love with their young men. The audience will not expect this type to be portrayed in much detail: at best (cf. §1) they will turn out to be free born and marry their lovers. On the other hand, there are the independent courtesans, foreign and hence non-citizen women, who depend for their livelihood on gifts or fees extracted from their lovers, and whose stock characteristics are mercenariness and greed (e.g. Erotium in Plaut. *Men.*, Phronesium in Plaut. *Truc.*, and Bacchis in Ter. *Heaut.*). Plautus concentrates on this latter type, and this is what the audience will generally expect to see. But Terence is rather more sympathetic, bringing out the difficulties of the courtesans' position as female non-citizens (as with Thais in *Eun.*) and tempering their self-interest with a genuine concern for other people (as with Bacchis in *Hec.*). The ancient commentator Donatus (on *Eun.* 198) praises Terence for varying the stock characterisation and introducing the 'good courtesan' (*meretrix bona*) into his plays. But this variation on the stock character is not in fact Terence's innovation; his 'good' courtesans have predecessors in Menander (notably Habrotonon in *Epitr.* and Chrysis in *Sam.*). On the *meretrix* see Duckworth 258-61.

§10. If the traditional attitude of Roman comedy to the *meretrix* is hostile, the reason may lie partly in a distinction between Roman society and Greek. The Greeks distinguished between the 'companion' (Gk *hetaira*), who could be a wealthy and accomplished woman, and the common prostitute (Gk *porne*), who was simply a source of sexual gratification. Roman society knew nothing of the *hetaira* (the comic dramatists use the one word *meretrix* to cover both categories) and thus had no sympathy with her problems; as for the prostitute, the general attitude seems to have been that, though the occasional visit by a young man could be tolerated, in the end affairs with such women were simply a source of financial ruin and loss of reputation.

§11. Another colourful minor stock character of comedy is the pimp (Lat. *leno*), who occurs in five plays of Plautus' and two of Terence's (*Phorm.* and *Ad.*). There are no pimps in the more complete plays of Menander's and only a few traces among the fragmentary ones, but there is no doubt that the character was taken over from Greek New Comedy. The pimp is essentially the owner of slave-girls whom he hires out for sexual favours or sells off to anyone who can pay the price of their freedom. As we see him in Roman comedy, he is always the villain of the piece, who has to be defeated if the *adulescens* in love with one of his girls is going to get access to her. The pimp is traditionally greedy, heartless, and unscrupulous; and he is always liable to sell the girl to a rival with ready cash if the young man is not able to produce the purchase price himself. In Plautus the character is often built up into an exaggerated comic caricature (the prime example is Ballio in *Pseud.*), and the audience will expect an unsympathetic characterisation. But Terence is more realistic. The pimp is still a villain, but his side of the question is allowed a hearing; he is after all a businessman and cannot be expected to wait endlessly for impecunious young men to produce their money.

On the pimp see Duckworth 262-4.

§12. Equally colourful is the character known as the 'parasite' (Lat. *parasitus*). The parasite is a development of the character originally known as the 'flatterer' (Gk *kolax*), so that flattery is a standard characteristic; at the same time the literal meaning of *parasitus* is 'one who eats alongside', which indicates another stock characteristic, namely a preoccupation with free meals. It is difficult to assess Menander's treatment of the character, since there are no fully developed parasites in his surviving plays. In Plautus parasites fall into three classes, (i) those who earn their free meals by witty conversation (e.g. Ergasilus in *Capt.* or Peniculus in *Men.*), (ii) those who do so by fawning and flattery, usually the hangers-on of soldiers (e.g. Artotrogus in *Mil.*), and (iii) those who are practical helpers and schemers (e.g. Curculio in *Curc.*). There are only two parasites in Terence's plays, Gnatho in *Eunuch*, who falls into the second of the above categories, and Phormio in *Phormio*, who falls into the third. Some parasites, especially those who scheme on behalf of the *adulescens*, win the audience's sympathy by their resourcefulness; others are less sympathetically drawn. The parasite (like the *hetaira*) was a feature of Greek life rather than Roman, so that the Romans must have regarded the parasite of comedy as a strange exotic figure; the nearest Roman parallel was the client of the noble patron, but the patron-client relationship was a much more formal one based on mutual obligations. On the parasite see Duckworth 265-7.

§13. The parasite is often associated with the 'swaggering soldier' (Lat. *miles gloriosus*), another stock comic type. The boastful soldier can be found in Aristophanes (Lamachus in *Acharnians*), but the stock character was developed in the fourth century B.C., when mercenary captains in the service of foreign kings became a common feature of Greek life. The main characteristics of the *miles* are blustering, boastfulness, lechery, stupidity, and cowardice; the soldier is also rich enough from the spoils of war to be a formidable rival to the *adulescens*. The most striking examples of the type are to be found in Plautus, where the character becomes an exaggerated caricature (notably Pyrgopolynices in *Mil.*). But there is only one swaggering soldier in Terence (Thraso in *Eun.*); and the surviving plays of Menander tend rather to offer sympathetically drawn soldiers (e.g. Polemon in *Perik.*), who represent deliberate inversions of the type. Again, the mercenary captain was not a feature of Roman life, since Roman armies were citizen armies commanded by citizen generals; some have argued that the Roman audience would see in the *miles gloriosus* a satiric portrayal of their own military commanders, but it seems more likely that he was regarded (like the parasite) as an absurd foreign type. On the *miles* see Duckworth 264-5.

§14. It remains to consider a group of minor female characters. The female household slaves of comedy are divided by the manuscripts into three principal groups, the *anus* ('elderly servant'), the *nutrix* ('family nurse'), and the *ancilla* ('maid'). The groups in practice overlap, since the *nutrix* may be elderly as well as the *anus*, though in most cases the *ancilla* seems to be regarded as younger. It is rare for a female slave in any of these categories to have a fully developed part; most appear in only a single scene. The chief function of the *nutrix* is to identify long-lost children (as Sophrona in Ter. *Eun.*), which normally necessitates only the briefest of appearances. The *anus* appears as the loyal supporter of a widow (as Canthara in Ter. *Ad.*) or as a long-suffering creature who is shamefully maltreated by her old master (e.g. Simike in Men. *Dysk.* or Staphyla in Plaut. *Aul.*), but neither of these roles requires much development of character. The best drawn female slaves are the *ancillae* of courtesans. Plautus has two striking examples (Milphidippa in *Mil.* and Astaphium in *Truc.*); and by far the fullest drawn female slave in Terence is Pythias in *Eunuchus*, who also belongs to this group. See Duckworth 254-5.

ETHICAL IDEAS

§15. We do not expect a comedy to be an ethical treatise, but any play which portrays human beings interacting in realistic human situations inevitably raises questions of human behaviour. Terence has been much praised for the 'humanity' (Lat. *humanitas*) of his plays. This is a good term to describe his general philosophy, which is that human beings should help each other, should treat each other decently, should forgive each other's failings, and should be aware that others can often see what is best for them more clearly than they can themselves. This philosophy is not original to Terence. Similar ideas were developed by the ethical philosophies of the fourth century B.C. (notably by the Aristotle and the Peripatetics, with their attempts to define true nobility, their ideals of moderation and the golden mean, and their concept of the 'reasonable man'); and these will have filtered through to Terence through the plays of Menander, who, as we have seen above (§2), was himself a pupil of the Peripatetic school. Humanity in Terence is linked with the concept of conduct worthy of a free man (*liberalitas*): to be born free (as distinct from being born as a slave) confers certain expectations and obligations in the moral sphere. In practice this seems to apply particularly to the nobly born, or at least to those born in relatively comfortable circumstances, so that the English translation is often 'gentlemanly', or 'gentleman'. It is often emphasised that the rich have a duty to behave properly towards the poor, who for their part easily take offence if the rich seem to be taking advantage. Sympathy for the honest poor is one of the many things that Greek New Comedy inherited from late fifth century tragedy (notably from Euripides' *Electra*): among the comedies where the rich-poor theme is prominent are Menander's *Dyskolos* and Plautus' *Aulularia.*

§16. A study of Terence's ethical vocabulary is illuminating, and is best done through the Latin words, since the Penguin translator does not use a constant English equivalent. Terence's most frequent ethical term is *aequom*, literally 'equal', hence fair, equitable, just. Other common words are *decet* (what is decent or fitting), *iustum* (what is just), *dignum* (what is worthy or deserved) and conversely *indignum* (what is unworthy or undeserved), *oportet* (what ought to be done), *officium* (duty), *fides* (loyalty to one's word), and *pudor* (a sense of shame or decency). Also prominent is the link beween *amicitia* (friendship) and *beneficia* (services); to the Greeks and Romans friendship was not just a matter of liking people but a relationship implying mutual obligations. This vocabulary is found chiefly in the mouths of the middle or upper classes in discussing their own behaviour; it is also used as a reproach by those who suffer at their hands, and even (as a humorous inversion) by such unscrupulous characters as pimps and parasites, if they can use it to their advantage. On the didactic element in comedy see Hunter 137-51; on moral tone Duckworth 300-4 (cf. Beare 109-112); on human relations in Terence Forehand 123-7.

§17. In the context of Terence's ethical ideas it is also worth noting a favourite device of his, namely the double plot, involving two young men, two girl-friends, and often two fathers and two slaves. Double plots are found in all of Terence's plays apart from *Hecyra.* In *Andria* it is clear that Terence created the double plot himself from a Greek original which had only a single love affair; but in the other plays the two halves of the double plot seem so closely integrated into the dramatic structure that it is hard to believe that both were not already part of the Greek model. Terence's preference for what has been called the 'duality method' must be significant. Double plots are of course a structural device, with various possibilities of balance, contrast, and interweaving. But they also enable Terence to contrast two kinds of young men and two kinds of love affairs and to invite moral comparisons; in some plays (notably *Ad.* and *Heaut.*) there is a further contrast between two kinds of fathers and two different attitudes to father-son relationships. The duality method thus allows Terence to offer a more complex view of human behaviour and relationships than would be possible with a single plot. On the double plot see Duckworth 184-90, Goldberg 123-48, Norwood (1931) 141-76.

STAGING, CONVENTIONS, FORMULAE

§18. Roman drama in the days of Terence was staged on temporary wooden stages erected in the forum or in other public places. In the absence of any archaelogical evidence, all that we can say with any certainty is that there was a stage building with three doors in its façade, normally representing neighbouring houses, and in front of this a wooden platform stage, normally representing a street. It follows that all the dialogue notionally took place in the one street; indoor scenes could not be portrayed, and all more distant action had to be narrated. This restricted setting gave rise to a number of conventions which seem artificial to us but were no doubt readily accepted by the Roman audience.

§19. The two side entrances to the stage had a fixed conventional significance. Unfortunately our evidence is confused, but the convention seems to have been that the right-hand entrance (from the audience's point of view) led to the forum (or city centre) and the left-hand one one away from the forum (i.e. to the harbour or the country). Characters entering from either side entrance are often seen and announced by characters on stage long before they are visible to the audience. If two characters enter together, they usually enter in mid-conversation. More often a single character enters, who typically utters a monologue of greater or lesser length before seeing or being accosted by the people already on stage; in most cases these bystanders offer aside comments on the monologue before making the newcomer aware of their presence. The 'overheard entrance monologue' is in fact one of Terence's most commmon ways of beginning a new scene. On the side entrances see Beare 248-55, Duckworth 85-7 (cf. Penguin p. 25); on the overheard entrance monologue Bain 135-44.

§20. The entry in mid-conversation and the overheard entrance monologue are equally possible for characters entering from the stage houses, but in this situation two further conventions are used. Entries from the houses are often announced by references to the sound of the doors opening. This is a convenient way to focus the audience's attention on the new character, and it enables the characters on stage to speculate for the audience's benefit on who is coming out. But there has been much debate on how or why the sound was supposed to be created. Real-life Greek and Roman houses (and presumably their stage counterparts) had double-leaved doors which opened inwards; they pivoted on long hinges which fitted at top and bottom to the lintel and sill at the junction with the doorposts. The doors could be locked by bolts and bars, but there is no reason to think that they were normally locked during the day. So, when a person opens the doors to come out of the house, the most probable source of noise will not be the unlocking of the doors but the rattling of the bolts and the squeaking of the hinges. Another convention for characters entering from the houses is the 'over the shoulder remark': a final remark is delivered back into the house to complete a conversation which has been going on indoors before any attention is given to the business on stage. This gives the audience some inkling of what has been said inside, and helps to provide some continuity between house and stage. On the doors see Beare 285-94, Duckworth 116-17; on entry conventions Duckworth 124-6.

§21. As the prominence of the overheard entrance monologue suggests, eavesdropping and asides are common on the Roman stage. They do not of themselves imply that the stage was of great length or equipped with suitable hiding places (such as side-alleys or porches); once the convention was established, the audience would accept that characters looking the wrong way or engrossed in their own thoughts would fail to see or hear others on stage. Eavesdropping scenes can be quite elaborate, sometimes going on for some length and sometimes involving four characters, with two commenting aside to each other on the conversation of the other two. Apart from the 'eavesdropping aside', where the aside speaker remains unseen, comedy uses two other types, the 'aside in conversation', in which one character turns aside to utter a remark unheard by the other, and the 'aside commentary', in which a third character stands aside and comments on the conversation of the other two. The effect of asides is often to amuse the audience, but it is rare for the audience to be addressed explicitly; this happens occasionally in Plautus, but Terence preserves the so-called 'dramatic illusion' whereby the characters are enclosed within the world of the play and do not directly interact with the spectators. On eavesdropping and asides see Bain 154-84, Duckworth 109-14.

§22. The monologue is much more prominent in Roman comedy than in modern comedies: it has been calculated that 12% of Terence's lines are spoken in monologue (and 17% of Plautus'). Monologues are used to narrate what has happened off-stage, or to offer reflections on the situation, or to deliberate on a course of action; some monologues fulfil more than one of these functions. A few monologues can be regarded as genuine soliloquies, where a character wrestles with some emotional problem, but most are artificial speeches delivered for the audience's benefit, though again the dramatic illusion is maintained. Monologues chiefly occur at the beginnings or endings of scenes. By far the commonest is the overheard entrance monologue (cf. §19); simple entrance monologues (that is, ones delivered on an empty stage with no eavesdroppers or asides) also occur but are not so frequent. At the end of the scene there are two possibilities, the 'link monologue', where a character stays on stage to lead into the next scene, and the less common 'exit monologue', after which the speaker departs leaving the stage empty. These relative frequencies are directly linked to Terence's preference for keeping his plays continuous; simple entrance monologues and exit monologues both presuppose an empty stage (either before or after), and Terence avoids having too many empty stages. On monologues see Duckworth 103-9.

§23. This brings us to a significant difference between Greek and Roman comedy. The Greek New Comedy of Menander and his contemporaries still had a chorus; this took no part in the plays, but it did perform interludes which (since there were four of them) had the effect of dividing the plays into five acts. The renaissance editors divided the plays of Plautus and Terence into five acts also, but this has no validity for the original performances: Roman comedies were written for continuous performance with no intervals. This often presented a problem of adaptation for the Roman dramatist, since the Greek interlude could represent the passing of off-stage time and could cover (for example) a journey to the town and back; and some of the awkwardnesses of staging in Roman comedy can be put down to the difficulty of bridging the Greek act-break. It thus becomes a matter of some interest to establish where the act-breaks in the Greek original actually came. As far as Terence is concerned, the Penguin translation presents the plays continuously; but the traditional act and scene numbering (II. iv etc.) provides a convenient framework for discussion and is followed here in the commentaries. On act-divisions in Roman plays see Duckworth 98-101 (out of date on Menander).

§24. There is another significant difference between Greek and Roman practice, which did not so much present a problem to the Roman writers as present them with an opportunity for expansion. It seems fairly clear that Greek New Comedy was restricted to three speaking actors, who had to cover all the parts between them. Roman comedy had no such restriction, and there are a number of scenes which have four or even five speaking parts. This means that the Roman dramatist could write in extra characters (e.g. Dorias in Ter. *Eun.*), expand the roles of existing characters (e.g. Antipho in Ter. *Phorm.*), or give speaking parts to characters who in the Greek play were non-speaking extras. There must have been a particular temptation to fill out the endings of the plays with extra speaking parts, since it is difficult to achieve a comprehensive ending with only three characters on stage. The general effect of these practices is to 'thicken' the play, though they sometimes lead to awkwardnesses of staging, where the extra character is left on stage unnoticed by the others and with no part in the dialogue. This is not to say that the number of actors in a Roman company was unlimited. In general the surviving Roman plays could be acted reasonably comfortably with a troupe of five or six actors doubling up the parts, and for simple economic reasons it is unlikely that troupes were much larger than this. On the number of actors at Athens and Rome see Beare 167, Duckworth 94-8 (again out of date on Menander), Gratwick 83, Sandbach 78-80, 111, Webster 82-4.

§25. At the head of the troupe of actors was the producer or 'actor-manager'. This person was an important figure in Roman drama, performing the plays with his own company and often taking the leading role himself. He also acted as an intermediary between the playwright and the state official in charge of the games at which the plays were performed. It seems that the producer bought the text of the play from the playwright, and was then paid by the state for putting on the performance. According to the 'production notices' which accompany the texts, the producer of all six of Terence's plays was Lucius Ambivius Turpio, who clearly played a significant part in promoting Terence's dramatic career and that of his predecessor Caecilius (see the third prologue of *Hec.*, pp. 293-4). A co-producer is named for four of the plays, Lucilius Atilius from Praeneste (a small town some twenty miles east of Rome), about whom we know little; he should be probably be regarded as the second leading actor of Ambivius' company. As for the actors, the evidence seems to be that (unlike their counterparts at Athens) actors at Rome were not highly regarded, and in fact generally belonged to the lower classes, including freedmen and even slaves. On actors and actor-managers see Beare 164-7, Duckworth 73-6, Gratwick 80-4, Sandbach 109-11.

§26. The production notices also record the name of the composer of the music for all six plays, Flaccus the slave of Claudius; it says something for the importance of the music that the composer's name is recorded at all, and it is interesting that, for Terence's plays at least, he was a slave. In Roman drama (as in Greek) there were three modes of delivery, speech, recitative, and song; recitative (which was declaimed rather than spoken) and song were accompanied by the pipe. Unfortunately we know almost nothing about the music. According to the production notices, Terence's plays were variously accompanied by 'equal', 'unequal', and 'two right-hand' pipes, with one of the plays (*Heaut.*) changing from 'unequal' to 'two right hand' in the middle. The choice of pipes presumably reflected the mood of the play, but is very difficult to interpret. The Penguin introduction (pp. 26-7) gives some account of the instruments and how they were played: 'two right-hand pipes' presumably means 'two treble pipes', though one was obviously held in the left hand. On Greek and Roman music see *OCD* 705-13 (esp. 710 on the pipe).

§27. The Penguin translation, being in prose, obliterates the distinction mentioned in the preceding paragraph between speech, recitative, and song. But it is important to have some idea of the musical and metrical structure of the play, which can be clearly established from the metres of the original Latin. In fact Terence differs from Plautus in his treatment of the three modes of utterance, and Plautus had departed considerably fom the practice of his Greek originals. Menander's plays were predominantly spoken and had only occasional scenes of recitative (the proportions in his two most complete plays are 83% speech and 17% recitative); the only song was that accompanying the dance of the chorus in the interludes, which were not an integral part of the play. In Plautus the proportions are 38% speech, 48% recitative, and 14% song; in other words, he turned what had been a mainly spoken drama into a predominantly musical performance, giving the actors lyric songs as well as a substantial amount of recitative.

§28. Terence maintained the same proportion of recitative as Plautus (48%), but virtually abandoned song (there are only three songs in his six plays, all of them very short); at the same time he introduced a further innovation by using mixed-metre recitative for some passages instead of a single metre as in Menander and Plautus. Spoken scenes are all in 'iambic senarii' (ia6), a six-foot line which is akin to English blank verse but with an extra foot. This is the nearest metre to ordinary speech, and the comic poets seem to have found it most suitable for narrative, for rapid dialogue, for scenes of plotting, and for low-key monologues. Terence uses several recitative metres, all of them 'long metres', consisting either of seven and a half feet ('septenarii') or of eight feet ('octonarii') in either iambic or trochaic rhythm. The most common is 'trochaic septenarii' (tr^7), followed by 'iambic octonarii' (ia^8), 'iambic septenarii' (ia^7), and 'trochaic octonarii' (tr^8). All that can be said about their effect is that they all in some way serve to raise the tone or heighten the utterance, and that trochaic septenarii, being the most common, are probably not as 'excited' or 'animated' as the others. As will be pointed out in the commentaries, Terence often varies his metres within a single scene, which provides a valuable clue to changes of pace and tone. On music and metre see Arnott 32-3, Beare 219-32, Duckworth 361-83, Sandbach 119-22; on the rhythmical structures of comedy Hunter 42-53.

§29. Another difference between the Latin text of Terence and the Penguin translation is that the conventions of Roman comedy did not provide for separate stage directions: those in the Penguin version are simply additions by the translator. It follows that the Roman dramatist had to write his stage directions into the text. Some of the implied stage directions are specific to a particular situation ('Here comes x in a hurry', 'Why are you shoving me?', 'Let go'); but many refer to standard stage movements, and a number of formulaic expressions were developed for this purpose, which the translator tends to be tone down or vary so that they do not seem so repetitive. The Latin text is in fact full of introduction formulae ('Look, there is x', 'Here comes x', 'Who's that coming? It's x'), door-knocking formulae ('I'll knock at the door', 'Who's knocking?'), eavesdropping formulae ('I will stand aside'), withdrawal formulae ('Come over here a little'), approach formulae ('I will go up'), action formulae ('I am delaying', 'Do I delay?'), leave-taking formulae ('Fare well', 'Anything else you want?'), and exit formulae ('I'll go in', 'Wait...I'll be back', 'Follow me'). Even so, Terence can be economical at times with his stage directions, leaving the producer to make the necessary inferences from the text and general situation.

§30. Similar to these stage-directional formulae are the formulae used when one character greets another on stage, namely the recognition formulae ('Who is speaking here?', 'Is it *x*? Yes it is', 'Why, there's *x*'), the greetings formulae ('Greetings', 'Hullo', 'Welcome', 'How are you?', 'How goes it?'), and the response formulae ('Greetings', 'The gods bless you', 'I was looking for you'). Sometimes formulae occur in clusters: overheard monologues, for example, are typically terminated by a sequence of recognition formula, approach formula, greetings formula. An extreme example of a set formulaic dialogue is the homecoming scene, where a character arriving back in the city from overseas or from the country is welcomed back. This proceeds as follows: 'Is it *x*? Yes it is. I will approach him. Good day', 'Good day', 'I'm glad to see you safely returned', 'I'm sure you are', 'Are you well', 'Yes, well enough', 'You must come and dine with us'. Plautus is not above spinning the formulae out for comic effect, and he also creates humour by making his characters take conventional questions (such as 'How goes it?' or 'Anything else you want?') literally. Terence also uses this latter technique, but in general keeps his formulae relatively brief and unobtrusive. He can also on occasion treat them with some subtlety, giving them some special point in the context, gently mocking them, or manipulating them to imply something about the attitudes of the characters involved. On stage-directional formulae see Bain 158-60, 179-82, Duckworth 114-21; on the homecoming scene Wright 138-51.

TERENCE AND HIS GREEK ORIGINALS

Two significant technical differences have already been noted between Greek and Roman comedy, with respect to choral interludes and the number of available actors (§23-4). Both of these necessarily led to adaptations by the Roman dramatists of their Greek originals. But there were wider questions of principle on how far adaptation of the Greek plays should go, and these were the subject of lively debate in Terence's own time.

§31. Terence several times refers in the prologues of his plays to a malevolent critic, whom he nowhere names but who is identified for us in the commentary of Donatus as one Luscius of Lanuvium (a small town some twenty miles south-east of Rome). Luscius, who had been the senior comic dramatist at Rome since the death of Caecilius in 168 B.C., mounted a determined opposition to Terence's dramatic career. This was no doubt due partly to personal jealousy, the established figure threatened by the emergence of a younger talent, but there was also a principle at stake. It seems that Luscius rejected the freedom with which the earlier Roman dramatists Naevius, Plautus, and Caecilius had 'Romanised' Greek comedy, and believed that Roman writers should instead present a faithful translation of their Greek originals. Terence did not believe in 'Romanisation' either, but he wanted to preserve the right of creative adaptation of the Greek plays in terms both of plot and of dialogue. Terence's six prologues give us a colourful, if not objective, account of this dispute: see especially those of *Andria* (p. 39), *Heauton* (pp. 101-2), and *Phormio* (pp. 227-8). On Luscius and his criticisms see Duckworth 62-5, Gratwick 116-17, Wright 78-9.

§32. There were basically two charges levelled at Terence by his critics, (i) 'spoiling' his Greek originals (Lat. *contaminare*) and (ii) 'plagiarism' or 'theft' (Lat. *furtum*). By 'contamination' the critics meant the spoiling of one Greek play by the addition of material from another. Terence admits to this practice in three of his prologues, in *Andria*, where he used parts of Menander's *Perinthia* (p. 39), in *Eunuchus*, where he introduced two characters from Menander's *Kolax* (p. 165), and in *Adelphoe*, where he imported a scene from Diphilus' *Synapothnescontes* (p. 339). Terence's aims in each case may have been different, though it looks as if, especially after the failure of *Hecyra*, he was concerned to introduce scenes of broader humour to keep his audience happy. By 'theft' the critics meant using a Greek play which had already been used by an earlier Roman dramatist. Terence counters this charge in *Adelphoe* (p. 339) by establishing that the particular scene transferred from Diphilus' *Synapothnescontes* had been omitted in Plautus' previous adaptation of that play, and in *Eunuchus* (pp. 165-6) by denying knowledge of the earlier Latin version and by asserting that the two borrowed characters were stock characters anyway, so that the allegation was pointless. The objection to *furtum* seems the more pedantic of the two; with contamination there was also the practical point that, if widespread, the practice of using two Greek plays to make a single Roman one would rapidly diminish the number of Greek plays available for Roman adaptation. See Penguin pp. 18-19, Arnott (1975) 48-50, Beare 95-108, Duckworth 202-8, Goldberg 91-7, Gratwick 116-21, Ludwig 171-5, Sandbach 139-41.

§33. The practice of contamination indicates that Terence was not a slavish translator: he was willing to make significant alterations to the structure of his Greek originals. And there seem to have been two further ways in which he created structural changes, though it is in practice very difficult to establish these in detail. It is commonly believed that Terence altered the openings of his Greek originals by omitting their expository prologues, and that, although he worked into his own opening scenes enough expository material for his plots to be followed, he nonetheless at times deprived the Roman audience of important information which its Greek counterpart had from the beginning. If this belief is correct, it follows that Terence rejected the opportunities for dramatic irony which the Greek audience's superior knowledge provided, but at the same time was able to exploit the

Roman audience's uncertainty to create suspense and surprise. All this depends on the assumption that his Greek models did have expository prologues, and this is a matter of conjecture rather than an established fact. But it is certainly true that all the surviving plays of Menander for which we have sufficient evidence do have expository prologues, and that several plays of Terence do produce surprise information at a late stage in a manner unparalleled in Menander. One arrangement of which Menander is particularly fond is worth noting, in that it is often assumed to have been used in the Greek originals of Terence's plays. This is the 'postponed divine prologue', in which a divinity corrects misapprehensions created by the opening scenes and fills in other details of the background (as in *Asp.* and *Perik.*); divine prologue speakers are particularly useful when there is a 'hidden identity' to reveal which is unknown to any of the human characters. For discussion see Arnott (1975) 51-3, Duckworth 227-31, Sandbach 141.

§34. The other possibility of structural change on Terence's part lies in the endings of the plays. It has been suggested above (§24) that Roman dramatists might be tempted to use their additional actors to fill out the finales of the Greek plays, and it is clear where they have in fact done so from the presence of four-actor scenes in the Roman versions. But Terence's alterations seem to have gone further than this: in two at least of his plays (*Ad.* and *Eun.*) there is an unexpected slant to the ending which is generally believed to derive from Terence rather than from the Greek original. If this is the case, one explanation may be that Terence was deliberately exploiting the surprise ending for dramatic effect, even at the expense of consistency. In a genre where there are a limited number of plots and the dénouement can generally be predicted, surprise is a useful weapon in the dramatist's armoury. But ethical considerations may also have played a part, granted Terence's interest in social and moral questions and the potential tension between Greek and Roman views (cf. §4); he may have wanted to bring the Greek play more into line with Roman attitudes, and, even where this was not the case, he may still have been trying to provoke the audience to think about the moral of the play by a change of direction at the end.

THE LANGUAGE OF TERENCE

§35. It is generally agreed that Terence's language lacks the exuberance of Plautus', but has a compensating simplicity and elegance. Julius Caesar in a famous judgment praised Terence for his 'natural' (or 'pure') language while at the same time lamenting his lack of vigour; and Cicero referred appreciatively to his 'quiet tone' (these comments are quoted by Suetonius in his biography of Terence: see the Penguin appendix, p. 393). The ancient commentator Donatus adds that the ancients found Terence's style inferior to the 'sublimity' of Menander's. It should be emphasised that Terence's language is not dull: it is varied from character to character, it has a wide range of imagery (some of which may seem familiar to us but was not so commonplace in his own day), it makes good use of proverbial expressions, it includes some striking exclamations and vivid terms of abuse. Some of the colour, and much of the neatness, of Terence's style is inevitably lost in a prose translation; the commentary draws attention to some of its features. On the language and style of Roman comedy see Duckworth 331-60.

The Eunuch

PRODUCTION NOTICE (p. 161)

The MSS of Terence include a 'production notice' (Lat. *didascalia*) prefaced to the text of each of the plays, except that the one for *Andria* is missing. These are not actual records of the first production, but were compiled later, probably by scholars of the first century B.C., from sources which we cannot now trace.

Megalensian Games: These had been instituted in 204 B.C., and were one of four festivals at which drama was performed in the days of Terence. The Megalensian games, held in April, opened the annual 'season'; in fact four of Terence's six plays were performed at them. See Beare 162-3, Duckworth 76-9, Gratwick 81.

curule aedileship: This was a relatively junior office of the Roman state but an important rung on the political ladder. The aediles were generally responsible for the public games, and could hope to gain political support for the future by lavish expenditure on them. Among their duties was the selection of plays for the festivals, and it was obviously in their interest to choose plays with popular appeal.

Lucius Ambivius Turpio and Lucius Atilius: Introd. §25.

Music composed by Flaccus: Introd. §26.

The author's second play: The ancient commentator Donatus makes *Eunuchus* Terence's third play, but modern scholars, on the basis of the consular dates given in the production notices, make it his fourth, produced in 161 B.C. after *Andria* (166), *Hecyra* (first performed 165), and *Heauton* (163). The discrepancies are no doubt due to some confusion in the sources between dates of composition and dates of performance or, where plays were repeated, between dates of different performances. See Beare 94-5, Duckworth 59-61, and (for an alternative view) Forehand 8-12.

SYNOPSIS (p. 162)

Synopses of Terence's plays, written in verse by Gaius Sulpicius Apollinaris (a scholar of the second century A.D.), are transmitted in the MSS along with the texts. They are of no particular interest.

CHARACTERS (p. 163)

The MSS of Terence do not have the lists of characters which the MSS of Greek drama prefix to their plays, though the illustrated MSS of the 9th to 11th centuries do offer a series of masks, framed in a 'shrine' (Lat. *aedicula*), which roughly correspond to the characters. The lists of characters in modern editions are compiled from the scene-headings in the MSS, which give for each scene the names and roles of the characters.

Of the twenty-three parts listed for *Eunuchus* in the Penguin edition, fourteen are speaking parts, which is the largest number in any surviving Roman comedy. Donatus, regards Parmeno as the leading role, Chaerea as the second, and Phaedria as the third (*Preface* 1. 4), though in fact it is the maid Pythias, who appears in eleven scenes, who has the second-longest part. The play would need at least seven actors to perform, doubling up the roles as appropriate. It is some indication of the degree to which Terence has adapted his Greek model that we cannot easily reconstruct a three-actor Greek original (on numbers of actors see Introd. §24).

Scene

The scene is not described in the MSS either; the details given here are deduced partly from the action of the play and partly from the conventions of the Roman theatre. *Eunuchus*, like many other plays, uses only two of the three doors of the stage building (Introd. §18); the unused door was probably covered by some sort of curtain. As for the side entrances (Introd. §19), the Penguin edition here assigns the harbour to the right-hand entrance along with the town centre (forum), but for no very compelling reason. This arrangement leaves the opposite entrance out of use for most of the play, and a different staging is followed in this commentary with the harbour in its conventional position on the left. The terms right and left are given (as in the Penguin edition) from the audience's viewpoint.

PROLOGUE (1-45, pp. 165-6)

[1] Terence's plays all begin with an artificial prologue, which is devoted not to explaining the plot but to a running battle with his literary critics. This is a new phenomenon for ancient comedy. Plautus does not use the prologue in this way, and the nearest parallel is to be found in Aristophanes, who occasionally uses the *parabasis* (spoken by the chorus in the middle of the play) to argue the merits of his own plays and to denigrate his rivals. In view of the evident need to engage the audience's attention at the beginning of the play (44 n.), Terence's polemical prologues are a bold innovation. Plautus' prologues generally take a familiar and jocular approach, which looks like a better way to involve his audience; Terence by contrast seeks sympathy by representing himself as the injured party in a quarrel and inviting the audience themselves to be the judges.

[2] The prologues of *Heauton* and *Hecyra* were spoken by

Ambivius Turpio himself, but it is clear from the opening lines of the former (1-3, p. 101) that this was unusual and that the prologue was normally spoken by one of the younger actors, which we can assume to have been the case with *Eunuchus*.

[3] It should also be noted that the prologue, like the rest of the play, is written in verse. Prologues are always in spoken verse (ia⁶) as distinct from recitative (on the metres see Introd. §27-8).

3 the poet: Terence.

4 if someone: i.e. Luscius of Lanuvium (Introd. §31).

something too harsh has been said: This presumably refers to Terence's previous prologues. At *Andr.* 21 (p. 39) Terence had accused his critics of 'dreary accuracy'; and at *Heaut.* 31-2 (p. 102) he had objected to his rival's use of the 'running slave' convention, something which Terence himself uses four times in six plays.

7 competence as a translator: Like the 'dreary accuracy' of *Andr.* 21, this seems to be a complaint about over-literal translation.

9 who has just given us *The Spectre*: Donatus gives us a summary of Menander's *Spectre* (Gk *Phasma*), and about a hundred lines have been found of the original text on papyrus. Terence implies that Luscius had somehow ruined the play, but offers no specific criticism.

10 his *Treasure*: The implication seems to be that this too was based on an original by Menander. In fact we know of six Greek plays with this title (Gk *Thesauros*), including ones by Menander and his two leading contemporaries Diphilus and Philemon. Luscius cannot have used Philemon's play, since this was the model for Plautus' *Trinummus*, without being himself guilty of 'theft' (23 n.).

11-12 defendant...plaintiff: The dispute was over a treasure buried in a tomb. The son of the dead man ('the plaintiff') claimed the treasure, even though he had sold the land containing the tomb to another man ('the defendant'), who claimed possession when the tomb was opened. The point is simply that it is customary in a court of law for the plaintiff to speak before the defendant, not vice versa. This is however a less than telling criticism on Terence's part: (i) it is not absolutely clear, in an arbitration between two rival claimants, which should have the prior right to put his case (in Men. *Epitr.* it is similarly the man in possession who speaks first), and (ii), if Luscius was as literal a translator as Terence makes out, the 'fault', such as it is, should be laid at the door of the author of the Greek original.

17 plenty of other things: In fact Terence had difficulty in finding specific counter-charges against Luscius (cf. 4 n.). Of his three later plays, the *Phormio* prologue (pp. 227-8) makes an oblique reference to Luscius' use of a rhetorical and pathetic style, and claims that, when one of his plays *was* successful, the credit was all due to the producer; the others makes no charges at all.

20 *The Eunuch* of **Menander:** We possess only a few scanty fragments of this play (Gk *Eunouchos*), which are little help in reconstructing the plot. We do know that Menander's names for the characters were different from Terence's (Daos for Parmeno, Chairestratos for Phaedria, and Chrysis for Thais): the satirist Persius (first century A.D.) has a version of the opening scene in one of his *Satires* (5. 161-75) in which Menander's names are used.

After the aediles bought it: It appears from the prologue to the third performance of Terence's *Hecyra* (57, p. 294) that the actor-manager bought the text of the play from the dramatist, in which case the aediles must have bought the production from the actor-manager. Suetonius records in his *Life of Terence* (see the Penguin appendix, p. 390) that *Eunuchus* was produced twice on the same day and earned 8,000 sesterces, which was the highest sum ever paid for a comedy. The proceeds of a successful play presumably went to the actor-manager rather than the dramatist.

22 the performance began: This is our only record of a preliminary performance of a Roman play before state officials. Since the play had already been bought, this performance cannot have been part of the normal selection process. Terence's account rather implies that Luscius had demanded a preview of the play in order to voice his criticisms of Terence's methods. We have no evidence whether such a preliminary vetting of plays was a common practice.

23 work of..a thief: On 'theft' (Lat. *furtum*) see Introd. §32.

25 a *Flatterer...*of **Naevius and Plautus:** On the surface this should mean either (i) that Naevius and Plautus collaborated on this play, which would have no parallel in the history of Roman drama, or (ii) that Plautus revised an existing play by Naevius, which would of course have been a precedent for the very 'theft' of which Terence is accused. The ancient commentators and lexicographers produce quotations from a *Flatterer* (Lat. *Colax*) of Naevius and from a *Flatterer* of Plautus: they were probably two separate plays.

p.166 **30 Menander's** *Flatterer:* We possess some 130 lines of this play (Gk *Kolax*) on papyrus, as well as a few quotations from antiquity. The remains are not sufficient to reconstruct the play or to establish what exactly Terence may have borrowed from it. But they imply that the plot revolves round a young man Pheidias, whose father has gone overseas leaving him with little means of support. Pheidias is in love with a girl owned by a pimp, and has as a rival lover a soldier Bias, who is accompanied by a flatterer Strouthias. Pheidias is helped by a slave Daos and (it seems) by a parasite called Gnathon (unless Gnathon and Strouthias are the same person).

32 transferred these characters: This apparently simple statement raises more problems than it solves. It would in principle be difficult to transfer characters from one play to another without at the same time transferring the action (i.e. the plot element) in which those characters participate. The possibilities in this case would seem to be:

(i) that the two characters bring with them from *Kolax* a detachable sub-plot which is additional to the basic plot of Menander's *Eunouchos*;

(ii) that they bring with them a plot element which has been fused with that of the original *Eunouchos* in such a way as to create a new plot structure;

(iii) that they simply replace a pair of corresponding characters in the original *Eunouchos* without significantly affecting the plot.

With the third possibility, the original characters must have fulfilled the same functions as the soldier and parasite do in Terence's play, namely to act as a rival to one young man for the favours of the courtesan and to bring with them the girl with whom the other young man falls in love. It has been suggested that the original characters were a different sort of rival (say, a rich trader) and his slave. The other possibility is that they were a rather less colourful soldier and parasite; and, since the commonest rivals of young men in comedy *are* soldiers, who do tend to be accompanied by parasites, this seems the more likely alternative. It is interesting that, in defending himself against a charge of 'theft', Terence is implicitly admitting to 'contamination' (Introd. §32); his obvious purpose is to enliven the play by the introduction of two larger-than-life stock characters.

33 these plays: The plural must refer to the two Latin versions of Menander's *Kolax*.

36-40 running slave...suspicion: This is a list of the stock characters and situations of New Comedy, all of which can be found in Terence. But again Terence is oversimplifying to make his point: it was an important part of his technique to create subtle variations on the stock characters and situations. It is should be noted that Terence here describes the traditional wife as 'virtuous' (Lat. *bona*) and the traditional courtesan as 'dishonest' (Lat. *mala*) (Introd. §5, 9).

43 what earlier writers have repeatedly done: In the context this should mean 'used stock characters and situations'. Terence is sidestepping the actual charge of 'theft'.

44 pay attention in silence: There are similar pleas in all of Terence's plays and in many of Plautus', underlining the fact that the Roman audience's attention was far from guaranteed. For the atmosphere of the Roman theatre see the prologues of Terence's *Hecyra* (pp. 292-4) and Plautus' *Poenulus*.

45 understand what *The Eunuch* has to say: Terence has used his prologue for literary polemics, rather than to set out the background of the plot. The 'exposition' thus has to be carried out more realistically in the opening scenes.

I. i: PHAEDRIA, PARMENO (46-80, pp. 167-8)

[1] The young man Phaedria enters in conversation with the

family slave Parmeno. Phaedria's mistress, having excluded him, is now inviting him back, and he does not know how to respond. Parmeno expresses some scepticism about Phaedria's ability to resist, and urges him to surrender.

[2] Since a curtainless theatre cannot simply disclose characters on stage at the beginning of a play, Phaedria and Parmeno must enter either from one of the stage houses or from the wings. The most likely entry is from the house of Phaedria's father, which is probably to be envisaged as the right-hand of the two stage houses (771ff n. 2).

[3] The play opens with a scene of dialogue. Terence opens his plays in various ways: no two plays exhibit exactly the same pattern, but he does have a distinct preference for dialogue over monologue for the opening scene (the latter occurs only in *Ad.*). Here the dialogue plunges the audience right into the middle of the situation, introducing two of the main characters and hinting at the basic situation. More detailed exposition is left for the following scene. This is in contrast to Terence's more usual practice, in which the first scene actually carries the exposition. It makes a lively and effective opening.

[4] The main interest of the scene lies in the two characters. Phaedria belongs to the type 'young man' (Lat. *adulescens*) and to the sub-type who fall in love with courtesans (Introd. §1). He is here portrayed as helpless and indecisive: it remains to be seen with what degree of sympathy he will be treated. The name 'Phaedria' (lit. 'the shining one') recurs as a young man's name in Terence's *Phormio*, but is not found in Menander; the corresponding character in Menander's *Eunouchos* was called Chairestratos (20 n.).

[5] Parmeno belongs to the type 'slave' (Lat. *servus*), and to the sub-type who assist their younger masters; the question immediately arises whether he will turn out to be a true 'tricky slave' (Introd. §7). In this scene Parmeno adopts a 'pedagogic' role, assuming a greater knowledge of the ways of the world and of the nature of love than his master: he is not unsympathetic towards Phaedria, but he is not over-deferential either (Introd. §8). At the same time it seems that Terence is poking fun at Parmeno's pretensions: his advice sounds impressive, but it is pompously and ambiguously expressed (50-6 n., 74 n., 77-8 n.). 'Parmeno' (lit. 'one who stands by') is a common slave name in Terence and Menander; the corresponding character in Menander's *Eunouchos* was called Daos (20 n.).

[6] The scene introduces the love affair of the *adulescens* as a major theme of the play. Two complementary views of love are offered. Parmeno represents what was to become the standard 'philosophical' view at Rome, found for example in Lucretius and Cicero, whereby love is a madness or disease which cannot easily be cured or controlled and is therefore best avoided. Phaedria's point of view is that of the 'elegiac' lover, as later developed in Roman elegy, emotionally dominated by a mistress from whom he finds himself

unable to escape. The scene was well known in antiquity and is quoted not only by Cicero and Quintilian (46 n., 57-63 n.) but also by the satirists Horace (*Satires* 2. 3. 259-71) and Persius (20 n.), who contrast the lover with the Stoic wise man who alone enjoys sanity and freedom. But the ultimate attitude of comedy to love is not as negative as this scene might suggest. Though Plautus caricatures certain types of lovers (such as the lecherous old man or the swaggering soldier), most plays contrive some sort of happy ending, and the attitude of Terence and Menander is basically one of sympathetic understanding of human foibles (Introd. §2).

[7] The scene (like the prologue) is in spoken verse (ia⁶). Terence never uses recitative for his opening scenes (Introd. §27-8).

46 what am I to do?: Terence directly translates the arresting opening phrase of Menander's *Eunouchos*; this is one of only three places in the play where Donatus actually provides the text of the Greek original (fr. 161). Cicero quotes this line (and line 49) in *On the Nature of the Gods* (3. 72) to illustrate the misuse of reason, and Quintilian quotes it no fewer than four times in his *Education of the Orator* to make various stylistic points.

48 insults from such women: The Latin for 'women' is *meretrices,* making it clear from the beginning that Phaedria's girl is a courtesan. In this opening scene Terence deliberately fosters the assumption that she is a typical wicked *meretrix* (71 n.); she toys with her lovers (55 n.), sheds tears to soften their anger ('a single tiny false tear' 67), and all the time makes them pay for the privilege ('Every penny...goes to her' 80).

50-6 Of course...think again: In the fourth or fifth century Bembine MS (which is the oldest MS of Terence) these lines are assigned to Phaedria as a continuation of his opening speech, so that, having resolved to refuse his mistress's invitation, he goes on to express doubts about the wisdom of refusal. In this version he is addressing himself in the second person in these lines, and the various 'sir's (which are the addition of the translator) should be ignored.

55 she'll stop play: This is one of the interpretations of the Latin *eludet* offered by Donatus, who suggests that the metaphor is from gladiatorial combat. But the sense is rather 'she will toy with you': the greedy courtesan is hardly likely to end the game when she has her lover at her mercy. The gladiatorial image is a rare and striking variation on the much commoner metaphor of love as warfare, which, though found rarely in Menander, is taken up by Plautus and Terence and then greatly developed in Roman elegy.

57 Reason can't solve...: If this whole speech is correctly assigned to Parmeno, he is guilty of an inconsistency here, which may be a deliberate part of his characterisation: it is not very logical to tell some one to 'think, and think again' (56) and then in the same breath assure him that reason can't solve his problem.

57-63 Reason...reason...method...method: The Latin is full of verbal repetitions and antitheses, ending with the oxymoron 'method for madness' (lit. 'go mad rationally'). The passage 59-63 is quoted by Cicero (*Tusculan Disputations* 4. 76) to illustrate the fickleness of love.

59-61 all these upsets...war then peace again: The idea that lovers' quarrels are brief, and renew love rather than destroying it, was proverbial in antiquity; it is found in Menander (fr. 567) and Plautus (*Amph.* 940-3) as well as elsewhere in Terence (*Andr.* 555, p. 65). Here it is couched in the imagery of love as warfare (55 n.).

65 I'll show her...let her try: The ellipses suggest the spluttering indignation of Phaedria.

70 Monstrous: Lit. 'unworthy deed' (Lat. *indignum*): on the concept of 'unworthy' behaviour see Introd. §16.

71 see her wickedness: This explicitly characterises the *meretrix* as *mala* (48 n.).

72 eaten up with love: Lit. 'on fire with love'. This is another of the metaphors for love which are common in Roman comedy and later in elegy but are not found in Menander (cf. 55 n.).

p.168 **74 Buy your freedom:** The metaphor (Lat. *te redimas captum*) seems to be that of buying back prisoners of war for a ransom (echoing the military imagery of 60-1). But the image is not altogether apt, since a lover can scarcely buy himself out of a courtesan's clutches, and in any case the general purport of Parmeno's previous speech advice was that Phaedria should not try to escape. If Parmeno means 'buy a peace with your mistress by giving her a not too expensive present', this is an ambiguous way of saying so.

77-8 Love provides...adding to them: Menander's version is here preserved in a quotation by the ancient anthologist Stobaeus: 'Do not fight the gods or add further tempests to your troubles but bear the ones you have to bear' (fr. 162). This neatly illustrates the point that, while Menander tends to regard love as an external divine force, Terence sees it as a purely human impulse. Again the advice is ambiguous, since 'not adding to [the troubles of love]' might equally mean 'giving in to your mistress' as 'rejecting her approaches'; again we have to assume that Parmeno intends the former.

79 Look, she's coming out: The transition to the next scene is achieved by an 'introduction formula' (Introd. §29).

blight on our fortunes: Lit. 'blight on our estate': the metaphor is of a blight attacking crops and eating away the profits of the family farm. The objection to young men's love affairs in Roman comedy is as often couched in financial terms as in moral.

I. ii: THAIS, PHAEDRIA, PARMENO (81-206, pp. 168-72)

[1] The courtesan, whose name is Thais, emerges from the second

of the two stage houses, and explains to Phaedria why she has excluded him. The soldier who was her former lover has unknowingly purchased as a gift for her a slave-girl who was brought up as her own sister on Rhodes, and she wants Phaedria to withdraw in favour of the soldier until the girl is safely delivered. The girl had originally been captured by pirates, and is thought to be of Athenian birth; Thais is hoping to restore her to her parents, and to gain from them the protection and support which she needs as a foreign woman in Athens. Phaedria reluctantly agrees to go away to the country for two days, leaving Thais to declare in a monologue that she is telling the truth about her love for Phaedria and about the girl, whose brother she has already tracked down.

[2] The scene is basically expository: the passage in which Thais explains her motives (99-149) is in effect an expository narrative. But Terence has avoided an artificial expository monologue: the narrative is enlivened by Parmeno's sceptical asides and by the occasional question from Phaedria, and the whole is 'framed' by two passages (81-98, 150-96) which realistically depict Phaedria's jealousy and helplessness. At first sight there is no reason to suppose that the whole scene has not been taken over in its existing form directly from Menander. Though all Menander's surviving plays have expository prologues (often postponed until after an opening scene of dialogue), it does not follow that he must have used one in his *Eunouchos*; if he did, it will have conveyed the background information here related by Thais, and it would follow that Terence has largely rewritten the scene to create a realistic dialogue. There are in fact some awkwardnesses here, apparent only later in the play, which some would see as evidence that Terence has tampered with the Greek opening: the statement that the girl is thought to be of Athenian birth (110 n.) should be noted, and also the precise details of Thais' dealings with the brother (203-6 n.). On Menander's prologues see Introd. §33.

[3] Thais belongs to the type 'courtesan' (Lat. *meretrix*: Introd. §9). We have had strong hints already in the opening scene (48 n.) that she belongs to the mercenary sub-type who exploit their lovers, and for much of this scene we may share the scepticism of her motives expressed by both Parmeno and Phaedria. But, since by convention monologue speakers do not lie, we have to take at face value her closing speech, in which she declares that she is telling the truth, and thus to revise our assessment of her character. Though she does elicit expensive gifts from Phaedria (169 n.), she also has some genuine affection for him ('no man is dearer to me' 201), and her concern to restore her 'sister' to her family is another good trait, though there is also a clear element of self-interest involved in that she hopes to win the protection of the girl's parents. So it seems that Terence is going to present, if not the unequivocally good courtesan that Donatus (on 198) suggests, a much more sympathetic variation of the type.

[4] Parmeno is aggressive towards Thais and rather superior in his remarks to his master ('Courage, sir...' 84-5, 'Well done, sir...' 154, 'He's weakening...' 178); he also indulges in some exuberant imagery worthy of the Plautine tricky slave (85 n., 105 n.). But our revised estimate of Thais' character will also affect our estimate of Parmeno's; in so far as he has misunderstood the situation, he may turn out to be not so much the tricky slave as the 'bungling slave', like his namesake in *Hecyra* (Introd. §7).

[5] The scene offers further perspectives on the nature of love: the portrayal of the 'elegiac lover' in the character of Phaedria is further developed, and the question of the nature of a courtesan's love is raised in relation to Thais. Phaedria trembles at the mere sight of Thais (83-4 n.), he longs for her to love him on equal terms (91-2), he complains that she does not reward him for his presents (163-71), he wishes that her protestations could be taken as sincere (175-7 n.), he withdraws to the country to endure his misery (187), he wants her to think only of him when she is with the soldier (192-5), and finally he wants her to give him her heart as she has his (196 n.). All of this has parallels in Roman elegy, and the whole amounts to a stock (but not unsympathetic) comic portrayal of the jealous lover. Thais' expression of her love for Phaedria is in contrast very guarded. There is no one whom she loves more (96 n.) and she will do anything rather than lose his affection (174 n.); but the only time that she says outright that she loves him is when he has just agreed to do her a favour (186 n.). In fact the vocabulary used by Thais very much suggests the concept of friendship (*amicitia*) as based on the exchange of mutual favours (*beneficia*) (cf. 147-9 n.), with the implication that the love of even a 'good' courtesan is liable to be as much practical as romantic. The portrayal of both Phaedria's love and Thais' in this scene is important for the appreciation of the ending of the play

[6] The spoken verse (ia^6) continues from the opening scene.

81-6 Oh dear...is that you?: The scene opens, as often in Terence, with an 'overheard entrance monologue' (Introd. §19), accompanied by asides and terminated formulaically (Introd. §30). In this case there are two aside speakers and there are a pair of 'recognition formulae' ('Who's that? Phaedria...is that you?' 86). But the whole sequence is kept brief and realistic: the monologue itself consists of only two lines.

83-4 sets me all trembling and shivering: This kind of description of the physical symptoms of love belongs to the lyric and elegiac tradition, best exemplified by a well known poem by Catullus (51) and its Greek model by Sappho (fr. 31).

85 fire...warm: This is an original use of the metaphor of the fire of love (72 n.) in that (i) it is neatly adapted to the idea of the shivering lover, and (ii) Thais herself is boldly personified as the fire.

88 Not a word....: Parmeno comments aside on the Thais-

Phaedria conversation, as also at 178 ('He's weakening...'). On the 'aside commentary' see Introd. §21).

95 my own, my darling: Lit. 'my heart'.

96 care for anyone or love anyone: The words imply not only physical love (Lat. *amare*) but also deeper affection (Lat. *diligere*).

105 full of cracks and leak all over: The comparison of Parmeno to a leaking vessel is a striking and apparently original idea. It is foreshadowed in 103 ('keep quiet'), where the Latin (*continere*) actually suggests 'hold my contents', and it is repeated at 121 ('leak out'); it is unusual for Terence to prolong an image to this length.

107 Samos...Rhodes: These were two of the leading Greek islands off the west coast of Asia Minor. Samian women are prominent in New Comedy: there are other examples of Samian courtesans who migrate to Athens in Menander's *Samia* and Plautus' *Bacchides*. The migration of Samian women in comedy seems to be related to the chequered history of the island in the fourth century B.C., when the inhabitants were expelled by Athens and replaced by Athenian settlers but were later restored.

110 from Attica / A citizen born? / I think so: Granted the conventions of comedy (§1), this interchange creates a strong presumption that the girl will indeed turn out to be citizen born, and will be duly married to one of the young men in the play; this is what happens to Glycerium in *Andria* who was similarly supposed to be the sister of a courtesan. It is important to note (i) that this conversation takes place in Parmeno's hearing and (ii) that the girl's citizenship is hinted at rather than established.

115 Sunium: This was a coastal town at the southern tip of Attica, about twenty-five miles from Athens; it had a prominent marble temple of Poseidon, which still survives..

119 a protector...who set me up: This person is not to be identified with the soldier friend of 125. The Latin actually says 'the one protector I had *then*, who *left* me all I have', with the clear implication that the man is now dead.

126 Caria: Caria, an area in the south-west corner of what is now Turkey, figured in the squabbles of the Macedonian generals after the death of Alexander the Great in 323 B.C. It is mentioned several times in New Comedy (e.g. in Men. *Sam.* and *Sik.*) as a scene of fighting for mercenary soldiers. Thais' soldier friend, like the other 'swaggering soldiers' of New Comedy, is a mercenary captain who hires out his services to foreign rulers (Introd. §13).

133 lyre: Lit. 'strings'; 'lute' would be a better translation (*Phorm.* 82 n.).

143-4 Is it more than a fancy? / No: This interchange has a significance beyond its immediate context. It is important to establish that the soldier has not actually slept with the girl, because

p.169

p.170

the loss of her virginity would not only spoil Thais' plan to restore her to her family but also make it difficult for Terence to contrive an honourable marriage for her at the end of the play.

147-9 I'm alone here...friends...kindness: This is not the only place where Terence shows a sympathetic understanding of the insecurity of the courtesan (cf. *Heaut.* 381-95, p. 118). Note that the concepts of friendship (*amicitia*) and kindness (*beneficium*) are explicitly linked (Introd. §16).

151 have first place: Lit. 'have the first part', a common metaphor derived from acting in a play.

p.171   **169 two thousand drachmas for the pair:** Phaedria clearly means to imply that his gifts are expensive ones. For comparison the real-life price of skilled adult slaves seems to have been only three hundred to five hundred drachmas, both in Menander's Athens and in Terence's Rome. We can expect real-life prices to be inflated in comedy: the *adulescens* is willing to pay even more to purchase his own girl-friend from the pimp (*Phorm.* 557 n.).

174 lose your affection: Lit. 'have you as my enemy'.

175-7 from your heart...really meant...sincere: The accumulation of synonyms underlines the intensity of Phaedria's emotion. The passage is imitated in a poem of Catullus (109) with reference to the protestations of his mistress Lesbia.

178 He's weakening: Donatus explains the Latin (*labescere*) as a metaphor from a tree falling under an axe. On the aside cf. 88 n.

p.172   **186 you're so kind:** This is probably no more than the traditional acknowlegement of a kindness, though there is a verbal link between the Latin phrase (*bene facis*) and the concept of friendship based on favours (*beneficia*).

187 endure my misery: The Latin has the colourful word *macerari*, originally a culinary term ('be steeped', 'be soaked'), and frequently used with connotations of 'be tortured' or 'be worn away'.

189 Very good, sir: This could be an exit line, with Parmeno going into his master's house to fetch the gifts at this point. We have to infer the precise exit points of characters, except where the dramatist chooses to include some kind of stage-directional phrase in the text itself (Introd. §29).

191 That's all then?: This is the standard leave-taking formula of comedy (lit. 'do you want anything else?') which demands at most a conventional reply before the speaker departs. Here Phaedria takes up the question literally, and thus detains Thais on stage (Introd. §30).

196 You have my heart: try to give me yours: This is a striking line, reflecting the depth of Phaedria's love and the mutuality which he longs for. The idea of giving one's heart to the beloved is less common in Roman comedy than might be expected (there is an example at Plaut. *As.* 141). But what Phaedria actually says here is '*be* my heart as I *am* yours'. If we pressed the implications of this, it would suggest not merely an exchange but the fusion of the two personalities, a conceit found later in love elegy which has no real parallel in comedy. But it may be merely an extension of the use of the vocative 'my heart' as equivalent to 'my darling' (95 n.). This looks like another exit line (cf. 189 n.): the natural assumption would be that Phaedria departs at this point for the country.

197-206 Oh dear...wait for him: Thais is left on stage to deliver an 'exit monologue', at the end of which she withdraws into her house. There are only two exit monologues in *Eunuchus*, compared with seventeen entrance monologues and three link monologues (Introd. §22).

198 judges my character by other women: Terence makes explicit his departure from the stock characterisation of the courtesan.

203-6 I have hopes...wait for him: The obvious interpretation of these lines is that Thais has contacted the supposed brother and arranged to meet him 'this very day' but has not so far done so.

206 I'll go in: This time Terence does use an unambiguous stage-directional phrase (Introd. §29). The renaissance editors placed the end of Terence's 'first act' here on the basis of the empty stage. As far as Terence is concerned, this is an academic point, since Roman plays were performed continuously (Introd. §23); but it is a reasonable speculation that the first act of Menander's *Eunouchos* did end at this point.

II. i: PHAEDRIA, PARMENO (207-31, pp. 173-4)

[1] Phaedria returns with Parmeno, repeating his instructions to deliver his presents to Thais as soon as possible. Phaedria then departs for the country, leaving Parmeno to reflect on his master's behaviour. The soldier's parasite Gnatho now approaches with the girl for Thais.

[2] The text gives no explicit help with the stage directions. We may be mildly surprised that Phaedria now returns to the stage (196 n.): we can only deduce in retrospect that he withdrew to his father's house at 196, from which he now emerges with Parmeno. The lack of clarity about the stage movements has been ascribed to Terentian adapation of his Greek original: it is a plausible speculation that in Menander the Phaedria character did depart for the country at the end of the previous scene and that the Parmeno character reappeared here to deliver a monologue.

[3] The scene allows Parmeno to express his scepticism both of the effectiveness of Phaedria's gifts and of his ability to 'stick it out' in the country; it also reveals that Phaedria was once a perfectly sensible young man, which tends to make his character more sympathetic and implies something about the destructive effect of love. The scene thus reinforces the ideas and characterisation of the opening scenes without adding anything very new.

[4] The scene is in recitative, after the spoken verse of the two

previous scenes. Mixed metres are used for the Phaedria-Parmeno conversation and a single metre (tr⁷), which is the commonest recitative metre, for Parmeno's closing monologue (see Introd. §27-8).

207 Do as I told you..: The scene opens in mid-conversation (Introd. §19). Phaedria's orders are an awkward repetition of those at 189, which has been taken as further evidence that Terence has tampered with the staging of the Greek original (above, n. 2).

p.174   **225 disease:** This is another common metaphor for love which seems to occur only rarely in Menander (55 n., 72 n.).

225-31 Heaven above...Thais herself: This is a 'link monologue' in that Parmeno remains on stage for the following scene (Introd. §22). The three link monologues in *Eunuchus* are all very brief, and all of them are spoken by Parmeno, who acts as something of a 'continuity man' while he is on stage.

228 who's that coming? ...it's Gnatho: The transition to the next scene is again achieved by an introduction formula (79 n.). It would be appropriate for Gnatho to approach from the right, since Phaedria has just departed to the left (i.e. for the country). It follows that the soldier's house, from which Gnatho is coming, is notionally located off-stage to the right (on the side entrances see Introd. §19).

hanger-on: This is the same word (Lat. *parasitus*) which was previously translated 'sponger' (26, 30, 38, p. 166).

230 what a beauty!: The immediate point is that Thais will be more impressed with the soldier's present than with Phaedria's. But beautiful girls also attract lovers.

II. ii: GNATHO, PARMENO (232-91, pp. 174-7)

[1] Gnatho enters congratulating himself on his technique as a parasite, and, after teasing Parmeno on Thais' transfer of affection from Phaedria to the soldier, goes into Thais' house to deliver the girl. As Gnatho departs to rejoin the soldier, Phaedria's younger brother Chaerea approaches from the harbour.

[2] This is the first of the scenes in the play involving the parasite and the soldier, who, according to the prologue were imported into Terence's *Eunuchus* from Menander's *Kolax* (32 n.). It advances the action in so far as (i) the girl is delivered to Thais and (ii) Thais is invited to dinner with the soldier. But the main function both of Gnatho's lengthy monologue and of the ensuing Gnatho-Parmeno dialogue is to amuse the audience The whole of the monologue must come from *Kolax*: it has no bearing on the plot, and its dramatic effect is simply to hold up the action and focus attention on the parasite. The dialogue, on the other hand, does achieve the delivery of the girl to Thais, and this must have had a counterpart in Menander's *Eunouchos*, if we accept that the girl raped by the 'eunuch' there was

brought to the courtesan by a rival lover (32 n.). The dialogue also contains the dinner-party invitation, but it will be best to postpone until later the question whether the soldier's dinner-party was also part of Menander's *Eunouchos*.

[3] Gnatho belongs to the type 'parasite' (Lat. *parasitus*) and to the sub-type who earn their free meals by fawning and flattery (Introd. §12). Here Gnatho's mastery of the art of flattery ('I [am] the inventor of the new method' 247) and his ability to secure invitations to dinner ('They always greet me, ask me to dinner, and bid me welcome' 259) are both emphasised; and a further quality is the arrogance by which he despises his less resourceful acquaintances ('He filled me with contempt' 239), sets himself up as the master of a school of flatterers (264 n.), and teases Parmeno on the basis of his superior gift to Thais ('How do you think Thais will like this present?' 275). To judge from later references the name 'Gnatho' (lit. 'Jaw': Gk *gnathos*) was a standard parasite's name, though the only other comedy in which it is actually found is Menander's *Kolax* (30 n.).

[4] Parmeno, who is at a disadvantage in relation to the respective gifts of Phaedria and the soldier, makes a spirited response to Gnatho, with some telling asides ('My word, that's a clever one!' 254, 'Look what can be got out of idleness...' 265, 'And men like this imagine...' 269-70), ironic rejoinders ('Standing on my feet' 271, 'Congratulations' 279, 'Witty, aren't you...' 288), and blunt retorts ('You' 272, 'I wasn't' 281). At the same time he has a trump card in that Thais has promised to take Phaedria back after two days: he hints at this in Gnatho's presence ('it's a world of ups and downs' 276), and exultantly proclaims it when Gnatho has gone into Thais' house ('Just you wait...' 283-5). The vehemence of this latter outburst indicates something about Parmeno's hatred for Gnatho; in his loyalty to Phaedria he begins to show some of the qualities of the 'loyal slave' (Introd. §7).

[5] This is another recitative scene. For his exposition of the technique of flattery Gnatho uses tr^7; but he changes to the less common ia^7 when he goes on to talk of the food sellers in the market ('During this conversation...' 255), and this metre then continues for the rest of the scene. On the metres see Introd. §28.

232-69 Ye gods...teasing the fellow: Gnatho's monologue is another overheard entrance monologue, accompanied by asides and terminated formulaically (81-6 n.). Donatus envisages Gnatho walking about the stage, and stopping from time to time to stare at the audience; as it later transpires, he has with him not only the girl but her maid. The monologue lasts for thirty-six lines, if we discount the two asides by Parmeno, which makes it the third longest monologue in the whole of Terence. At first sight, it differs from Terence's other long monologues in being detached from the action; it is much more in the tradition of Plautus, who is quite happy to hold up his plots with inorganic set-piece monologues and who gives several of his parasites discursive self-introductory speeches. Gnatho's monologue, however, is different from those of Plautus' parasites in the philosophical posture which it adopts (264 n.); it lacks the Roman allusions in which Plautus' parasites tend to indulge (255-7 n.); and, though it is presumably taken over by Terence from Menander's *Kolax*, we had better suspend judgment on its thematic relevance to Terence's play. The language of the speech is worthy of note: beneath its informal surface it uses a host of rhetorical devices, such as antithesis ('fool... man with brains' 232), pairs of synonyms ('rank and position' 234), triplets ('unshaven, dirty, and wretched' 236), a variety of metaphors (235 n., 236 n., 247 n., 268n., 274 n.), paradox ('I've nothing...and lack nothing' 243), repetition ('praise ...praise...No...No...Yes...Yes' 251-2), and word-play (264 n.).

235 guzzled: Lit. 'licked up', a vivid metaphor.

236 a ragged old man: Lit. 'overgrown with rags and years'; the implied agricultural metaphor is a rarity in Terence.

244 playing the fool or taking a beating: This view of the parasite's lot appears also in the fragments of Greek New Comedy and in Plautus (e.g. *Capt.* 88-90, 470-2), but the parasites who actually appear in the surviving plays are treated rather better.

p.175   **247 setting our traps:** i.e. to catch birds (Lat. *aucupium*).

the inventor of the new method: This is meant to be seen as a pompous exaggeration on Gnatho's part: it is a commonplace of Greek and Roman literature to record the 'first inventor' of things. The technique of flattery was certainly not original to Gnatho. It had already been exemplified on the Roman stage in the time of Plautus (e.g. by Artotrogus in *Mil.*), and on the Greek side it can be traced back all the way to the Old Comedy of the fifth century B.C., where we possess an exposition of it by the chorus of Eupolis' *Flatterers*.

252-3 If they say No...agree with everything: These lines are quoted by Cicero (*On Friendship* 93) as part of his condemnation of flattery, especially among friends. Donatus also takes a moralising view, assuming Terence's purpose to be satirical and comparing *Andr.* 67-8 (p. 42): 'Agree with everything nowadays, if you want friends: truthfulness only makes you unpopular.'

255-7 confectioners...spratsellers: Donatus suggests that there is a comic intention here in that a Roman market is being described when the context of the play is Greek. It is true that the terminology here is thoroughly Roman, but the incongruity, if perceived at all, is not a glaring one. Plautus' parasites by contrast refer quite specifically to Roman locations (Ergasilus in *Capt.* mentions both the Triple Gate of Rome and the oil market in the Velabrum). In general Plautus delights in incongruous Romanisms, Terence avoids them.

264 Gnathonists: The obvious analogy is with 'Platonists' as a term for followers of Plato (Lat. *Gnathonici / Platonici*).

265 But I must hurry on: This is a common 'action formula' (lit. 'do I delay?') used by characters in comedy when some action is perceived to be overdue (Introd. §29). By using it here, Terence is implicitly admitting that Gnatho's monologue has been longer than its dramatic function warrants.

267 Why, there's Parmeno: The transition from monologue to dialogue is made by a recognition formula (81-6 n.).

268 having a cool reception: The expression is more striking in the Latin (lit. 'the fellows are freezing'); the metaphor is common enough in later Latin, but it may be original to Terence, since there are no parallel examples in Plautus or Greek comedy.

p.176   **270-1 bids a warm welcome to his dear friend:** This is ostentatiously effusive when a simple 'hullo' or 'greetings' (Lat. *salve*) would have sufficed.

How do I find you?: This is a conventional question which demands at most a conventional response. Here Parmeno signifies his objection to Gnatho's effusiveness by taking the question literally and giving a facetious reply (Introd. §30; cf. 191 n.).

274 He's warming up / That's just where he's wrong: This exchange provides an extension of the simple 'aside in conversation' technique (Introd. §21). Gnatho's remark (lit. 'I am burning him': again a bolder image than in the English translation) is spoken aside from Parmeno, who nevertheless hears it and replies with an unheard aside of his own. Granted that the whole business of asides is a dramatic convention, it is entirely up to the dramatist whether a particular aside is heard or not.

277 six whole months: This could be simply a round figure for the length of Thais' affair with the soldier; but there may be some implication of a contract for a specific period, similar to those between soldiers and courtesans in Plautus' *Asinaria* and *Bacchides*.

p.177   **284-5 little finger...kicking:** The vividness of the language indicates the vehemence of Parmeno's feeling. Doing something with one's little finger was a proverbial expression for acting with effortless ease, but the violence of 'kicking at them' (lit. 'leaping on them with your heels') is striking. It is clear from the context that Gnatho must deliver the girl into Thais' house during Parmeno's speech, but there are no explicit stage directions in the text (cf. 189 n.).

288 Witty, aren't you: The last two utterances of Gnatho's have been ironic.

289-91 Now I do believe...: Gnatho's exit, again not precisely signalled in the text, leaves Parmeno to deliver a brief link monologue (225-31 n.) as Chaerea approaches. Gnatho departs in the same direction as he had entered (right: 228 n.), allowing Chaerea, who is coming from the harbour, to enter from the opposite side (left). On the location of the harbour entrance see Introd. §19.

290 on guard duty at the docks: Terence actually mentions the Piraeus in the text, which many of his Roman audience would presumably have recognised as the harbour of Athens, but refrains from using the technical Greek word ('ephebe') for Chaerea's military service. Young Athenians were required to serve as ephebes for two years from the age of eighteen, during which time they underwent military training and performed guard duties both on the coast and in the country. Chaerea can be assumed to be in military dress, which in comedy typically involves a hat, cape, tunic, and sword.

today: Better 'at present' (Lat. *nunc* = 'now'): military service would keep the ephebes away from Athens for long periods rather than on a day-to-day basis.

291 in such a hurry and searching everywhere: This is in effect a stage direction for the Chaerea actor (Introd. §29).

II. iii: CHAEREA, PARMENO (292-390, pp. 177-82)

[1] Chaerea enters lamenting that he has lost track of a beautiful girl whom he had seen in the street. Parmeno realises that this must be the girl brought by Gnatho, and jokingly suggests that Chaerea should change places with Phaedria's eunuch to gain access to Thais' house. Chaerea insists on taking up the suggestion, much to Parmeno's consternation, and they go inside to effect the exchange.

[2] The arrival of Chaerea indicates that this is going to be a double plot involving two young men and two love affairs, which is a favourite structure of Terence's (Introd. §17). In the absence of an expository prologue (45 n.) this is our first inkling of Chaerea's existence, though the more perceptive of the audience may have foreseen a second love affair from the hints already dropped about Pamphila's social status (110 n.) and beauty (230 n.).

[3] Chaerea is another *adulescens* (Introd. §1). Like most of the type he is hopelessly in love, and like most he looks to the family slave for help. But the contrast with Phaedria is immediately made explicit by Parmeno's remark that Chaerea's 'frenzy' is likely to make Phaedria's look like 'just fooling' (300-1), and Chaerea displays a resourcefulness and vitality on his first appearance which mark him off as different. Modern verdicts on Chaerea's character and behaviour have ranged all the way from 'detestable' to 'an engaging scamp': it remains to be seen how his character will be developed in the rest of the play. In this scene Terence emphasises:

(i) his infatuation with Pamphila ('I've written off all other women' 296; 'I've completely lost my head' 306; 'I don't care how, so long as I have her' 320; 'help me to possess her' 362);

(ii) his preoccupation with physical attractiveness ('Oh she's a beauty' 296; 'This isn't an ordinary girl' 313; 'Natural complexion, firm figure..plump and juicy' 318; 'is she as lovely as they say?' 361);

(iii) his contempt for the older generation (including the misguided mothers of 314-7, the slobbering old man of 335-42, the horrible old eunuch of 356-7);

(iv) his impetuousness, which leads him to take up Parmeno's suggested exchange instantly ('Splendid...Quick...this minute' 376);

(v) his readiness to justify his conduct with plausible arguments ('*Wrong?*...a deed well done' 382-7).

Chaerea's language too is more colourful than that of most Terentian *adulescentes* (303 n., 312 n., 318 n., 354 n., 383-5 n.). The name 'Chaerea' occurs in several plays of Menander's, though not otherwise in Plautus and Terence; it suggests 'man of joy'.

[4] There is a clear development in the character of Parmeno in this scene, picking up hints which were dropped earlier (46ff n. 5, 81ff n. 4). His general air of superior wisdom is here undercut by his attempt to retract the eunuch suggestion ('I'm a damn fool' 378) and his inability to talk Chaerea out of taking it up, so that in the end all he can do is lamely try to avoid the responsibility ('Only don't go putting the blame on me' 388-9). This is a reversal of the true tricky slave character (Introd. §7).

[5] The scene extends the variety of attitudes to love which the play presents. Chaerea's view, based on purely physical attraction, is clearly different from Phaedria's 'elegiac' view, based on the ideal of mutual devotion (46ff n. 6), and from Thais' 'courtesan's' view, based on practical considerations (81ff n. 5). It is in fact unusual to see young men in comedy in the first flush of physical infatuation; normally they have fallen in love before the play begins, and the dramatist is more concerned to explore their reactions to the problems of the affair than their initial symptoms. Parmeno offers a negative view of Chaerea's love, which he calls a 'frenzy' (301 n.) even before he has heard the details. But this may not be Terence's final verdict (Introd. §2).

[6] The scene displays extraordinary metrical variety, and is a good example of how Terence uses metre to distinguish different sections of the dialogue and their different tempos (Introd. §28):

(i) Chaerea's opening monologue and Parmeno's asides are in excited mixed-metre recitative;

(ii) Chaerea's enthusiastic description of the girl and his plea to Parmeno to help are in one of the more animated recitative metres (ia^8) (from 'Damned if I know' 306);

(iii) his narrative of how he lost track of the girl is in more matter-of-fact spoken verse (ia^6), as most narratives in drama tend to be (from 'That was what I was cursing myself for' 323);

(iv) Parmeno's account of the girl who came with Gnatho is in the standard recitative metre (tr^7), which raises the tempo a little after the spoken verse (from 'She was brought here' 352);

(v) the rest of the scene reverts to the more animated ia^8 of the second section, as Chaerea warms to the prospect of playing the eunuch (from 'he'll speak to her' 367).

292-304 Hell!...hullo, Parmeno: Once again, the scene begins with an overheard entrance monologue, accompanied by an aside and terminated formulaically (232-69 n.).

301 frenzy : Lat. *rabies*, a coarse word, often applied to the savagery or lust of animals and with a distinctly satirical or contemptuous tone when applied to the love of humans (e.g. Lucretius *On the Nature of Things* 4. 1083, Horace *Epodes* 12. 9).

303 paying attention: Lit. 'giving a straw', a common idiom which is part of the colourfulness of Chaerea's language.

304 look who's there - hullo, Parmeno: Chaerea's recognition and greeting of Parmeno consists of two simple formulae 'look' and 'hullo' (Lat. *salve*). This makes an interesting contrast to Gnatho's effusive outpouring (270-1 n.).

p.178   **308-10 You know the promise...secretly to your room:** This is a charming vignette of the relations between the young master of the house and his pedagogue (Introd. §8).

311 Don't be so silly: The tone is one of friendly reproach (Lat. *inepte*).

312 make the effort: Lit. 'strain your sinews'.

313-18 This isn't...plump and juicy: Chaerea's remarks offer an interesting glimpse of ideals of female beauty in the classical world. The passage is probably derived from the Greek original: there is no good reason for regarding the dialogue as original to Terence or the attitudes as Roman rather than Greek.

315 looks like a prize-fighter: Juvenal's *Satires* display similar scorn for females with a propensity for traditionally male sporting activities (wrestling 2. 53; athletics, sword-fighting, gladiating 6. 246-67; weight training 6. 418-21).

318 juicy: Chaerea's language is again colourful.

sixteen: This is one of only three passages in Roman comedy where the age of the girl loved by the *adulescens* is given. Selenium is said to be seventeen at Plaut. *Cist.* 755, and Phanium seems to be only fifteen at *Phorm.* 1017-18 (p.279).

p.179   **327 Archidemides:**   This is perhaps a stock name for an old friend of the father of the *adulescens* (cf. Plaut. *Bacch.* 284).

340 to support me: The Latin is *advocatus*, but the reference is not to professional advocates, who are a later development at Rome, so much as to friends who would help each other as advisers in legal business (for advocates in action see *Phorm.* 446-59, p. 248).

341 an hour: This is an evident exaggeration on Chaerea's part, though Terence does have to cover the time taken up by Gnatho's long monologue.

p.180   **347 spongers:**   Lat. *parasitus* (228 n.).

348 dead and buried: Lit. 'the final laments have been uttered', an idiomatic phrase derived from Roman funeral procedure.

354 doesn't leave my brother much of a part: The metaphor is from the theatre (151 n.). In Plautus such metaphors are often metatheatrical, that is, they call attention to the fact that they are uttered by an actor and can be applied to the acting of the play in which they occur. But this is scarcely the case here: the statement is not meant to refer to Phaedria's part in the play.

359 She hasn't for long: This is news to the audience, who have had no reason to suppose that Thais is a new neighbour of Chaerea's family. Terence is covering the rather improbable stage convention whereby two families live next door to each other and even so are not very well aware of what is going on in the neighbouring house (cf. *Ad.* 649 n.). In this case Chaerea's absence on guard duty (290 n.) makes his ignorance more plausible.

p.181 **373 touch her, play with her:** These are additions by Parmeno to Chaerea's own list of the pleasures that the eunuch might enjoy (366-7). Chaerea was talking of proximity, which Parmeno extends to physical contact; it is not explicit that either at this point envisages rape, though 'sleep by her side' is not entirely innocent.

374 None of the women there can recognise you: This detail is important for the whole eunuch trick, and Terence has prepared for it with some care. Chaerea's absence from home on guard duty means not only that he does not know his new neighbours (359 n.), but also that they do not know him

p.182 **379 shoving me...have me down:** This is in effect a stage direction (Introd. §29: cf. 291 n.), suggesting some comic business as Chaerea tries to bustle Parmeno into the house. The action underlines Chaerea's impetuosity.

381 it'll be me who smarts for it: The Latin has a more colourful proverbial expression (lit. 'your bean will be threshed on me').

382 wrong: The Latin word expresses strong moral disapproval (*flagitium:* lit. 'disgrace', 'outrage'), which raises the question what precisely it is that Parmeno has in mind.

(i) On the assumption that he foresees that Chaerea will rape the girl, it is often pointed out that he fails to use an obvious argument. Parmeno was present when Thais suggested to Phaedria that the girl might turn out to be an Athenian citizen (110 n.); and, since the rape of a citizen girl would have been an outrage and indeed a criminal offence, the mention of this possibility might have been enough to deter even the ardent Chaerea. Some have seen this as evidence of a Greek original in which Parmeno was not present when Thais made the suggestion (81ff n. 2), but there may be an easier explanation; in Terence's version Parmeno is generally sceptical of Thais' story and may have simply dismissed the whole idea as a fiction.

(ii) This line of argument is based on the assumption that the 'wrong' envisaged by Parmeno is one perpetrated on the girl. But it is not explicit that Parmeno foresees a rape (373 n.), and there is the other possibility that he sees the 'wrong' as one perpetrated on Thais.

On the supposition that the girl is a slave and Thais is her new owner, it would be wrong to gain entry to Thais' house by false pretences and make use of her property. There is a similar case at *Ad.* 88-92 (p. 343), where Aeschinus' action in breaking into a pimp's house and carrying off one of his girls by force is regarded as a 'scandal'.

383-5 pay back those tormentors: Lit. '...those crosses', a bold personification. Chaerea certainly sees his plan in terms of striking a blow against Thais; and this seems to support the second interpretation of Parmeno's objections given above, unless we are to credit Chaerea with deliberately mistaking the slave's meaning. In regarding Thais as a typical evil courtesan and tormentor of the young, Chaerea is reinforcing the tension between this stereotype and the true character of Thais as presented by Terence (48 n.).

386 Would you rather...?: Lit. 'is it right that I should rather...': Chaerea appeals to the concept of *aequom* (Introd. §16).

I duped my father: This is the standard practice of the young man of comedy, who not only deceives his father about his love affairs but often, with the help of slave or friend, swindles the old man of money (as in *Heaut.* and *Phorm.*). This would have seemed particularly outrageous at Rome in view of the traditional Roman respect for the *paterfamilias* (Introd. §4).

390 Follow me: With this common exit formula (Introd. §29) Chaerea leads Parmeno into their house, and the stage is left empty. The renaissance editors put the end of Terence's 'second act' here, which may again correspond to Menander's act division (206 n.).

III. i: THRASO, GNATHO, PARMENO (391-453, pp.182-5)

[1] Gnatho returns with Thraso (right: 228 n.), flattering him absurdly and reassuring him of Thais' love.

[2] This is the second of the scenes involving the two characters imported from Menander's *Kolax* (32 n.). Like the earlier Gnatho scene (232ff n. 2), much of it has nothing to do with the plot, and the scene is to that extent detachable; it serves to introduce Thraso, but is otherwise an amusing interlude, which adds to the broad humour of the play. The whole scene must come from Menander's *Kolax*; there was probably no corresponding scene in Menander's *Eunouchos*.

[3] Thraso belongs to the type 'swaggering soldier' (Lat. *miles gloriosus*: Introd. §13). He displays the traditional gullibility of the *miles*, emphasised by the asides of Gnatho and Parmeno ('what a hopeless fool the man is' 418-19) and by his own inability to see when his boasting is being undercut ('I thought it was an old one' 428) or when Gnatho's adulatory responses are double-edged (393-4 n., 397 n., 403 n., 409 n., 452 n.). But his boasting takes an interestingly different form. Whereas the traditional *miles* boasts of his military and amatory successes (the opening scene of Plaut. *Mil.* is well worth reading for comparison), Thraso prides himself on his ability to

please others ('I have a real knack...' 395-6) and on his his wit at other people's expense (the elephant trainer's 412-15 and the Rhodian's 419-26); and his almost pathetic desire to be loved by Thais (446 n.) contrasts with the usual absurd confidence of the character in his own irresistibility. There is also the question to what extent Thraso is based on Bias in Menander's *Kolax* (30 n.). There are surviving fragments of *Kolax* (frs. 2-4) which show Bias as priding himself on three things, his drinking ability, his wit, and his success with women: Terence has imitated the second of these but not the other two. So, in this scene at least, Thraso is neither the stock type nor an exact replica of Menander's Bias. The names of soldiers in comedy tend to reflect their military pretensions: 'Thraso' mean 'Bold', and echoes names like 'Thrasonides' and 'Thrasyleon' found in Menander.

[4] Gnatho in this scene puts into practice the art of flattery about which he boasted in his opening monologue, with Parmeno's asides ('a wicked liar' 419, 'To hell with you' 431) underlining the effrontery of the technique. But at the end of the scene (434 n.) he takes on another role, that of advising his master on love (as does the parasite at Men. *Dysk.* 50-80), thus moving out of the second class of parasites (flatterers) and into the third (practical helpers and schemers) (Introd. §12). In his language Gnatho maintains the colourfulness of his previous scene (232-69 n.) with vivid images (406 n., 417 n., 438 n., 439 n.) and extravagant forms of flattery (401-2 n., 452 n.).

[5] The metre reverts to spoken verse (ia⁶), which is the most appropriate metre for swift witty dialogue (Introd. §28).

391 Thais really sent me many thanks?: Thraso and Gnatho enter in mid-conversation (207 n.). Cicero (*On Friendship* 98) quotes Gnatho's response 'heartfelt thanks' as an example of the flatterer's technique of 'increasing' what the hearer wants to hear.

393-4 That's a real triumph for her: This remark on the surface flatters the soldier but underneath bears an ironical secondary implication. For the Romans a triumph was the the spectacular home-coming procession of a victorious general in which his booty and some of his vanquished enemies were paraded. Ostensibly the meaning here is 'an occasion for celebration', but there is also the suggestion that Thais is the victorious general who has Pamphila for her booty and Thraso as her victim.

p.183   **397 That is something which has always struck me:** This sounds polite, but can be interpreted sarcastically ('So I've noticed').

The king: Terence does not feel it necessary to specify which king Thraso is supposed to be serving; there is a similarly anonymous reference to serving 'in the king's army' at *Heaut.* 117 (p. 105). The implied reference is to one of the Hellenistic kings who came into power after the death of Alexander the Great in 323 B.C.; in a similar context the soldier at Plaut. *Mil.* 75 is serving king Seleucus (312-

281 B.C.), who founded the Seleucid dynasty in Syria.

401-2 held you...in high favour: Lit. 'carried you in his eyes'. Gnatho is straining for superlative expressions.

He did indeed: The premature interruption underlines Thraso's absurd eagerness to be praised.

403 How wonderful!: The secondary meaning is 'amazing, unbelievable'.

405 as if - do you know?: Thraso, for all his alleged quickness of wit, cannot summon up the appropriate phrase.

406 rid his mind of: Gnatho uses the colourful image 'spue out' (Lat. *exspuere*).

409 *Very* select: Lit. 'a man of no friends'. The implication of the Latin is either that the king must be desperate if he chooses Thraso, or that Thraso scarcely counts as a friend.

413 Indian elephants: War-elephants formed an important part of the armies of the Hellenistic monarchs, and tend to figure in the exotic boasts of the swaggering soldiers of comedy (cf. Plaut. *Mil.* 30). Elephants had appeared in Italy in the invading armies of Pyrrhus and Hannibal in the third century, and were beginning to be used sporadically by the Romans themselves in Terence's day.

417 You had him by the throat: The image is vivid; it may be drawn from warfare or from the gladiatorial arena.

p.184 **419 a wicked liar:** Lit. 'a committer of sacrilege', a term of abuse used only twice by Plautus, both times of pimps (*Pseud.* 363, *Rud.* 706), but more widely by Terence.

420 dealt with: This is another image of single combat (lit. 'touched', i.e. 'stung', 'scored a hit on'), this time in Thraso's mouth.

that man from Rhodes: It appears from two surviving fragments of Menander's *Kolax* (frs. 3 and 8) that in Menander's version (i) the soldier's wit was directed not at a Rhodian but at a Cypriote, and (ii) the witticism took a different form, namely a reference to the proverbial Cypriote ox which fed on dung ('you Cypriote ox' = 'you dung-eater'). Terence has changed the witticism to one more likely to be intelligible to a Roman audience (426 n.) and also the nationality of the victim: the Rhodians were in the news at Rome in Terence's time because of political quarrels following the Rhodian behaviour during the Second Macedonian War (171-167 B.C.).

426 Why should you be a hare who runs with the hounds?: Lit. 'You are a hare: do you pursue delicacies?'. According to Donatus the point of the saying is 'You are seeking in another what can be found in yourself': a hare, which is itself a delicacy, should not itself be seeking delicacies (or, being game itself, should not be seeking game). The implication is that the Rhodian youth is himself sexually desirable, and should not be making advances to Thraso's girl. According to a late Roman writer known as Vopiscus, soldiers in comedy were in the habit of telling old jokes as part of the stock characterisation. Vopiscus quotes this line as an example, but ascribes it to Livius Andronicus (the founder of stage drama at Rome) instead of to Terence. Whether the line occurred in one of Livius' plays or not, the implication seems to be that this is an old Roman witticism which the audience would recognise as such, even though Thraso is claiming it as his own.

434 By the way...: These words mark the transition from the comic banter of the first three quarters of the scene to the more relevant matter of the last quarter. They pick up the theme of Thraso's alleged fancy for the girl (143-4 n.), and Gnatho's suggestion that he might invite her to dinner just to annoy Thais foreshadows a future development of the plot.

438 It galls you: Lit. 'it burns you'. Gnatho again uses fire imagery (274 n.).

p.185   **439 one way of stopping it:** The image this time is medical (lit. 'only one remedy': Lat. *remedium*), with an allusion to the metaphor of love as a disease (225 n.).

440 Pamphila: Not only does Pamphila not appear in the play but she is named only five times, being otherwise referred to chiefly as 'the girl' (Lat. *virgo*, lit. 'maiden'). The implication is that she is regarded as an element in the plot rather than as a character with whom we are meant to identify or sympathise (Introd. §2). The name 'Pamphila' (lit. 'all-loving') recurs as a young girl's name in *Phormio* and *Adelphoe*.

445 cut her to the quick: Lit. 'bite her' (Lat. *mordere*).

446 If only she really loved me: This adds a pathetic touch to Thraso's character. Donatus offers a long note, which is worth considering, even if in the end it seems misguided: 'This line illustrates the character of the soldier and Gnatho in an economic manner: it makes it plausible that the soldier can readily bear Thais' preference for Phaedria, in that he has always realised that she does not love him. For, if it were not so, either Phaedria has to be excluded from her favours or the conclusion of the play becomes tragic because of the grief of the soldier...We should remember that comic poets do not present their ridiculous characters as entirely stupid or unfeeling, for there is no pleasure for the spectator when the person who is being deluded is a complete idiot.' To judge from his *Miles*, Plautus would not have agreed with the last sentence.

451 True: I hadn't thought of that: This response underlines Thraso's lack of comprehension. Gnatho's remark is true but only up to a point. Loving the soldier's presents is not the same thing as loving the soldier, but Thraso is unable to make the distinction.

452 you hadn't given your mind to it: The scene ends with a patently absurd piece of flattery.

III. ii: THAIS, THRASO, GNATHO, PARMENO, PYTHIAS
(454-506, pp. 185-7)

[1] Thais emerges from her house and is pressed by Thraso to accept his invitation to dinner. Parmeno seizes the opportunity to deliver Phaedria's presents. Thais takes these inside, and departs with Thraso, after telling her maid Pythias what to do if Chremes appears.

[2] This third soldier-parasite scene does advance the plot in two respects: it moves the action one stage nearer to Thraso's dinner-party, and it achieves the entry of Chaerea into Thais' house. It is not clear how much of the scene derives from Menander's *Kolax*, how much from his *Eunouchos*, and how much from Terence's own invention. Three things are reasonably certain: (i) the Chaerea character must have entered the courtesan's house at this point in Menander's *Eunouchos*; (ii) at least one line of the scene comes directly from *Kolax*, since by chance we possess the corresponding line of the Greek play (498 n.); (iii) neither Menander's *Eunouchos* nor his *Kolax* can have had five speaking characters here, granted the restriction of the number of speaking actors in Greek New Comedy to three (Introd. §24): this looks like evidence that Terence has combined characters from both plays into a single scene.

[3] The scene adds little to the characterisation, now that the outlines of the main characters have been firmly established. Thais' main motive is to keep on the right side of the solder until her hold on the girl is secure. She goes along with Thraso's invitation ('When you like; I won't keep you waiting' 460), even though she is waiting for the girl's brother to call (206, p. 172), and she is not too eager to receive Phaedria's gifts under Thraso's nose (463 n.). Thraso is impatient of delays ('Must we stand around?' 465, 'Are - we - going?' 492, 'Can't we go?' 506) and scornful of his rival's presents (471 n.); and there are several hints of the traditional swaggering soldier in his lecherous remark about the eunuch ('I know what I'd do to that eunuch' 479), his alleged parading of his battles and scars (482-3 n.), and his inability to perceive when he is being mocked (497 n.). After his scene with Chaerea, Parmeno reverts to acting as the loyal slave of Phaedria, praising his gifts (472-8) and contrasting his reasonableness with Thraso's absurd demands ('And the donor of *these* gifts...' 480-5); he also gives as good as he gets in the slanging match with Thraso and Gnatho ('The man's sub-human' 460, 'you scum of the earth' 489). Gnatho has comparatively little to say in this scene; there are allusions to the parasite's traditional greed for food (458 n., 491 n.) and to the flatterer's traditional mockery of his patron (498 n.).

[4] The spoken verse (ia⁶) continues.

454-9 I'm sure I heard...why delay?: This is presumably the first time that Thais and Thraso have met since the soldier returned to Athens with Pamphila, since the communication in lines 137-42 (p. 170) reads as if it was carried out by messenger; so the stage is set for a formal homecoming scene (Introd. §30). Terence uses some of the conventional formulae here ('I'm sure I heard...there he is...Welcome' 'how are you?'. 'come along to dinner'), but in the end cuts the formalities rather short; this is not for arbitrary reasons but to reflect the unseemly haste of Thraso and Gnatho (457 n., 458 n.). Moreover, the dinner invitation is amusingly inverted, being here given *by* the returning travellers instead of to them. So Terence is not merely using the conventions here but exploiting them to particular effect.

456 my sweetheart: Lit. 'my kiss' (Lat. *savium*), an effusive term of endearment suited to the soldier. The word is not used elsewhere in Terence, and appears only in exaggerated contexts in Plautus (e.g. *Poen.* 366).

457 the girl: Thraso uses the word *fidicina* ('string-player': 133 n.) for Pamphila, which is some indication of how he regards her (i.e. as an entertainer); this contrasts with the term *virgo* used by Thais and Chaerea (440 n.).

There's gallantry!: Parmeno is being ironic. Thraso has cut short the conventional greetings in his haste to claim credit for the gift of Pamphila.

458 come along to dinner: why delay?: Gnatho, like the typical parasite, is eager to eat.

460 sub-human: Lit. '[not] born of human stock'. This vivid insult is prompted by Gnatho's unseemly haste for food (458), and has of itself no deep philosophical significance. But it is perhaps worth noting that behind the rhetoric there lies Terence's favourite concept of 'humanity' as the basic ideal of human behaviour (Introd. §15).

461 Here's my cue: Lit. 'I will go up', the standard 'approach formula', here used to terminate an overheard dialogue (Introd. §29).

463 I'm obliged to you: This remark has puzzled commentators even since Donatus, who suggests that Thais, taken aback by Parmeno's appearance, can only offer an empty politeness. But presumably, having gone to some trouble to remove Phaedria from Thraso's sight, she does not wish to be approached by Phaedria's slave in Thraso's presence. In effect she is saying 'Nice to see you, Parmeno, but not now'.

p.186   **469 Here, hurry along:** These instructions are shouted to unnamed fellow slaves inside the house (the Latin verb is plural).

471 Three hundred drachmas: This is obviously meant as a derisory amount for a supposely exotic slave-girl, and is no evidence for the price actually paid by Phaedria (169 n.).

473 looks like a gentleman: The Latin is *liberalis*, lit. 'free born' and hence 'well born' (cf. Introd. §15).

476-7 literature, music, athletics: These were the three traditional areas of Greek education. But to the Romans the accomplishments would seem more exotic, since neither music nor athletics was part of the Roman educational system.

any young gentleman's: 473 n.

482-3 recount his battles and display his scars: Parmeno assumes that Thraso is the typical swaggering soldier (cf. 391ff n. 3).

p.187 **491 steal from a corpse:** Lit. 'take food from the flames', a proverbial expression alluding to the practice of burning food and drink together with the bodies of the dead. A vivid illustration is provided by a poem of Catullus (59), which describes an old whore pursuing a loaf of bread as it rolls away from a funeral pyre, only to be caught and beaten by the undertaker. The point is that Gnatho must be ravenous if he has to flatter a person like Thraso to get a meal.

493 I'll be back in a minute: Thais' brief exit into her house with the gifts is clearly signposted, as is her return at 499 ('But here comes Thais' 499) But there is nothing in the text to indicate Parmeno's departure after 496 or to suggest where he is supposed to be going (cf. 189 n.).

497 What are you laughing at: In the Latin text this is preceded by *hahahae*, given to Gnatho, who is laughing at Parmeno's last remark and has to cover up with a hastily invented explanation.

498 that tale about the man from Rhodes: This is a neat back-reference to the previous scene (419-33, p. 184). As it happens, the corresponding line from Menander's *Kolax* is preserved, spoken by Strouthias to Bias (fr. 3: 'I laugh when I think of the tale about the Cypriote'), which (i) confirms that Terence is using Menander's *Kolax* here and (ii) shows that the device of the back-reference is also from Menander.

500-3 Look after them well...: Thais' instructions to Pythias are presumably spoken aside from Thraso, who, if he heard them, might suspect that Chremes was yet another rival lover.

501 Chremes: This is the first indication of the name of Pamphila's supposed brother.

506 You follow me: The 'you' is plural, which is the evidence that Thais emerged with (at least) two maids at 500, as in the Penguin stage direction. With this formulaic exit line (390 n.) Thais and her maids depart for Thraso's house (right). What happens to Pythias is not so clear: the Penguin translation makes her re-enter the house, but the scene-headings in the MSS imply that she remains on stage during Chremes' following monologue.

III. iii: CHREMES, PYTHIAS (507-38, pp. 188-9)

[1] Chremes arrives, voicing his suspicions of Thais' designs, and is greeted by Pythias. He grudgingly agrees to go to see Thais at Thraso's, and leaves with another maid Dorias.

[2] The direction of Chremes' entry cannot easily be established.

It appears that he has a country estate at Sunium (519 n.) and is due to return there the next day ('I shan't be in town' 533), but this does not prove that he is just arriving from the country. On the contrary he has already been in Athens for his first visit to Thais (below, n. 4), and it later transpires that he has a residence in the city where the old nurse of the family can be found. It suits the staging of the play best if this town house is notionally situated off-stage left; and, if we imagine Chremes now arriving from it, he will enter from the opposite side to that on which Thais has just departed (right).

[3] With Chremes' arrival, the focus is firmly fixed on Pamphila's identity. Chremes' scepticism about Thais' questions echoes Parmeno's scepticism of her whole story in the first act, but the effect is to create some amusing dramatic irony rather than to sow any seeds of doubt. The Roman audience would in any case be predisposed to accept the identification of Pamphila as Chremes' sister (110 n.), and the various hints dropped here by Chremes confirm the identification beyond a shadow of doubt. It cannot be coincidence that Chremes has a property at Sunium, and that he lost a sister some time ago who, if alive, would be exactly the same age as Pamphila (519 n., 526 n.). The dramatic question now is not who Pamphila will turn out to be, but how and when and with what results her identity will be established.

[4] There is a puzzling discrepancy between Chremes' account of his dealings with Thais and what Thais herself told us at the end of the first act (203-6 n.). Contrary to the impression given there, Chremes here makes it quite clear that he has already visited Thais ('When I called...' 512, 'Now she's sent for me again' 528, 'I'm damned if I'll come a third time' 530). Since it is hard to twist Thais' words at 203-6 to imply that the first visit has already taken place, Terence seems to be guilty of careless writing, and the suspicion arises in cases like this that the discrepancy is due to faulty adaptation of the Greek original. Some have seen this awkwardness as confirmation that Terence recast Menander's first act to remove an expository monologue (81ff n. 2), with lines 203-6 as a hastily written stopgap to provide an exit speech for Thais. The alternative is to suppose that Terence invented or expanded Chremes' speech here without proper consideration of what he had written in 203-6. But neither of these approaches provides a very satisfactory solution.

[5] Chremes is described as an *adulescens* in the scene headings of the manuscripts (and by Thais: 204, p. 172), but does not fit very easily into the traditional character type (Introd. §1). He is not a young lover, nor (as some young men in comedy are) the friend and helper of a young lover, and the role that he plays (that of the 'recognition agent' who solves the problem of an an unknown identity) is more often played by an elderly relative (like Crito at *Andr.* 796ff, pp. 78-9) or a slave or old nurse of the family. So the audience will for once have had no clear preconceptions about his character. In this

scene Terence chooses to emphasise Chremes' suspiciousness ('this was all a plot' 515, 'I said there was a plot' 532) and his unwillingness to cooperate ('I'm damned if I'll come a third time' 530); his language to Pythias ('Impossible', 'Certainly not'. 'Go to the devil' 534-6) is brusque to the point of rudeness. Donatus (on 507) sees 'rusticity' as the hallmark of the character, which he explicitly says is derived from Menander; there is a parallel of a sort in the suspicions of the young rustic Gorgias in Menander's *Dyskolos* when faced with the more sophisticated townbred Sostratos. It is interesting that the name 'Chremes' occurs elsewhere in Terence as the name of an old man (in *Andr.*, *Heaut.*, and *Phorm.*), which is how it is regarded by later writers such as Horace (*Epodes* 1. 33, *Satires* 1. 10. 40); it does not occur in extant Menander or in Plautus.

[6] Pythias falls into the category of *ancilla* ('maid') (Introd. §14). She has relatively few lines in this scene, but establishes herself as a 'bold, lively, little hussy' (to quote one modern description); her language is much more intimate and alluring than in the Penguin translation (531-7 n.). The name 'Pythias', which occurs in Menander but not elsewhere in Roman comedy, is used by Horace as a typical name for a scheming female slave (*Art of Poetry* 238).

[7] The spoken verse continues for the third successive scene.

507-31 The more I think...It's Chremes: Chremes delivers an entrance monologue, which is partly narrative, partly reflective in character. If Pythias is still on stage (506 n.), this is another example of an overheard entrance monologue, but Chremes does not see Pythias, nor does she make any asides. If Pythias has gone inside, Chremes' monologue is delivered on an empty stage, which is comparatively rare in Terence: there are only two other examples in *Eunuchus* (Introd. §22).

511 (In case any of you...know the woman): The bracket here might be taken to imply a conscious address to the audience, but this is not in Terence's manner. Chremes is thinking aloud, and the Latin says 'anybody' rather than 'any of you'.

512 she found an excuse for keeping me waiting: Better 'she found an excuse for *detaining* me'. Thais was eager to interview Chremes, and had no reason to keep him waiting.

513 she'd been at her prayers: Better 'had just completed a sacrifice'. Sacrifices were regularly followed by a dinner, and it was common practice on such occasions to invite visitors to join in the meal (cf. Plaut. *Rud.* 342-4). Thais was thus inviting Chremes to a prolonged discussion over dinner.

519 Sunium: 115 n.

526 no more than sixteen: 318 n.

531 Hi there, is anyone at home? It's Chremes: This is a formulaic way to terminate an entrance monologue delivered on an empty stage. If Pythias has been on stage all the time, she does not emerge from the door but approaches Chremes (unexpectedly) from the side, which would be a bolder and more effective staging.

531-7 Oh, my dear young man...where she is?: Pythias speaks in highly alluring tones: hence Chremes' brusque replies. The words here translated 'dear' (Lat. *lepidus*) and 'please' (Lat. *amabo*) are words particularly associated with courtesans: the tone might better be represented by the English 'nice' and 'my darling'.

p.189 **538 Dorias:** Thais had specifically instructed Pythias herself to escort Chremes to the soldier's party (501-3, p. 187), and Terence gives no explicit reason for the change of plan. It is a reasonable conjecture that in Menander's version Pythias did accompany Chremes; Terence, with more actors at his disposal, has 'thickened' the plot by adding Dorias as an extra character (Introd. §24). Chremes and Dorias depart right in the direction of the soldier's house (228 n.); Pythias must go back inside Thais'.

III. iv-v: ANTIPHO, CHAEREA (539-614, pp. 189-93)

[1] Antipho, a fellow guardsman from the Piraeus, arrives to look for Chaerea, who is supposed to have arranged a dinner for his friends. Chaerea emerges from Thais' house in the eunuch costume, and tells Antipho about his new girl and his successful use of the eunuch disguise. They go off together to Antipho's house, so that Chaerea can change out of his eunuch costume.

[2] Antipho is another *adulescens*. He belongs to the sub-type 'friend and helper of young lover' (507ff n. 5), but has little real character: he appears only in this scene, and his sole function is to provide a listener for Chaerea's story. Donatus expressly tells us that Antipho 'was invented to avoid a long monologue by Chaerea as in Menander', which must mean that the character was introduced by Terence. Antipho's utterances are restricted to brief questions and exclamations (the name should mean 'one who speaks back'), but there is an obvious gain in liveliness and humour.

[3] The characteristics established for Chaerea on his previous appearance (292ff n. 3) are here reinforced. He is infatuated with Pamphila ('I fell for this one' 567, 'To cut it short, I'm in love' 568, 'how I can make this girl my own' 613-14); he is preoccupied with physical attractiveness ('I've a connoisseur's eye for a lovely woman' 566); he is impetuous ('a suggestion which I jumped at' 571, 'Was I to lose the chance offered me...?' 604-6); and he is ready to embrace plausible arguments (591 n.). The rape of Pamphila leaves him 'excited and happy' (555) and with not a shred of guilt, even though of the traditional young men's excuses he can claim neither wine nor darkness (Introd. §2). The whole idea of rape offends our modern susceptibilities, but there is no sign in this scene that Terence means his audience to react with revulsion, Chaerea evidently intends a

continuing relationship; our final verdict will depend on his reaction when he discovers Pamphila's true birth .

[4] The metre reverts to recitative, as in Chaerea's previous appearance (292ff n. 6); it is a mark of the excitement of the scene that even the narrative portions are in recitative. Metrically speaking, the scene falls into four sections (on the metres see Introd. §28):

(i) Antipho's opening monologue is in the relatively uncommon ia^7;

(ii) Chaerea's elated entrance speech (from 'Anyone here?' 549) is in mixed recitative metres;

(iii) the first part of Chaerea's narrative (from 'I beg you' 562 to 'He could and gladly' 591) is in ia^8, the most excited recitative metre;

(iv) the rest is in ia^7, as in the opening section.

539-48 Some of the lads...see if I can find out: This is another example of an entrance monologue delivered on an empty stage (507-31 n.). Antipho, coming from the harbour, must enter from the left (289-91 n.); he thus avoids meeting Chremes and Dorias as they depart right (538 n.).

539 docks: i.e. the Piraeus, as the Latin explicitly says (290 n.).

540 club together for dinner: There are several other references to this practice in Roman comedy, but always by its Greek name (*symbola*), so that the practice itself must be Greek.

546 is it him or isn't it? It is...I'll just step back: At first sight Terence seems to be playing with recognition and eavesdropping formulae in a Plautine manner (Introd. §30), but here Antipho's hesitation is justified: Chaerea is not immediately recognisable in his eunuch costume.

549 Anyone here? Nobody: This is an ironic touch: speakers of overheard entrance monologues do not usually look for eavesdroppers, let alone wrongly declare that there are none present.

551 face death while I can bear it: This utterance bears an interesting resemblance to that of another ecstatic lover, Pamphilus at *Andr.* 960-1 (p. 88), who declares '...my immortality is won so long as trouble doesn't interrupt my happiness'. Donatus specifically says that the latter passage is taken over from Menander's *Eunouchos,* where it must have come either from Chaerea's speech here or from his later exultation at his forthcoming marriage (1031-49, pp. 215-16). The two sentiments are similar but different: here Chaerea is willing to face death before his happiness is spoiled, in *Andria* Pamphilus feels himself immortal.

p.190 **557 I'll go:** This is the standard approach formula 'I'll go up' (461 n.).

do him the service I see he wants...: This must be ironic, since Chaerea has just expressed pleasure that there are no busybodies to question him.

560 welcome: Lat. *salve* (304 n.).

561 The very man I wanted to see: Antipho does not count as a busybody, and Chaerea is now delighted to find a friendly listener for his story. Terence has neatly transformed Menander's monologue into a dialogue situation (above, n. 2).

.191 **581-2 leaving a few new young ones to wait on the girl:** This looks like a relic of Menander's version in which Pythias accompanied Chremes to the soldier's (538 n.). In Terence's version, Pythias remains behind but is not present at the time of the rape. We have to assume that the rape took place while Pythias was outside talking to Chremes (531-8, pp. 188-9), which gives little time unless we assume that she was on stage for the whole of the Chremes scene (506 n.).

584-5 Jupiter pouring the shower of gold...: Danae was the daughter of Acrisius, king of Argos, who in response to an oracle that he would be killed by Danae's son, imprisoned her in an underground chamber (or, in some versions of the legend, in a tower) to prevent her becoming pregnant. Zeus, however, visited Danae as a shower of gold, and Danae duly bore a son, Perseus, who killed Acrisius. The reference to this picture presumably comes from Menander, and is interesting evidence for the kind of painting that might be found in an Athenian courtesan's house. Chaerea's view of Jupiter 'turning himself into a man and crawling secretly across another man's roof, coming down...through the skylight' (588-9) is not strictly compatible with entry into Danae's chamber as a shower of gold, though there are wall-paintings from Pompeii which show both the shower of gold and Jupiter in human form.

589 skylight: Lat. *impluvium*. This detail suggests a Roman house rather than a Greek (Roman houses had a rectangular hole in the roof to catch rainwater and let out smoke), so that Terence has translated Chaerea's descrition into Roman terms.

590 who shakes the topmost towers...: The parody of the Roman tragedian Ennius (see the Penguin footnote) must also be the work of Terence: we cannot tell whether there was a similar parody of a Greek tragedy in Menander.

591 Couldn't a mere man like me...?: Donatus' comment (on 584) is worth quoting: 'It was a good idea to introduce the picture suddenly to motivate the attack on the girl, since Chaerea had not come with the intention of raping her straight off but of seeing, hearing, and being together with her' (cf. 574). This is one of several remarks of his (cf. 604-5 n.) designed to exonerate Chaerea from the charge of premeditated rape. It is possible that Donatus has correctly interpreted Terence's intention (cf. 373 n.), though it would be in character for Chaerea to seize upon a plausible excuse for his behaviour (above, n. 3).

.192 **602 like this:** A stage direction, suggesting some comic posturing by Chaerea.

604-5 lose the chance offered me...so unexpected: Donatus comments: 'For he had envisaged something else...not what the picture and the opportunity persuaded him to do'.

608 Where? At your house? / No, no, at Discus's: There
is no real conflict here with lines 541-2, where a place had been fixed
but nothing was ready there. Chaerea must have decided (for reasons
unspecified) to transfer the location to Discus', and Antipho's 'At your
house?' must be simply a guess.

609 What a way!: The location of Discus' house some distance
away has a dramatic point: it keeps Chaerea off stage long enough (in
fact to 840, p. 205) for the news of the rape to come out and also for
the Thais-Chremes-Thraso aspect of the plot to be developed.

610 Where can I change?: There is a practical problem here
which Terence chooses to ignore. Chaerea has given his own clothes
to the eunuch (572), who is still wearing them when he appears in the
next act (701, p. 197). Chaerea can scarcely have taken a spare set of
clothes with him when he entered Thais' house, and he does not now
dare to go home to get some. There is no mention here of the obvious
solution, to borrow some clothes from Antipho.

614 Right you are: Antipho and Chaerea probably exit left
(i.e. Antipho's house is notionally situated in the direction of the
harbour), so that they do not meet the returning Dorias at the beginning of the next scene. The act-break marked here for Terence by the
renaissance editors probably again corresponds to the act-break in the
Greek original (390 n.).

IV. i: DORIAS (615-28, p. 193)

[1] Dorias returns from Thraso's house (right), explaining that
Chremes' arrival there had caused a row between Thais and Thraso.

[2] The effect of the scene is to divert attention away from the
Chaerea-Pamphila affair back to the Thais-Thraso relationship, which
is now centred on the party at the soldier's house.

[3] Dorias' speech is an entrance monologue on an empty stage
(507-31 n.). Her excitedness is emphasised by the use of recitative
instead of the usual spoken verse for narrative, mixed metres at first
and then tr^7 for the second half (from 'Thraso imagined' 623).

621 about his sister: Dorias takes Chremes' relationship to
Pamphila for granted. The audience will not question the identification, even though it has yet to be confirmed (507ff n. 3).

623-5 brought in a rival...told a boy to fetch Pamphila:
This is a back reference to the earlier scene where Gnatho advised
Thraso to retaliate in this way if Thais brought Phaedria to dinner
(434 n.). The substitution of Chremes for Phaedria as the rival creates
a pleasing irony: some have supposed that in Menander's version it
was actually the Phaedria character who arrived at the party. Note the
suggestion that the soldier has after all not yet renounced all claim to

Pamphila: it is this which relates the whole dinner-party episode to the Chaerea-Pamphila half of the dual plot.

625-6 That girl at a dinner party?...Certainly not: Pamphila was an accomplished lute-player (133 n.), and Thraso obviously wanted her to perform as an entertainer at the party. But this was not a respectable occupation for citizen girls, and Thais would not want Chremes to see his 'sister' behaving in this way.

627 removed her jewels: This action has puzzled commentators since Donatus: most probably Thais feared physical violence from the soldier and gave the jewels to Dorias for safe keeping.

628 slip away from the party: We might have expected Dorias to go into Thais' house at this point to put the jewels in a safe place, in which case her monologue would have been a rare example of an entrance-and-exit monologue. There is no indication in the text that she sees Phaedria approaching or that he notices her, and she does not appear in the scene headings of the MSS in the following scene. But in fact she must remain on stage, since she suddenly speaks again at 656 (p. 194) and there is no sign of an exit and re-entry before this point. As we have seen earlier in the case of Pythias (506 n.), Terence is not always clear about exits, but the awkwardness of staging confirms the suspicion that Terence has added the part of Dorias to the play (538 n.). If there was a corresponding speech in Menander's *Eunouchos*, it was presumably spoken by Pythias, who would have gone intside at the end of it and discovered the rape of Pamphila.

IV. ii: PHAEDRIA, DORIAS (629-42, pp. 193-4)

[1] Phaedria returns from the country (left), longing for a glimpse of Thais.

[2] Phaedria's return marks another shift in the focus of the plot. He has been off stage since 224 (p. 174), ostensibly to allow Thais to complete arragements with Thraso for the delivery of Pamphila. Terence has used his absence to introduce two complications to Thais' plans, the rape of Pamphila by Chaerea and the quarrel at the soldier's party over Chremes. We are now ready to return to the Phaedria-Thais relationship with which the play started.

[3] The immediate effect of Phaedria's monologue is to reinforce the contrast between his character and Chaerea's. After seeing the exuberant Chaerea in action, we are reintroduced to the introspective Phaedria, who is as indecisive as ever ('I suppose it doesn't matter...but it does' 638).

[4] Phaedria's monologue resembles Chremes' at 507-31 in that (i) it is partly narrative, partly reflective, and (ii), though apparently delivered on an occupied stage, it is not interrupted by asides. The metre reverts briefly to spoken verse (ia^6) to underline the change of mood from Dorias' monologue.

633 passed our farm: It is a standard situation of Roman comedy that a family whose town house is located on the stage also owns a country farm, which is conceived of as being no great distance from the city. Phaedria's original intention had been to go and work on the farm (220, p. 173) to forget his troubles.

636-7 Must I really spend two days alone...?: Phaedria boasted that he could stay away for *three* days (223, p. 173); it is no surprise that he has failed to fulfil his boast.

p.194 **640-1 A long-distance view of love:** Lit. 'to love from the most distant line': it is not clear what precise image Terence has in mind. Donatus (on 367) talks of seeing, talking to, being with, etc., as the five 'lines' of love, which he implies go in a fixed sequence.

642 Why the devil is Pythias rushing out...?: cf. 291 n.

IV. iii: PYTHIAS, PHAEDRIA, DORIAS
(643-67, pp. 194-5)

[1] Pythias rushes out of Thais' house, having discovered the rape of Pamphila, and blames Phaedria for giving the eunuch to Thais. Phaedria goes into his own house to look for the eunuch.

[2] Phaedria's return does not after all herald any development in his own relationship with Thais; instead he is himself swept into Chaerea's business, and the focus returns to the Chaerea-Pamphila affair. So the Phaedria-Thais half of the dual plot remains subordinate, though, as often, Terence is linking the two halves by involving one young man in the love affair of the other (Introd. §17).

[3] As a consequence we see a different side of Phaedria's character: he is no longer the helpless elegiac lover but the active investigator of his brother's behaviour. But it is Pythias who dominates the scene; she continues to be vividly drawn (507ff n. 6), though her language takes on a different colour. Most striking is the violence of her abuse against the eunuch as perpetrator of the rape ('Brute, monster' 643, 'I'd scratch his eyes out, the poisonous snake!' 648) and even against Phaedria as the giver of the gift ('you go to hell' 651-2). There is some suspicion that she is exaggerating the eunuch's crimes: whether or not Chaerea actually tore Pamphila's hair and clothes after the rape (645-6 n.), he certainly did not steal things from the house (661). Dorias plays a very minor role in the scene, simply offering two exclamations about the enormity of the deed (656, 664).

[4] The scene offers a different perspective of the rape of Pamphila from that offered by Chaerea himself after the event (539ff n. 3). The major emotions expressed by Pythias and Dorias are

(i) a sense of outrage at the wickedness of the crime ('a wicked thing' 644, 'to add insult to injury' 645, 'it's monstrous' 664),

(ii) sympathy for Pamphila ('the poor thing' 646, 'The girl does nothing but cry...' 659), and

(iii) a sense of amazement that a eunuch was able to perpetrate such a deed ('it's fantastic' 656, 'I never heard of such a thing' 664, 'It certainly never crossed my mind' 666).

Phaedria, who is sceptical of the whole story ('*How* could a eunuch...' 657), for the moment keeps his views to himself.

[5] The metre reverts to recitative to reflect Pythias' emotional state, mixed metres at first and then ia⁷ (from 'The girl does nothing but cry' 659).

645-6 to add insult to injury...: The obvious interpretation of these lines (advanced by Donatus) is that the girl resisted the rape and that in Chaerea's struggle to overpower her he tore her dress and hair. But there is the problem (also perceived by Donatus) that the text actually says '*after* he'd wronged the girl...', making the tearing of dress and hair an act of gratuitous violence after the event. This could perhaps be regarded as a deliberate exaggeration by Pythias (who was not in fact present: 581-2 n.) of the enormity of Chaerea's behaviour. It should also be noted that the tearing of the girl's dress and hair is a standard feature of lovers' quarrels in Latin love poetry (e.g. Ovid *Amores* 1.7).

650 I'll go and ask her: cf. 557 n.

655 felt like I do: Pythias seems to mean, not drunk but angry because the victim of outrageous behaviour.

656 My dear Pythias...: Dorias, who has been silent since her monologue at 615-28 (p. 193) suddenly interrupts the Pythias-Phaedria conversation (628 n.).

.195 **663 please go and see:** The word translated 'please' is *amabo* (better 'my darling'); the seductive tone used by Pythias in her scene with Chremes reappears briefly (531-7 n.).

IV. iv: PHAEDRIA, DORUS, PYTHIAS, DORIAS
(668-726, pp. 195-8)

[1] Phaedria reappears with the reluctant Dorus, whom Pythias and Dorias do not recognise. When Dorus admits that he changed clothes with Chaerea, Phaedria tries to cover up the situation, and takes Dorus back into the house to torture him. The maids decide not to tell Thais what has happened.

[2] The scene moves the Chaerea-Pamphila half of the plot a step further towards the unmasking of Chaerea. Its effect depends partly on dramatic irony as Pythias and Phaedria gradually discover the truth of the eunuch substitution, and partly on its slapstick humour as Phaedria abuses, threatens, and beats the hapless Dorus. Four speaking actors are involved. It seems likely that Dorias is the one who was not in the Greek original (538 n.): she has very little to say until the end of the scene, and there it is a little surprising that the more forceful Pythias turns to her for advice.

[3] Phaedria is much more assertive than he has been previously; note his abusive language (668-70 n., cf. 'dumb brute' 696, 'scoundrel' 717), his physical violence to Dorus (715 n.), and his series of techniques for dealing with the situation (700 n., 706 n., 709 n.). Commentators have remarked that Phaedria says nothing in this scene about Pamphila's supposed citizen birth, and have used this omission to reconstruct an opening for the Greek original in which Phaedria did not hear this suggestion (81ff n. 2); but it would have been entirely inappropriate for him to refer to it in Pythias' hearing when his main intention is to cover up the situation.

[4] The scene begins in spoken verse (ia⁶), but reverts to recitative (tr⁷) at 703 (from '*Now* will you believe...'), where the truth about the eunuch substitution is finally established.

668-70 scoundrel...rotten bargain...brute: The Latin in fact has four terms of abuse, *sceleste* ('you scoundrel'), *fugitive* ('you runaway'), *male conciliate* ('you rotten bargain'), and *carnufex* ('you butcher', 'you hangman'). It is unusual for Terence to pile up abuse in this way, whereas Plautus is fond of doing so for comic effect (for an extreme example see *Pseud.* 357-69). In fact there is more abuse in *Eunuchus* than any other play of Terence's, mostly centred on the eunuch trick (cf. 643ff n. 3) and mostly occurring in the second half of the play.

674 Have you caught him, sir?: Here 'sir' is a translation of *amabo*, one of Pythias' favourite words (663 n.).

p.196 **682 gentlemanly and good looking:** These words echo Parmeno's description of Chaerea as the eunuch (473-4, p. 186).

683 in coloured clothes: The ancient commentator Eugraphius asserts that eunuchs generally wore multicoloured clothes. In the illustrated medieval MSS of Terence Chaerea as the eunuch is depicted in a brilliant striped outfit of red and green and brown.

688 worn-out, wrinkled, senile: Pythias' language is even more expressive in the Latin, with a triplet of alliterated words (*uietus, uetus, ueternosus*).

689 the colour of a weasel: Presumably, grey. According to Donatus Terence has misunderstood the Greek original here: Menander actually wrote *galeotes geron* ('a lizard of an old man') with reference to the eunuch's blotched or freckled skin, but Terence confused the Greek words *galeotes* ('lizard') and *gale* ('weasel').

693 a lad of sixteen: In fact Chaerea must have been eighteen to be serving as an ephebe (290 n.). Pythias is exaggerating to emphasise the contrast with Dorus.

697 My brother?...Just now: These six speeches all fit into one six-foot line of Latin verse. Terence's dialogue can be very rapid.

p.197 **700 Then how did you know that he was my brother?:** Phaedria is interrogating Dorus like an advocate in court, in the hope that the story may be proved wrong.

706 Just come over here a little: This is a stock 'withdrawal formula' (Introd §29). Phaedria continues to interrogate Dorus; but, since he has now lost hope that the story may be wrong, he does not wish the maids to hear.

709 the wanton impudence of the man!: If this is said aloud, the reference must be to Dorus, not to Chaerea: Phaedria is now embarking on a new tactic, designed to persuade the maids that Dorus is lying. Alternatively, this is an exclamation aside, referring to Chaerea, which Pythias is not meant to hear.

710 a wicked trick: Lat. *indignum* (70 n.).

713-14 can't tell the truth without torture: The evidence of slaves was admissible only under torture in both Greek and Roman law, the assumption being that they would otherwise lie through excessive loyalty to (or fear of) their masters.

Come along with me: Lit. 'follow me' (506 n.).

.198 **715 Go in at once:** This is followed in the Latin by a cry (*oiei*) from Dorus, which is represented in the Penguin edition by the stage directions. Dorus disappears from the play at this point; he is the only eunuch in Roman comedy, and is predictably a feeble character.

716 without losing face: This suggests that Phaedria is as much concerned with preserving his own reputation (especially with Thais) as with any unselfish covering up for his brother.

718-726 Sure as I live...what's happening: This dialogue represents what was presumably a link monologue by Pythias in the Greek original (in the absence of Dorias: 538 n.). It fulfils two useful functions: (i) it foreshadows Pythias' revenge on Parmeno ('pay him back' 719) as a new development of the plot, and (ii) it postpones the revelation of the rape to Chremes and Thais until Terence is ready to develop its consequences.

721-2 know nothing of what you know: This is advice proverbially offered to slaves (cf. *Heaut.* 748, p. 137).

723 win her gratitude: The 'her' is ambiguous. The obvious reference (suggested by Donatus) is to Pamphila, whose chances of an honourable marriage will be ruined if she is known to have lost her virginity. Some have seen a reference to Thais, but Thais needs to know what has happened to Pamphila and will scarcely be grateful for Pythias' silence.

726 You go and put away those jewels: This is a rather awkward back-reference to 627 (p. 193), which confirms the suspicion that Terence has done some re-stitching in this part of the play.

IV. v: CHREMES, PYTHIAS (727-38, pp. 198-9)

[1] Chremes returns from Thraso's house, rather drunk, and is surprised that Thais, who left before him, has not yet arrived.

[2] We now return to the Thais-Thraso relationship and to the soldier's dinner-party. After Dorias' monologue, we have been expecting Thais to appear, so that the return of Chremes is something of a surprise: the only new point that he brings is that is that he himself had been ejected after Thais had left. The scene adds some more slapstick humour, as the drunken Chremes makes a pass at Pythias (730-2), though it is not nearly as funny as some of the drunken scenes in Plautus (e.g. *Most.* 313-47, *Pseud.* 1246-1334).

[3] Chremes' drunkenness is another unexpected factor. It might possibly be explained in terms of his alleged 'rusticity' (507ff n. 5): as a rather naive countryman, he has been as unable to cope with the temptations of wine as he had been with the wiles of a courtesan and her maid (cf. 736 n.). But we might well suspect that the drunkenness was introduced by Terence as a further means of enlivening the play.

[4] The scene is in ia^8, one of the liveliest of the recitative metres, as befits a drunken scene.

727 a cheat...and a swindle: Chremes refers to the effect of wine, rather than to any deliberate deception by Thais or Thraso.

730 Who's there?: The recognition formula again has a special point in the context (546 n.): in his drunken state Chremes does not recognise Pythias at first glance.

You're a beauty: This is an amusing reversal of Chremes' attitude in his previous scene, where he was suspicious of Pythias' alluring tones. Here Pythias does nothing to encourage him.

p.199 **732 Love needs a bite...:** It is interesting that, when Cicero quotes this same proverb (*On the Nature of the Gods* 2. 60), he refers it specifically to Terence.

736 wasn't that enough for you?: It is another sign of the naivety of Chremes that he did not know how to interpret Thais' nod.

737 I wonder where I got ahead of her: Having left first, Thais should have arrived first. Terence acknowledges the implausibility but offers no explanation. It is no doubt dramatically more effective if Thais is the last to return; Terence could have made her leave last and avoided the problem.

IV. vi: THAIS, CHREMES, PYTHIAS
(739-70, pp. 199-201)

[1] Thais returns from Thraso's, and warns Chremes that Thraso will be coming to remove Pamphila by force. She just has time to send Pythias in to fetch the tokens which will prove Pamphila's identity, before Thraso is seen approaching with an army of followers.

[2] The scene is very much a link scene; it leads into appearance of Thraso to take Pamphila back, which looks like being the climax of the plot element centred on the soldier's dinner-party.

[3] The main interest of the scene is in its characterisation. Thais'

scorn for the soldier is now made abundantly clear ('I can put up with his stupid ways and bragging words...I'll have him horse-whipped' 741-2); and she makes no secret of her contempt for Chremes ('you're not afraid, are you?' 756, 'What a man to defend me!' 770), manipulating him as easily as she has already manipulated Phaedria. The dominant nature of her character is thus firmly established. Chremes' cowardice is a new trait, emphasised by his pathetic pretence of bravery ('Nonsense. Who's afraid? Not me.' 756-7) and his attempt to justify his behaviour ('I'd rather we took preventive action than have to retaliate...' 762); his drunkenness seems to have disappeared.

[4] The recitative is maintained, with changes of metre dividing the scene into three: (i) tr^8 for the initial conversation, (ii) mixed metres for the talk about the sister (from 747 'Where is she?'), and (iii) tr^7 for the soldier's approach (from 755 'Good god, look...').

740 I'll scratch his eyes out: Pythias had made the same threat against the eunuch (648, p. 194). Donatus suggests that this is a particularly female threat and used against lustful males.

743 I was looking for you: This is a common 'response formula' (Introd. §30), typically used (as here) by an overheard monologue speaker to respond to the greetings of an eavesdropper.

745 Me? How?: These abrupt questions suggest the same suspiciousness that Chremes had earlier shown towards Thais (507ff n. 5). He is evidently unaware of the Thais-Thraso-Pamphila situation, nor has he realised that Thraso takes him for a rival lover of Thais.

your sister: Thais talks of Pamphila as Chremes' sister, and Chremes accepts the identification at face value, even though neither was sure of it before and they did not have chance to discuss it further at the soldier's party ('it wasn't the right moment...': 621, p. 193).

746 and a lot more beside: Thais is presumably referring to her quarrel with Phaedria, unless she is simply exaggerating to emphasise Chremes' debt to her.

747 What?: A courtesan's house is scarcely the ideal place for a young well bred girl.

748 I've looked after her: This remark is overlaid with dramatic irony, given that Pamphila has been raped. Duckworth (234) claims that 'the irony is not comic, but pathetic, almost tragic'.

the right thing: Lat. *dignum* (Introd. §16).

p.200 **749 I don't expect a penny in return:** This is disingenuous: Thais does in fact expect a return (in the form of support from Chremes' family: 147-9 n.), and Chremes' reply (750) recognises this.

753 the little box with the proofs: In comedy children who are abandoned or sold or abducted at an early age commonly have with them 'trinkets' or 'tokens' by which their true parentage can be established. Such tokens are a regular feature of the recognition scenes of comedy, notably in Menander's *Epitrepontes*, where the central scene features a dispute over the trinkets found with an abandoned baby, or in Plautus' *Cistellaria*, which is named after a casket (Lat. *cistella*) of identifying trinkets. The best illustration of the nature of the trinkets is provided by the casket of Palaestra at Plaut. *Rud.* 1156-71, which contains a tiny gold sword bearing her father's name, a tiny gold axe bearing her mother's name, a tiny silver sickle, a tiny pair of clasped hands, and a golden locket given by her father on her birthday. There has been no previous mention of any such casket belonging to Pamphila in *Eunuchus*, but the existence of one scarcely comes as a surprise.

754 Look, he's coming: In fact Thraso and his 'army' do not appear for another seventeen lines: the convention is that characters on stage can see people approaching while they are some distance away and still invisible to the audience (Introd. §19).

In the chest: Pythias must exit after this line, though there is no precise indication in the text (cf. 493 n.).

757 My God: Lat. *attat*, an exclamation expressing sudden alarm.

759 dealing with a foreigner: The comic *miles* is typically represented as Greek but not Athenian, so that he has no citizen rights, and few friends, at Athens. The immediate implication is that Thraso will be easy meat for Chremes, but the remark has added significance in the mouth of Thais, who is in exactly this position herself.

764 I'd like some help: The Latin is for 'help' is *aduocatos* (340 n.): Chremes is expecting to find friends in the forum who will provide legal advice and support if it comes to a wrangle with Thraso.

765 Let go: This is in effect a stage direction: Thais physically restrains Chremes as he tries to run off.

p.201   **767 Here they are:** Pythias reappears with the tokens; her return is signalled rather more clearly than her departure (754 n.).

768 give him in charge: i.e. take him to court.

770 champion: The Latin word is *patronus*: there is thus an ironic reversal of the real situation that Chremes is the citizen and it is Thais herself who is seeking a patron. It is part of the characterisation of Thais that she is stronger than the young men on whom she relies.

IV. vii: THRASO, GNATHO, SANGA, CHREMES, THAIS
(771-816, pp. 201-4)

[1] Thraso arrives with Gnatho, and deploys his motley army of servants outside Thais' house. He decides to negotiate before using force; but Thais rejects his complaints about Chremes, and Chremes defies him to touch Pamphila. Chremes departs to show the tokens to the nurse Sophrona, Thais goes into her house, and Thraso withdraws.

[2] Thraso and his army enter from the right: it would leave space for the army to be deployed if Thais' house was located on the left-hand side of the stage (46ff n. 2). The rest of the stage directions

in the Penguin edition are best ignored. There is no indication in the text that Thais and Chremes go into the house at the end of the previous scene. We must imagine them remaining on stage outside the house (784 n.), which is how they are shown in the miniatures of the medieval MSS (these, however, have Thraso and his army on the left and Thais and Chremes on the right). All references to the window should be deleted: there is no evidence that the stage houses of Roman comedy had windows.

[3] This is the fourth of the scenes imported into *Eunuchus* from Menander's *Kolax*. Like the others (232ff, 391ff, 454ff), it adds some broad humour to the play, this time visual as well as verbal; in fact in performance it must have been the visual highlight of the play. We are now in a better position to judge how well integrated the Thraso-Gnatho scenes are into the plot of *Eunuchus*. The dinner-party sequence, with the siege scene as its natural climax, has in fact loomed quite large in the third and fourth acts; it has contributed to both halves of the dual plot in that it has cleared the way for Phaedria to resume his affair with Thais and for Chaerea to retain access to Pamphila. But there is a real problem in envisaging how Terence has put the two Greek plays together. The siege scene must come from Menander's *Kolax* but there is no sign of a soldier's dinner-party in the fragments of that play; and in any case it would be difficult to reconstruct a plausible development for Menander's *Eunouchos* if the dinner-party sequence was deleted. So it seems to follow that the rival in Menander's *Eunouchos* must also have had a dinner-party and must also have come to demand his girl back, and that Terence has expanded and enlivened this sequence by adding the siege scene from *Kolax*. But certainty is impossible. What we can say is that the siege scene in *Kolax* cannot have had five speaking actors (plus the three non-speaking parts) as does Terence's scene here. The Sanga equivalent will have been at most a mute part in the Greek play, and Chremes (who is clearly a *Eunouchos* character, not a *Kolax* one) will have been absent; it is hard to imagine the scene without any of the other three characters.

[4] As for the characterisation, Thraso is the expected combination of bluster ('Better death than dishonour...First, I'll storm the house' 772-3) and cowardice ('I'll take up my position behind the front line' 781, 'A wise man should try everything before he has recourse to arms' 789); he ends by meekly withdrawing his army with nothing achieved. Gnatho continues to flatter Thraso ('Right, sir', 'Very good, sir', 'Splendid, sir' 773-4) and to undercut the flattery with asides ('A formation designed to give him a safe place' 782) and sarcasm ('Every minute spent with you is something learned' 791); he stands up for Thraso by verbally abusing Chremes ('you cur' 803), but in the end is ready to counsel retreat ('Go home' 811). Thais scornfully ignores Thraso's complaints about Chremes ('What if I

did?...What's that to you?...Well, I wanted to' 793-6), and remains generally in control of the situation, referring to Thraso as 'a great booby' (785) and finally dismissing him with an emphatic exit line (810 n.). Chremes, after an unpromising beginning ('I was right about bolting the door' 784), shows unexpected boldness, with his combination of vivid threats ('Clear off, or I'll break your head' 803) and abuse ('you dirty brute' 798 n.), but this is only after Thais has reduced Thraso to size; even then Chremes finds an excuse to leave the scene before the soldier's army is withdrawn (809 n.).

[5] The recitative continues, beginning in excited ia^8 but settling into tr^7 at the point where Thraso first sees Thais ('Look there' 788) and the confrontation begins.

771-91 Am I to put up with...something learned: As a variation on the standard overheard monologue opening, the scene begins with an overheard dialogue, and the accompanying asides are also double rather than single (Chremes and Thais). This structure requires four actors, and thus does not occur in Greek comedy.

772 Simalio, Donax, Syriscus: 'Thug-slaves' or 'whip-men' (Lat. *lorarii*) appear frequently in Plautus and in three plays of Terence (the other examples are Dromo at *Andr.* 860-5, p. 52, and Parmeno at *Ad.* 167-75, p. 346) but not at all in surviving Menander. They often have expressive names: here Simalio suggests 'Snub-Nose' and Donax 'Piper'; Syriscus by contrast is a form of the common slave name Syrus, meaning 'the Syrian'. The *lorarius* is a man of few words, whose main function is to provide slapstick comedy by beating, threatening or tying up his master's opponents.

776 Sergeant Sanga and his kitchen squad of thieves: Sanga is evidently a cook ('My mind's been on my saucepans' 816), and cooks are notoriously thieving. It is not clear that we are to envisage more non-speaking characters to represent the 'squad': the response 'Present, sir' is in the singular in the Latin. The military terms 'sergeant' (Lat. *centurio*) and 'squad' (Lat. *manipulus*) are intentially incongruous.

780 Sannio: This is the name of a colourful pimp in *Adelphoe*; here it belongs to a mere household slave.

p.202   **783 Pyrrhus:** King Pyrrhus of Epirus (roughly modern Albania) invaded Italy in 280 B.C. to help the Greek cities of South Italy against the Romans. The reference here might possibly derive from Menander, since Pyrrhus was consolidating his kingdom in Menander's lifetime. But it is much more likely to be Terence's addition. Pyrrhus was a well known figure of Roman history: the phrase 'a Pyrrhic victory', denoting a victory won at too great a cost, derives from his indecisive battles against the Romans in 280 and 279.

784 I was right about bolting the door: This is a back reference to 763 (p. 200). The Latin here uses the present tense ('It is a good idea...'): the line does not imply that the door has already been bolted or that Chremes and Thais are now inside the house.

786 Well, what now?: The blustering commander is already reduced to asking his subordinate to suggest a plan of action. Gnatho's reply is carefully calculated to play up to Thraso's cowardice without conveying any overt criticism.

788 How soon do we attack?: The question is mischievous: Gnatho is well aware that Thraso's confidence has evaporated.

.203 **798 you dirty brute:** Lit. 'you fork-bearer', a vivid term of abuse referring to the practice of punishing a slave by tying a Y-shaped piece of wood to his neck and binding his arms to the projecting ends. It is a favourite word of Plautus', which occurs three times in *Eunuchus* and only once in Terence's other plays.

805-6 freeborn...a citizen of Attica...and my sister: Chremes boldly makes this claim to Thraso, even though he has not finally established Pamphila's identity (745 n.): he has the 'proofs' in his hand, but still needs the old family nurse to authenticate them.

807-8 fetch the nurse Sophrona...show her the proofs: The nurse (Lat. *nutrix*) is often crucial to the recognition of long-lost children in comedy (Introd. §14), and it is no great surprise that one is brought in here. 'Sophrona', which implies 'prudent', is a common nurse name; it occurs in *Phormio* and in several plays of Menander's.

809 I'll stop you all right: This is evidently an exit line (though there is no explicit stage direction). Chremes departs to fetch Sophrona; this will be to the left, which is where his town house can be assumed to lie (507ff n. 2), and thus in the opposite direction from Thraso's army. It would have been more courageous of Chremes to stay until Thraso's army was withdrawn.

.204 **guilty of theft:** Gnatho is stretching a point in suggesting that Chremes has 'stolen' Pamphila: his aim is to provide Thraso with an excuse to withdraw.

810 Find someone else to answer you: This is a telling exit line; Thais turns her back on Thraso and goes into her house.

811 Now what do we do?: Thraso again feebly asks his subordinate for advice (786 n).

812-13 I know women and their ways...: The fickleness of women was proverbial in antiquity: cf. 'these women are like children - no sound sense at all' (*Hec.* 312, p. 304).

814-15 as a true soldier should: The addresses of Roman generals to soldiers before battles are full of reminders that they are fighting for 'hearth and home': Terence parodies this by making Sanga take the idea of 'hearth' literally.

816 Follow me, my men: Thraso and his men depart, leaving the stage empty. This is the last but one empty stage in the play, and may well represent the end of Menander's fourth act..

V. i: THAIS, PYTHIAS (817-39, pp. 204-5)

[1] Thais and Pythias enter in conversation from Thais' house. Thais has discovered Pamphila in distress and the eunuch missing, and Pythias admits that the eunuch turned out to be Chaerea in disguise. They see Chaerea approaching.

[2] The focus returns to Chaerea and his unmasking, after three scenes concerned with the soldier's dinner-party. It is notable that, as we move into the fifth act, neither half of the double plot has reached a conclusion. The marriage of Chaerea and Pamphila has been clearly enough foreshadowed, but we still need final confirmation that Chaerea (and his father) will be willing and that the rape will be condoned. The way is clear for Phaedria to return to Thais, but there is no obvious permanent resolution for this affair, granted that marriage is out of the question. There is also the problem of how Thais will find a patron in Athens, since her plan to restore Pamphila to her parents has been spoiled by the rape. And it has not been finally established what will happen to Thraso and Gnatho, though at this stage we must be expecting Thais to reject Thraso outright. There is thus still plenty of suspense left as we proceed to the dénouement.

[3] This scene shows Thais in a new light, with the emphasis on her anger with Pythias, underlined by a string of abusive vocatives (818 n., 825 n., 829 n., 832 n.), and her sense of shame at being deceived (827 n., 832-3 n.). She does refer twice to the girl crying (820, 829), but more because this is evidence of what has happened than to express sympathy for Pamphila. Pythias is for once caught on the back foot: she is forced to abandon her previous resolve to say nothing about the rape (720-4, p. 198), but still tries to hide behind phrases like 'They say' (822), 'I suppose' (827), 'I think so' (829).

[4] The metre reverts to spoken verse (ia⁶) after three and a half scenes of recitative.

818 You wretched woman: Lat. *scelestus*: 668-70 n..

p.205   **824 young brother:** Lit. 'ephebe brother' (290 n.).

825 You scandal-monger: Lit. 'you poisoner'. Pythias had herself used this word of Chaerea at 648 (p. 194).

827 I shall die of shame: Lit. 'I am lost'. In fact there is no reference to shame in the Latin here, and Thais may be referring rather to the ruination of her plan to restore Pamphila to her parents.

829 you liar: Lit. 'you committer of sacrilege' (419 n.).

832 You wretch: Lat. *scelestus* again (818 n.). According to Chaerea (576-7, p. 191) Thais herself put the girl into his care, so that it is unreasonable of Thais to blame Pythias on this score.

trusting the wolf with the lamb: The expression is proverbial. Animal imagery in Terence is confined to proverbs: for other wolf proverbs see *Phorm.* 506 (p. 252) and *Ad.* 537 (p. 363).

832-3 I'm so ashamed of being taken in: On the surface Thais seems to be thinking more of herself than of the suffering of the girl. The Latin concept here ('ashamed') is *pudor* (Introd. §16).

835 There's our man...Look left: This is one of the few occasions in Roman comedy when the text itself establishes which side entrance is being used. Here there are interesting implications. Chaerea enters from the actors' left, i.e. the audience's right. At first sight, this seems to conflict with the location of Antipho's parents' house (for which Chaerea was heading when we last saw him) to the audience's left (614 n.). But it transpires that Chaerea has not come direct from this house, having fled from one alley to another to avoid being recognised (845-7, p. 206), and this might reasonably account for his return to the stage from the opposite side to the one by which he departed, contrary to the normal convention.

V. ii: CHAEREA, THAIS, PYTHIAS (840-909, pp. 205-8)

[1] Chaerea returns, still in his eunuch's costume, and, on hearing that Pamphila is a free citizen, declares his wish to marry her. He is forgiven by Thais, much to Pythias' disgust, and invited inside her house. Chremes approaches with the nurse Sophrona.

[2] The scene clears the way for the marriage between Chaerea and Pamphila, and thus brings us close to the resolution of this half of the dual plot. All that is now needed is the final confirmation of Pamphila's identity and the assent of Chaerea's father; but, granted the conventions, neither is likely to cause any problem.

[3] Chaerea's willingness to marry the girl whom he has raped will come as no surprise to the audience: all young lovers in comedy marry their girls if they can. The young man is in love; marriage is now possible; from the girl's point of view it is socially desirable; and Greek and Roman comedy probes no deeper than this. This scene in effect delivers the play's final verdict on Chaerea's behaviour (esp. 864-88): it was wrong, but it was due to love, and, since love (as we all know) is a powerful force, it can be forgiven, if the young man proves his good faith by marrying the girl. Questions that might occur to a modern reader (such as, whether the young man is 'really' in love or whether he will make a good husband) are simply not raised, nor, for that matter, is the question of the girl's feelings. All this has to be seen in the context of a society in which arranged marriages are the norm and of the generally lenient view of young men's escapades which comedy takes (Introd. §2). In the end, Terence is endorsing this general verdict rather than questioning it .

[4] A further question is whether Terence is able to make this solution credible in terms of Chaerea's characterisation. He has so far been portrayed as impulsive, plausible, and irresponsible (292ff n. 3, 539ff n. 3). When first challenged by Thais, his first response is to try to bluff his way out of the situation, still pretending to be a eunuch

and using a typical slave's plea for lenience (852-3 n.). But, when the situation changes, in that (i) Pythias declares Pamphila to be a free-born citizen (857-8) and (ii) Thais reveals that she knows Chaerea's identity (864), Chaerea's response changes with it. It is now possible for him to marry Pamphila, and this is what he instantly decides to do, using all his persuasive skills to win over Thais ('...there will be a lasting bond of good feeling between us' 872-3, 'I hadn't any intention of insulting you' 877-8, 'I love you too' 882, 'I put myself in your hands' 886) before asking for the girl's hand in emotive terms ('I shall die if I can't marry her' 888). So the characterisation is in fact perfectly consistent: Chaerea remains a plausible rogue and his desire to marry is as impulsive as his previous behaviour.

[5] Thais' treatment of Chaerea has to be seen in the light of her plan to win patronage and protection for herself in Athens by restoring Pamphila to her family (81ff n. 3). Chaerea has jeopardised this plan by robbing Pamphila of her virginity; the only way in which the plan can now succeed is for Chaerea to restore Pamphila's honour by marrying her. By the end of the scene Thais has gained this object, not by asserting herself over Chaerea as she has over Chremes and Thraso but by using considerable finesse. She teases Chaerea for a while by pretending to accept the eunuch disguise, choosing her moment to drop the pretence ('this must stop' 864) and rebuke him for what he has done (864-71). This rebuke is carefully couched. Instead of exuding righteous indignation, Thais simply reproves Chaerea for letting himself down ('your conduct was unworthy of you' 864-5), and even admits the possibility that as a courtesan she deserves this kind of insult (865-6 n.). She then appeals for his sympathy in her predicament over Pamphila (870-1 n.), and finally forgives him on the basis that she too has experienced the power of love (880-1 n.). It would be unwise to talk of 'noble forgiveness' on Thais' part, or even to overemphasise her 'humanity'; it is very much in her own interest to secure the marriage and indeed a connection with Chaerea's family (872-4 n.). Once Chaerea has declared his eagerness to marry, Thais returns immediately to the practicalities of obtaining his father's consent (889 n.) and detaining Chaerea himself until the recognition is completed. The scene ends, as it began, with Thais teasing Chaerea ('Are you bashful?' 907); once again she has demon-strated her ability to manipulate the men with whom she is involved.

[6] Pythias is amusingly drawn, in keeping with her previous characterisation (643ff n. 3). She retains her anger against Chaerea, using the same abusive language as before ('you brute' 860, 'the beast' 862 n.) and making similar threats of physical violence (859-60 n.), and she is predictably aghast when Thais proposes to let him back inside her house. She thus acts as a foil for Thais' cool handling of the situation, and provides much of the humour of the scene.

[7] The spoken verse (ia^6) continues.

p.206 **845-6 down an empty alley...from one to another:** As the Penguin footnote says, the Latin word here used for alley is *angiportum*. But the alleys here mentioned are clearly at some distance off-stage; they do not imply a back lane running parallel to the stage behind the houses' (as the footnote seems to suggest), and they have nothing to do with the supposed *angiportum* leading back at right angles between the houses (cf. *Phorm.* 891 n.).

850 here you are: Lat. *salve* (270-1 n.).

852-3 Please overlook this one lapse...: This is a typical slave's plea: cf. 'Let him off just this once': *Phorm.* 141-2 (p. 232).

858 I took her for a fellow slave: Chaerea has just heard for the first time that Pamphila is free born, which competely alters the implications of the rape. But the word 'fellow' shows that he is not so taken aback as to abandon the pretence that he is a eunuch.

859-60 keep my hands off your hair: At 648 (p. 194), when she did not know the eunuch's identity, Pythias was threatening to scratch his eyes out.

863 Only pretending to be your slave: The precise point remains obscure, and different translations of the Latin are possible. But the gist is clear: 'if I did tear his hair, I suppose I wouldn't get away with it'.

p.207 **862 the beast:** Lit. 'fork-bearer' (798 n.).

865-6 right...wrong: Lat. *dignus* and *indignus* (70 n.). It is interesting that Thais sees Charea's 'wrong' as perpetrated on herself rather than on Pamphila (382 n.). In admitting the possibility that, as a courtesan, she has deserved such treatment, she is being very conciliatory.

870-1 the right thing...some solid advantage: These lines are calculated to appeal to Chaerea's better nature, but accurately reflect Thais' actual mixture of motives, i.e. genuine concern for the girl overlaid with a strong element of self-interest. The Latin terms are *aequom* (386 n.) and *beneficium* (147-9 n.).

872-4 lasting bond...close friendship: Chaerea has taken Thais' point, and is hinting at a permanent tie of friendship between Thais and his own family, rather than one with that of the girl's parents.

880-1 I'm not...lacking in human feeling: This is another allusion to the Terentian concept of 'humanity' as the basic ideal of human behaviour (460 n.). Here it is explicitly based on the sharing of a common human experience, namely love, and the moral is that we should be ready to forgive common human failings.

883 you'd better watch out: Pythias is alluding to Chaerea's treament of Pamphila.

886-7 I put myself in your hands...Be my protector: Lit. 'be my patron' (Lat. *patrona*). This is a neat variation on the typical behaviour of the helpless *adulescens*, who commits himself into the hands of his slave *(Heaut.* 351, p. 116) and even addresses his own slave as his patron (Plaut. *Rud.* 1266). There is also an echo of Thais' previous assertion that Chremes needed a patron (770 n.).

p.208 **889 What about your father?:** The father's consent, which was in practice necessary for a young man to marry both in Athens and in Rome *(Phorm.* 232 n.), often presents a stumbling-block in comedy. The likely objection from the father is the low social status of the girl and the inability of her family to provide a satisfactory dowry *(Phorm.* 120 n.). Apart from this, fathers are generally happy to see their sons married, if only because marriage marks an end to the squandering of the family's wealth on courtesans (cf. *Ad.* 149-53, p. 345).

905 here comes her brother: Chremes approaches from the left (809 n.) with the nurse

908-9 Go in, I'll follow. Wait here...: The stage directions in this part of the play are very precise.

V. iii: PYTHIAS, CHREMES, SOPHRONA (910-22, p. 209)

[1] Pythias questions Chremes and Sophrona and ushers them into Thais' house. She then goes in herself as Parmeno approaches.

[2] This is a rather perfunctory linking scene, completing one plot element, the recognition of Pamphila and leading into a new one, the foreshadowed revenge of Pythias on Parmeno (718-26 n.).

[3] The appearance of Sophrona is something of an anticlimax, granted that Terence has taken some care to set up the recognition. She has no individual character (her only characteristic is that she is slow-moving: 912), and she speaks only a single word ('I am moving' 913); her recognition of the tokens has taken place off-stage, and it is conveyed to the audience not by her but by Chremes. The role of the nurse in *Heauton* is almost as slight; in *Phormio* on the other hand she is involved in an extended scene (729ff, pp. 262-5).

[4] Pythias' language continues to be colourful, with abuse (911 n., 921-2 n.), sarcasm ('our worthy friend' 918) and threats ('torment-ing him' 920, 'terrify the life out of him' 922) for Parmeno; at the same time she still speaks alluringly to Chremes (915 n.).

[5] The spoken verse (ia^6) continues.

911 that scoundrel: Lit. 'that committer of sacrilege' (829 n.), i.e. Parmeno.

913 you don't move *on*: Chremes ventures on an uncharacteristic word-play.

915 please: Lat. *amabo* ('darling': 663 n.).

916 I'm fond of the girl: Cf. 643ff n. 4.

918 here comes...Parmeno: Parmeno left the stage at 496, with no indication of where he was going. Since Chremes has just appeared from the left, it would balance the staging best if Parmeno appeared from the right.

921-2 I'll just pop indoors...and then be back: Again the stage movements are precisely signalled (908-9 n.). Pythias' speech turns out to be an an exit monologue, one of only two in the play (197-206 n.). But the action is in fact continuous: the stage is empty only momentarily before Parmeno's appearance.

for his wicked lies: Lit. 'the committer of sacrilege' (911 n.).

V. iv: PARMENO, PYTHIAS (923-70, pp. 209-11)

[1] Parmeno enters congratulating himself on the success of the eunuch scheme, but is alarmed when Pythias tells him that the girl is a free-born citizen and that her brother is threatening to punish Chaerea as an adulterer. He decides that he had better tell the father the truth.

[2] Pythias' revenge on Parmeno seems at first to constitute a minor sub-plot, which risks delaying the dénouement of the play, but it is cleverly linked to the appearance of the father, who is necessary to the solution of the Chaerea-Pamphila affair (817ff n. 2), and to the eventual fate of Parmeno, whose role in the play has been significant enough to need bringing to a satisfactory conclusion. This is an amusing scene which depends for its humorous effect on the dramatic irony provided by Parmeno's ignorance of the true situation.

[3] Pythias takes a vindictive pleasure in her revenge. She continues to show a biting tongue, with a further series of abusive terms ('you rascal' 941, 'that vile Parmeno' 944, 'impudence' 948); she also indulges in some smooth ironic mockery (961 n., 962-3 n.). Her wiliness is also to the fore as she deceives Parmeno with her 'faked' monologue (943 n.).

[4] Parmeno's opening monologue suggests pomposity on his part (46ff n. 5) and a capacity for self-deception. He now takes the credit for the eunuch ruse, though at the time he had tried to dissuade Chaerea from following it through, and, even more improbably, for introducing Chaerea to the sleazy world of prostitutes as a way of teaching him to steer clear of them. It is thus difficult to sympathise with him as he is mocked by Pythias. But he does show himself essentially loyal to his young master at the end of the scene, both in his attempt to invoke his older master's authority ('I tell you this young man is my master's son' 962) and in his decision to tell the father the truth in order to save the son. Loyalty is an important part of Parmeno's character (232ff n. 4, 454ff n. 3); at the same time the decision to tell the father the truth puts him fairly clearly into the category of the bungling slave, in contrast to the true tricky slave who maintains his deception to the end (Introd. §7).

[5] The scene begins in spoken verse (ia^6), but changes to recitative (tr^7) as Pythias begins her 'faked monologue' (943 n.).

924 If he's played his cards well: Parmeno has no means of knowing how the eunuch ruse turned out, but is complacently assuming the best.

927 a greedy professional: Lat. *meretrix*: Parmeno sticks to his previous misconception of Thais' character (81ff n. 4).

930 my real masterpiece: Lit. 'deserving of the palm': it is uncertain whether the image derives from acting (354 n.) or chariot-racing.

934-40 Met outside...young man's salvation: This description of sordid 'professionals' has nothing in common with the portrayal of Thais and her household in the play, and shows how misconceived Parmeno's view of them is.

p.210   **941 I'll see you suffer for these words...:** Pythias has evidently heard some or all of Parmeno's monologue, and yet there is no previous indication in the text of her return to the stage. It is unusual for characters to come on stage unannounced; and there is therefore some suspicion that Terence has altered the staging from the Greek original, though it is hard to see his reason for doing so. There was no real need for Pythias to go in at the end of the previous scene when she saw Parmeno approaching (921-2 n.), since Chremes had already confirmed the recognition; the obvious staging would have been for her to stay outside to eavesdrop on Parmeno.

943 Heavens above: Pythias launches into a 'faked' entrance monologue, with the deliberate intention of being overheard. There is a close parallel for this at Plaut. *Mil.* 991-9, where the courtesan's maid delivers a faked monologue to deceive the lecherous soldier.

944 What's that?: This is evidently an aside: Parmeno does not address Pythias until 947.

947 I'll ask her: Lit. 'I'll approach her', the usual formula.

953 I don't know, I'm sure: This non-committal response does not clarify how seriously Parmeno had taken Thais' original claim about Pamphila's birth (382 n.).

956 though Thais begged him not to: Pythias is putting her mistress in a good light; at the same time she is destroyinging any hope that Thais will be able to forestall Chaerea's fate.

p.211   **957 as they do adulterers:** As the Penguin footnote says, castration was the traditional punishment for adulterers: the final scene of Plautus' *Miles* has a cook flourishing a knife and threatening to castrate the soldier there for adultery. In Athenian law, which Teence is here following, adultery (Gk *moicheia*) included sexual assault on unmarried girls.

960 adultery in a house of this reputation: Parmeno has a point here in Chaerea's defence, in that Athenian law expressly excluded prostitutes from the sphere of *moicheia*.

961 I don't know, I'm sure: Pythias mockingly echoes Parmeno's response in 953.

962-3 Gracious, you don't say so!: Pythias continues to

tease: she knows Chaerea's identity well enough (823-4: p. 205).

967 coming back from the country: The father approaches from the left-hand entrance.

V. v: DEMEA, PARMENO (971-1001, pp. 211-13)

[1] Demea is told by Parmeno of Phaedria's eunuch gift and of Chaerea's supposed fate, and rushes into Thais' house to investigate.

[2] The scene introduces Demea, and thus advances the plot in two ways, (i) towards Demea's consent to Chaerea's marriage and (ii) towards his punishment of Parmeno. By the end of the scene the latter looks more probable than the former, but, as the audience will be well aware, comedies traditionally have happy endings.

[3] Parmeno is amusingly depicted as the bungling slave desperately trying to cover up for himself. He is tongue-tied and shaking when confronted by Demea ('I'm struck dumb with fear' 977, 'You're shaking' 978); his first concern is to exculpate himself even before telling the story ('whatever's happened here, it wasn't my fault' 980); he passes over the rape and the fact that the girl is a citizen (985 n.); he denies any part in the eunuch scheme, though in the previous scene he had claimed the credit for it ('I didn't put him up to it' 988); and he finally tries to transfer the blame on to Thais and her household ('It just shows the impudence of these women' 994), consoling himself with the thought that he will at least have the satisfaction of seeing Thais suffer at Demea's hands (998-1001).

[4] Demea belongs to the type 'old man' (Lat. *senex*: Introd. §3). Our first impression is that, though Chaerea was confident that he would agree to the marriage (889-90, p. 208), Demea actually belongs to the sub-type of the 'stern father' (*senex durus*); his utterances are nearly all incredulous questions, expressions of dismay ('That'll finish me' 984, 'I'm ruined' 985, 'Oh, no, no!' 993), or threats ('I'll see to *you*, you scoundrel' 989-90). It is in fact unlikely that 'Demea' is the father's name in this play; Donatus tells us that, whereas Menander named the father 'Simo', Terence did not give him a name at all. One branch of Terence's MS tradition lists him as 'Demea' and the other as 'Laches', but these must represent mere guesses: both of these names occur elsewhere as old men's names in Terence and in several plays of Menander's. The absence of a name reflects the very reduced part that the father plays in *Eunuchus*.

[5] The scene reverts to spoken verse (ia⁶). This is the last spoken verse in the play, the remaining scenes being in recitative.

971 a country place near town: Donatus comments that all villas in comedy are suburban (cf. 633 n.).

976 I'm glad to see you safely back: Terence again makes imaginative use of the conventions of the homecoming scene (454-9 n.). In spite of his evident panic, Parmeno manages to trot out the appropriate welcome formula. But, instead of making the usual acknowledgement ('I'm sure you are'), Demea simply repeats his question; his tone has rapidly changed from contentment to suspicion that something has gone wrong during his absence.

978 You're shaking: There is an implied stage direction here for the Parmeno actor.

983 Who's she?: Better 'To whom?' Demea is simply clarifying that Thais is meant: he already knows all about Thais and her household (1000 n.).

984 Two thousand drachmas: There is a discrepancy here with Phaedria's earlier statement (169, p. 171) that he paid two thousand drachmas for the eunuch and the Ethiopian slave-girl together, but Parmeno is in a flustered state here and may be misrepresenting or oversimplifying the facts.

985 I'm ruined: Like most of his type Demea is as much concerned with the financial loss incurred through his son's affairs as with the disgrace (79 n.).

in love with a girl in this house: Parmeno uses the word *fidicina* (457 n.), with the implication that the girl is a *meretrix*; he is avoiding the question of Pamphila's citizen status.

987 one calamity after another: The phrase is proverbial.

988 Don't look at me like that: This is another stage direction written into the text.

989 scoundrel: Lit 'fork-bearer' (798 n.).

p.213 **995 disaster or disgrace:** The word translated 'disaster' (Lat. *damnum*) has strong connotations of financial disaster, and has reference to Phaedria (985 n.); 'disgrace' applies to Chaerea.

996 Then I shall go straight in: Lit. 'do I delay to burst in?', a version of the common action formula (265 n.), with the word 'burst' emphasising Demea's anxiety. Donatus comments that it is the fear for his son's life engendered by Parmeno's story that makes Demea so ready to agree to the marriage.

1000 The old man has been looking for an excuse: This is a rather cryptic remark, which establishes that Demea is well aware of what goes on in Thais' house (983 n.) and seems to contradict the statement that Thais had only recently come to live in the neighbourhood (359 n.). Donatus tells us that in the Greek original Menander explained more clearly that the old man, having long been angry with the *meretrix* for corrupting Phaedria, had now at last found an excuse for punishing her.

V. vi: PYTHIAS, PARMENO (1002-24, pp. 213-14)

[1] Pythias emerges from Thais' house laughing at the success of her story, and taunts Parmeno with the prospect of punishment from

both father and son.

[2] This scene completes the minor Pythias-Parmeno sub-plot (923ff n. 2). Pythias has gained her revenge, and now departs from the play, leaving Parmeno to contemplate his impending punishment. It is an amusing little scene, which depends on the clash of characters, the clever spiteful Pythias, combining mockery, threats ('you'll be the one to be strung up' 1021), and irony ('It's your reward for faithful service' 1023), and the loyal but bungling Parmeno (1009-11 n.), who is now reduced to his lowest point ('It's the end for me' 1023).

[3] The recitative resumes, in one of the less common metres (ia⁷).

1005-6 Where...is he? / There he is, I'll...: The Latin actually says 'I'll approach'. The recognition sequence is overplayed but to some point: if Pythias does not at first see Parmeno, it is because she is so overcome by laughter

1007 What are you laughing about? Can't you stop?: This is another example of a stage direction written into the text.

1009-11 A sillier man...a smart clever fellow: Pythias makes this contrast to add to Parmeno's humiliation. At the same time it seems that Terence is deliberately drawing attention to the reversal of the tricky slave character, since the word here translated 'smart' (Lat. *callidus*) is a common epithet for the 'tricky slave' (Introd. §7).

.214 **1017 You're still laughing?:** Another stage direction.

1021 strung up: Slaves were commonly tied to posts or pillars to be whipped (cf. 'strung up and flogged': *Phorm.* 220, p. 237).

1024 betrayed like a mouse with my own squeaking: Donatus explains that this is a proverbial expression for those who betray themselves, based on the shrew-mouse which squeaks loudly while eating and thus betrays its presence to pursuers even in the dark. This would make a good exit line, but there is no indication that Parmeno leaves the stage at this point.

V. vii: GNATHO, THRASO, PARMENO
(1025-30, pp. 214-15)

[1] Thraso returns (right) with Gnatho, and is about to surrender himself to Thais, when Chaerea bursts out of Thais' house.

[2] This (the fifth scene involving the two *Kolax* characters) is another rather perfunctory transition scene (cf. 910ff). There is an awkwardness of staging, in that Parmeno, who is apparently still on stage (1024 n.) even though he does not appear in the scene headings of the MSS, neither sees Thraso and Gnatho nor is seen by them (cf. 628 n.). The awkwardness may be related to the fact that Terence is interweaving *Kolax* scenes here into the original *Eunouchos* plot, and has chosen to bring Thraso and Gnatho back before the solution of the Chaerea-Pamphila affair is finally announced.

[3] Thraso is reduced to abject surrender after the failure of his attack on Thais' house, but does manage an impressive mythological parallel (1027 n.). Gnatho has apparently not been consulted ('What are you trying to do?' 1025); he offers his usual flattery ('a worthy precedent' 1027), accompanied by a typically sarcastic aside ('I hope I'll see her take a slipper...' 1028).

[4] The recitative continues, with a return to tr⁷.

1027 Hercules turned slave to Omphale: Terence does not feel it necessary to explain the story (see the Penguin footnote), which implies that the myth was already familiar to the Roman audience, as presumably was the Jupiter-Danae story (584-5 n.). In fact Terence has very few allusions to Greek mythology in his plays. But there are a fair number of such allusions in Plautus, who clearly expected his audience to understand them, and so we have to assume a reasonable familiarity with Greek mythology among the Romans of this period: one source of knowledge would have been the Latin adaptations of Greek tragedy which had been performed on the Roman stage since 240 B.C. It is likely that the Hercules myths, along with the Trojan War cycle, were among the most familiar at Rome in Terence's day; sacrifices to Hercules at the Great Altar at Rome traditionally went back to the days of the foundation of the city.

1029 I can hear her door opening: Introd. §20.

p.215   **1030 I've never seen him in my life:** In fact Thraso had seen Chaerea when he was delivered to Thais in the eunuch costume (p. 186). The obvious explanation of the contradiction is that Chaerea is now wearing his own clothes, as is suggested in the Penguin stage direction, and this would be appropriate symbolically in that Chaerea has now abandoned the eunuch pretence and is about to marry Pamphila in his own person. But there are practical problems with this interpretation (cf. 610 n.). Chaerea was still wearing the eunuch's clothes when he went into Thais' house (907, p. 208; cf. 1015-16, p. 214), and he has still had no chance either to recover his original clothes or to borrow some elsewhere. Donatus rightly assumes that Chaerea is still wearing the eunuch's costume; he suggests that what deceives the soldier is his 'virile confidence', i.e. the change in his demeanour from the submissiveness of the eunuch.

rushing out in such a hurry?: Another stage direction.

V. viii: CHAEREA, PARMENO, GNATHO, THRASO
(1031-49, pp. 215-16)

[1] Chaerea rushes out of Thais' house, elated that his father has agreed to the marriage and has also taken Thais under his protection. He sends Parmeno to fetch Phaedria.

[2] The scene seems to tie up all the loose ends, and to bring the

play to a satisfactory conclusion (817ff n. 2). With Demea's consent to the marriage (1036 n.) the final detail of the Chaerea-Pamphila half of the plot is settled, and the announcement that Demea has taken Thais under his protection seems to provide security for Thais and at least a short-term solution for the Thais-Phaedria affair. Parmeno is thanked effusively by Chaerea (1035 n.), and will presumably escape his threatened punishment; and Thraso will be 'kicked out' (1041), which seems to be what he deserves.

[3] This is the sixth scene in the play incorporating the two characters from *Kolax*. Once again (as at 454ff and 771ff) the result is a scene with more than three actors. If Terence is still closely following Menander's *Eunouchos* at this point, Menander's scene will have involved the Chaerea and Parmeno characters and possibly the Thraso character (i.e. the rival); there will have been no space for the Gnatho character.

[4] The recitative continues, with a change to ia^8 (which is one of the more excited recitative metres) to match Chaerea's elated mood.

1032-3 all the powers of heaven are on my side: This echoes Chaerea's assertion to Thais that 'it may be heaven's will' that has brought them into contact (875, p. 207). Chaerea has more faith in heaven than most young men of comedy.

1034 Now why's he so pleased with himself?: There is no indication that Parmeno has just returned to the stage, which confirms that he must have remained on stage unseen and unspeaking during the preceding Gnatho-Thraso scene (1025ff n. 2).

1035 author...instigator...perfecter: Chaerea expresses his thanks to Parmeno in a resounding rhetorical triplet.

1036 I'm going to marry her: Lit. 'she has been betrothed to me'. This line implies that Demea's consent has been given; the consent of Pamphila's guardian (i.e. Chremes, there being no mention of her father) can be taken for granted.

1037 Did you hear that?: Gnatho comments aside to Thraso. The scene consist entirely of two characters eavesdropping on two others (771-91 n.).

Phaedria's love affair has weathered its storms: Lit. 'is in a calm [sea]'. The metaphor of love as a voyage on a dangerous sea, found also (but rarely) in Menander and Plautus, becomes common in later Latin love poetry: the best known example is Horace's Pyrrha ode (*Odes* 1. 5).

1038 one happy family: This will consist of Demea, his two sons Phaedria and Chaerea, his protegé Thais, and his daughter-in-law Pamphila.

1039 under our patronage: Lit. 'clientship' (Lat. *clientela*), with explicit reference to the Roman patron-client relationship. But this is not to be seen as an incongruous Romanism in a Greek context (255-7 n.), any more than the earlier references to 'patrons' (770 n.,

886-7 n.): in Athens Thais would similarly have been seeking a protector (Gk *prostates*), and Terence is simply representing the Greek technical term by the Roman equivalent.

1044 No doubt at all, I fancy: This seems to spell the end of Thraso's hopes.

1044-9 Where shall I begin?...will continue: This is technically a link monologue, but differs from normal link monologues in that there are other people (Gnatho and Thraso) still on stage.

p.216   **1046 Fortune who guided me:** Chaerea is now ascribing his happiness to a combination of human and divine agencies (1032-3 n.). Fortune is here personified (lit. 'Fortune the helmswoman'), in contrast to the two other occurrences of the word *fortuna* in the play where it is simply translated 'Luckily' (134, p. 170) or 'By a stroke of luck' (568, p. 190). There is obviously a thin dividing line between fortune conceived of as an impersonal force and Fortune personified as a deity. The concept of Fortune as a goddess became widespread in Greece in the time of Greek New Comedy: Menander makes Fortune (Gk 'Tyche') the prologue speaker of *Aspis*, and there is inscriptional evidence for a shrine to Good Fortune at Athens in Menander's day. There were also shrines to Fortune at Rome from early times.

1047 so many vital matters...in a single day: There may be a sly allusion here to the fact that the action of a comedy traditionally takes place within a single day. There is only one play in the whole of Roman comedy, namely Terence's *Heauton*, in which a night intervenes ('Dawn's breaking' 410, p. 119).

1048 kindness and good humour: Demea turns out to be a *senex lenis* after all (971ff n. 4).

1049 heaven's blessing will continue: On Chaerea's elation in this scene cf. 551 n.

V. ix: PHAEDRIA, CHAEREA, THRASO, GNATHO
(1049-94, pp. 216-18)

[1] Phaedria emerges from Demea's house, delighted with the news of Thais' acceptance by his father, and threatens Thraso if he ever dares set foot in the street again. Gnatho however persuades him to accept a compromise whereby Thraso is allowed to stay on as a rival lover to pay for Thais' expensive tastes.

[2] The final scene provides a surprise conclusion to the play, for which there has been no real preparation (1031ff n. 2). In fact, the conclusion seems to go against the characterisation that Terence has developed in the course of the play. To take Thais first, it is true that she has exacted gifts from both Phaedria and Thraso; but the idea that she is simply the typical greedy and expensive courtesan, though repeated here ('you must always be paying out to her' 1075), has been repeatedly scotched. It has been made quite clear that she does have

some genuine feelings for Phaedria, and that her ultimate motive is to obtain status, not gifts. She has also been shown to be an independently minded and resourceful woman, well able to manage the men with whom she has to deal, so that it is strange to see an arrangement for her future being concluded behind her back and without her consent. As for Phaedria, he has been portrayed as the jealous lover, unable to tear himself away from his mistress and unhappy to think of anyone sharing her favours, so that it comes as a surprise that he is willing accept the soldier as a continuing rival. And the basically unsympathetic characterisation of Thraso and Gnatho is maintained in the final scene, so that there seems no need to make concessions to them in the end, even granted the traditional festivity of the comic finale. Thraso continues to be portrayed as the conceited but feeble swaggering soldier ('he's a silly idiot, a lazy dim-wit...' 1079), who deserves to be humiliated at the end (whatever Donatus says: 446 n.), like the soldier in Plautus' *Miles*. And, though some parasites (such as Phormio in *Phormio*) are resourceful endearing rogues whose triumphs the audience can share, Gnatho has been merely the slick self-serving flatterer ('all that I'm doing is primarily in my own interests' 1070): why then should the play end on a note of victory for Gnatho?

[3] One approach to the problem of the ending is to deny that it exists or at least to minimise its seriousness. It is certainly possible that we are creating or magnifying the problem by looking at the play with modern susceptibilities. We are in particular danger of sentimentalising Thais as a disadvantaged but deserving woman who succeeds by her own resourcefulness in establishing some sort of position for herself at Athens. She is after all a courtesan, and, by definition, a courtesan does not restrict herself to one man. There are other Roman comedies in which courtesans' favours are shared (examples are Plaut. *Bacch.* and *Truc.*); and, though it is clear that Thais despises Thraso, will she really be affronted by an arrangement in which he is kept around to provide gifts and dinners? As for Phaedria, it is not clear that the Romans would necessarily have shared our sympathies for his romantic ideals of love. He has been portrayed as helpless and indecisive over Thais; and, if his blustering threats to Thraso in the final scene are easily undermined by Gnatho, this may not be too much out of character. In the case of Thraso, the final solution is not presented as an act of generosity to him, even though he may think that he has gained by it; it is a just reward for his stupidity (1088 n.), in that he is simply going to be used as a source of finance and amusement. But there are still two problems left, neither easy to explain away, namely the victory of the undeserving Gnatho and the way in which Thais' affairs are arranged behind her back.

[4] There is a mechanical explanation of the problem of the ending which needs to be taken into account, even though it is unlikely to be the whole story. This lies in the fact that Terence is not writing

an original play but adapting a Greek original. We cannot simply assume that, if Terence's ending offends our taste, Menander's must have been different, since the ending of Menander's own *Dyskolos* has also offended modern susceptibilities. But there is an evident possibility in the case of 'contaminated' plays like *Eunuchus* that Terence has been unable to combine his two Greek models into a harmonious whole. We have no independent evidence for the ending of either Menander's *Eunouchos* or his *Kolax*. But we do know that in the *Kolax* the young man was impecunious and that the *meretrix* was not an independent courtesan but a slave in the power of a pimp (30 n.), so that an ending where the parasite gained some sort of settlement for himself and the soldier without consulting the girl might have been quite appropriate. So it is at least a tenable hypothesis that the problem of the ending has been created by Terence's substitution of the *Kolax* ending for that of Menander's *Eunouchos*.

[5] There still remains the question whether Terence intended by his ending to make some serious point. If the play is about love (and we have seen that various kinds of love are portrayed), the point of the ending would be the negative one that love is not in the end a matter of the heart but of making suitable arrangements; and this point could then be extended by implication to Chaerea's case. Another suggestion is that the play is about the impossibility of human independence: in this case the point of the ending would be to show that, for all Thais' resourcefulness, the independence of the *meretrix* is illusory, and that, for all Phaedria's romantic ideas, an *adulescens* cannot hope for a permanent or exclusive relationship with a courtesan. On this interpretation, the victory of Gnatho has a special relevance in that the parasite is the supreme example of human dependence. Thirdly the play may be about human selfishness. If the arrangements made by Phaedria for Thais in the ending are regarded as selfish, this would mirror the selfishness shown in various ways by Thais, Chaerea, and Gnatho in the rest of the play, with the ironic point that only Gnatho is honest enough to proclaim self-interest as his primary motive. The last two interpretations have the advantage that they make Gnatho's an integral part the structure; but the problem with all three is that they give the play a much more negative attitude to human behaviour than Terence (or Menander) usually shows. In the end it may be unwise to exaggerate the didactic effect of the finale. There is always the possibility that Terence was deliberately sacrificing consistency for dramatic effect (Introd. §34); and the majority of the audience may well have seen the final scene simply as an amusing tailpiece designed to send them away in good humour, rather than offering any deep moral or social comment. For discussion see Forehand 72-80, Goldberg 105-22, Hunter 93-4, Konstan (1986), Sandbach 142-5.

[6] The possibilities of the four-actor scene are here skilfully exploited (cf. 1037 n.). The scene begins with two separate two-actor

conversations (Phaedria-Chaerea and Thraso-Gnatho), in which neither pair overhears the other; then (from 'Who's that?' 1060) passes to a four-way conversation; then (from 'Just move off' 1068) to a three-way one with Thraso excluded; and ends (from 'you can come here now' 1088) with all four actors involved, the whole being carefully articulated by the stage-directional phrases. The technique is different from, and more complex than, the other four-actor technique in which two characters comment aside on the conversation between two other characters before being identified (771-91 n.).

[7] This is the fourth successive scene of recitative, with a change back to tr[7]. All Terence's plays end with recitative (and all with tr[7]), just as they all begin with spoken verse (46ff n. 7).

1049 Good God: Phaedria's entry is very abrupt, with obvious dramatic effect. Not only are there no introductory formulae, but he interrupts Chaerea in mid-line in the Latin, which is a comparatively rare phenomenon (*Ad.* 81 n.).

1051-2 No one deserves to be loved more than...Thais: This is a clear affirmation of the good qualities of Thais, and makes a stark contrast with the view that Gnatho is about to propound of the typical greedy courtesan. Chaerea's enthusiasm may be a product of his own elation, but, in view of the way the play has developed, there can be little doubt which view Terence intends us to accept.

1052 she has done so much for all our family: Of those in the new extended family (1038 n.), the direct beneficiaries of Thais' actions (apart from herself) are Pamphila and Chaerea, though by persuading Demea to take her under his protection she has indirectly benefited Phaedria.

1059 I need never wait for an invitation: This is a typical parasite's remark.

1061 Good evening.../ Perhaps you don't know: Phaedria fails to return Thraso's greeting, as if to imply that he scarcely deserves the normal courtesies (976 n.).

p.217 **1063-6 Shall I tell you...I mean it:** Backed by the knowledge that his father has taken Thais under his protection, Phaedria displays more resolution here than at any other stage of the play. There are however some uncertainties in the MSS about speaker assignation in this scene, which makes it difficult to interpret the characterisation: one branch of the MS tradition gives the the 'Shall I tell you...' speech and the following 'I mean it' to Chaerea.

1068 Let's hear him: This remark is the first stage in the weakening of the young men's position. It clearly belongs to whichever of the brothers is taking the softer attitude. One branch of the MS tradition assigns it to Phaedria. But the Penguin edition is probaly right to give it to Chaerea, whose own interests are not at stake and who might be assumed to be in a generous mood after the successful outcome of his own affair.

Just move off a little way over there: This stage-directional formula sends Thraso out of earshot, a variation on the staging in which one character draws another aside to carry out a private conversation without being overheard (706 n.).

p.218 **1081 What shall we do?:** The MSS assign this question to Phaedria, which in fact seems the more likely characterisation: this is the point at which Phaedria begins to waver.

1085 I've had uphill work...with that clod: Lit. 'I've been turning that stone'. This looks like an allusion to Sisyphus' punishment in the underworld (see the Penguin footnote), in which case it is another example of a mythological reference in Terence (1027 n.). According to Donatus the phrase is proverbial.

1087 I offer you...Thraso: Lit. 'I propose him to you as a toast'.

for the laughs and everything else...: Lit. 'to be eaten up and laughed at'.

1088 He deserves it: i.e. to be used and humiliated.

1088-93 For pity's sake...as I told you: The play ends neatly with a final sample of Thraso's conceit and Gnatho's shameless flattery, taken no doubt from Menander's *Kolax*.

1094 This way, please: The actors must exit into the stage building, and the appropriate house is Thais', where all the other characters (except Parmeno) are now gathered.

Farewell, and give us your applause: All Terence's plays end with a request for applause (Lat. *plaudite*), which is preceded in the MSS by the mysterious Greek letter omega. Who actually spoke the final *plaudite* is not at all clear. According to Horace (*Art of Poetry* 155) it was spoken by the *cantor* ('singer', perhaps the musician who accompanied the play), but the matter is still disputed. For some plays of Plautus' the MSS indicate that the final words were spoken by the whole cast, and this cannot be ruled out for Terence. The Penguin translation takes the simplest course, by giving the *plaudite* to the actor who speaks the immediately preceding line.

Phormio

PRODUCTION NOTICE (p. 223)

See the notes on the Production Notice of *Eunuchus*.

Roman Games: These took place in September and were the third of the four annual dramatic festivals in Terence's time, the others being the Megalensian Games in April, the Apolline in July, and the Plebeian in November. The Roman Games were by far the oldest of the Roman festivals, going back probably to the sixth century B.C. Scenic performances are recorded there for the fourth century, and the first Roman drama was performed there in 240 B.C.

Lucius Ambivius Turpio and Lucius Atilius: Introd. §25.

Music composed by Flaccus: Introd. §26.

unmatched pipes: Unmatched (or 'unequal') pipes may imply some sort of harmony, or melody plus accompaniment, or perhaps even an extended scale, but it is difficult to gauge how this affected the mood of the play (see the Penguin introduction, pp. 26-7).

***The Claimant* by Apollodorus:** Terence used Apollodorus as the model for two of his plays (*Phorm.* and *Hec.*), the other four being based on Menander. Apollodorus was not one of the 'top three' New Comedy dramatists (Menander, Diphilus, and Philemon) as recognised by the scholars of antiquity, nor do many quotations or papyrus fragments of his work survive, though he did win the first prize five times in the Athenian dramatic competitions. He is generally supposed to have been a pupil of Menander's; in so far as we can judge from Terence's adaptations, his style and approach were similar.

The author's fourth play: Modern scholars make it his fifth, if the first performance of *Hecyra* is included. *Phormio* was produced in the same year as *Eunuchus* (i.e. 161 B.C.) but five months later.

SYNOPSIS (p. 224)

See the note on the Synopsis of *Eunuchus*.

CHARACTERS (p. 225)

See the note on the Characters of *Eunuchus*

Phormio has thirteen speaking parts, which is well above he average for Roman comedy. The longest role is that of the slave Geta, who is on stage for fifteen scenes, but the ancient commentator

Donatus (*Preface* 1. 4) gives Phormio as the main part, Geta as the second, and Demipho (who appears in eleven scenes) as the third. It is clear enough that leading role is that of Phormio, even though he appears in only seven scenes: Terence himself in the prologue (27) says that Phormio will play the leading part, and the role was entrusted to Ambivius Turpio in the original production, if we can believe Donatus' amusing story (on 315) of how Ambivius played Phormio's entrance scene drunk. The play is written in such a way that the Phormio actor could also play Phaedria; it is otherwise curious that Phaedria, who in the end profits from Phormio's machinations, never actually meets his benefactor on stage. There are also ample signs of a three-actor Greek original, in which the first actor played not only Phormio and Phaedria but also Phaedria's father Chremes, the second played Geta, and the third combined Demipho and Antipho (again father and son).

Scene

See the note on the Scene of *Eunuchus*.

Phormio probably uses only two stage houses, namely those of the two fathers Demipho and Chremes: there is just a hint (712 n.) that Chremes' house is the left-hand of the two. It is possible that Dorio's house is also on stage, as the Penguin translator assumes, but the evidence is self-contradictory (484 n., 829 n.). For this play the Penguin edition adopts the conventional treatment of the side entrances, with the harbour to the audience's left and the town centre (forum) to their right, and this arrangement is followed in the commentary.

PROLOGUE (1-34, pp. 227-8)

See the introductory notes on the Prologue of *Eunuchus*.

1 the old playwright: Luscius of Lanuvium (Introd. §31).

the poet: Terence.

5 feeble language and weak composition: This is a different charge from the stock charges of 'contamination' and 'theft' (Introd. §32), both of which are concerned with fidelity to the Greek models. Luscius is now attacking Terence's style, apparently on the grounds that it is relatively plain, as compared with the colloquial exuberance of Plautus and the other Roman comic dramatists (Introd. §35).

6-8 love-lorn youth...to save her: Terence counterattacks by criticising Luscius' style as extravagantly rhetorical and pathetic.

10 the credit should...go to the producer: *Eun.* 17 n.

17 the prize of victory: Lit. 'the palm'. Though the Greek theatre had highly organised competitions with prizes for the playwrights and actors, we are not well informed about the Roman stage. There are references to competition for the 'palm' (and to unfair devices used to secure it) in two prologues of Plautus' (*Amph.* 64-74,

Poen. 36-9), but there is a suspicion that these are later prologues composed for revival performances when theatrical conditions may have changed. There is also a statement by the later writer Pliny (*Natural History* 21. 4) that a curule aedile of 211 B.C. was the first to present gold and silver crowns in the theatre. If there were regular competitions in Terence's day, we might have expected to hear much more about them: the 'palm' here may be simply metaphorical.

22 I shall stop talking about him: There are no specific references to Luscius in any of Terence's subsequent prologues, though there are allusions to 'enemies' (*Hec.* 22, p. 293), 'unjust men' (*Hec.* 54, p. 294), and 'unfair critics' (*Ad.* 2, p. 339).

24 for the first time: i.e. there have been no previous adaptations of *The Claimant* on the Roman stage: Terence is forestalling any charge of 'theft' (Introd. §32).

The Claimant: Gk *Epidikazomenos*, lit. 'the man who goes to law to establish a claim'. Terence has replaced the technical term by the name of the leading character: this is the only one of Terence's six plays where he has changed the title of the Greek original.

28 adventurer: Lat. *parasitus* (Introd. §12).

plays the leading part and directs most of the intrigue: *Phormio* resembles several plays of Plautus', which are also named after dominating masters of intrigue, usually tricky slaves (*Epidicus* and *Pseudolus*) but including another parasite (*Curculio*).

228   **30 Pay attention...in silence:** *Eun.* 44 n.

32 drove our company from the stage: See the *Hecyra* prologues (pp. 292-4).

33 thanks to the courage of our producer: This confirms that the prologue is not here spoken by Ambivius Turpio himself (as in *Heaut.* and *Hec.*) but by another actor of the troupe. On the importance of the producer (or 'actor-manager') see Introd. §25.

I. i-ii: DAVOS, GETA (35-152, pp. 229-33)

[1] A slave Davos arrives with money to repay a debt to a fellow-slave Geta. Geta explains that his master Demipho and his master's brother Chremes have gone overseas, leaving their respective sons Antipho and Phaedria in his care. Phaedria has fallen in love with a music-girl belonging to a pimp, and Antipho with a poor orphan girl, whom he has contrived to marry with the help of the parasite Phormio. A letter from Demipho has just arrived at the customs, which Geta departs to collect.

[2] These are presented as two scenes by the MSS, the convention being that the entry of a new character constitutes a new scene, but it is more convenient to treat them as one. Between them they carry the basic exposition of the plot, setting out the existing situation, and introducing all the main characters. Davos disappears from the play after his conversation with Geta, and is thus what is known as a

'protatic' character, i.e. one who appears only at the beginning of a play to assist in the exposition. Terence uses this device in two other plays (*Andr.* and *Hec.*), and Plautus uses it in four (*Epid.*, *Merc.*, *Mil.*, and *Most.*); it can be traced back through Menander (Chaireas in *Dysk.* is the nearest parallel) to Aristophanes, who has protatic slave characters in three plays (*Knights, Peace, Wasps*). The effect is to transform what would otherwise have been an expository monologue into an expository dialogue, which is likely to make a more interesting opening.

[3] Many scholars have assumed that Apollodorus' play had a formal expository prologue, following the common practice of Menander's. This is because there is a crucial fact (namely the real identity of the orphan girl), unknown to Geta, which emerges only comparatively late in the play. A divine prologue could have revealed this to the audience, and thus created some effective dramatic irony; as it is, Terence is able to achieve a surprise effect by bringing out the information later. If Terence has omitted a divine prologue from Apollodorus' play, he must have incorporated most of the expository material from it into the Geta-Davos dialogue. But it is not easy to reconstruct a convincing opening to the Greek play with a divine prologue (whether this opened the play or was postponed in Menander's manner), nor are there any major awkwardnesses in Terence's opening scenes which would suggest that he has tampered with the Greek original. On the general question see Introd. §33.

[4] The opening scenes already make it clear that this is another double plot, according to Terence's usual practice (Introd. §17). Like *Eunuchus*, the play involves two young men, each with a different kind of love affair, though this time they are cousins rather than brothers; unlike *Eunuchus*, it also involves two fathers, who may (or may not) turn out to have contrasting attitudes to their sons' behaviour. It remains to be seen what links, apart from the blood relationships, are forged between the two halves of the dual plot. None of these four characters appears in the opening scenes, but a few hints are given about their characterisation. Of the young men, Phaedria is the 'head over heels' type (like Chaerea in *Eun.*), falling madly in love with a girl whose social status will not permit marriage ('All he could do was feast his eyes on her...' 85); Antipho is less independent, relying on Phormio's help and 'terrified of his absent father' (118). Of the fathers, Demipho has 'wealth enough and to spare' but nonetheless undertakes an overseas trip on the promise of 'mountains of gold' (68-9); he is not the sort to agree to his son's marrying 'a girl with no dowry and no family' (120 n.). Chremes, who is the older of the two fathers (63), remains very shadowy, except that 'both fathers' had ensured that 'there wasn't a penny' to spend on girl-friends (84). The scene also gives us a vivid introduction to Phormio, described as a 'real adventurer' and 'an impudent rascal' (122 n.), with the fictitious court

case a clear proof of his boldness and ingenuity. We are not told Phormio's motive for helping Antipho, but it seems that he is willing to risk his own skin to do so ('I'll be in trouble, but no matter' 133).

[5] Davos and Geta both belong to the type 'slave' (Lat. *servus*: Introd. §7). As a protatic character, Davos' main function is to ask questions and make appropriate comments. But he does come across with a clear character, honest, loyal to a fellow slave, and rather cynical about the behaviour of the rich ('Unfair I call it...' 41) and about general standards of honesty ('We've come to the point of being most grateful if a man does no more than pay his debts' 55-6). Geta is rather more important to the play. At our first acquaintance, he is neither the 'tricky slave' nor the 'bungling slave' (compare Parmeno in *Eun.*), but a long-suffering pedagogue (72 n.), who is whipped when he tries to restrain his charges (76 n.) and who in the end takes the easy course by '[falling] in with all their wishes' (78-9). Davos and Geta are both common slave names in Greek and Roman comedy: there is also a Davos in Terence's *Andria* and a Geta in his *Adelphoe*. Like Syrus (*Eun.* 772 n.) the names Geta and Davos denote ethnic origins: both the Getae and the Davi seem to have been Thracian tribes.

[6] As in *Eunuchus*, it looks as if love will be the main theme of the play, though the prominence given to the fathers here suggests that father-son relationships will also be important. But it is another common theme of comedy, relationships between rich and poor, which dominates these opening scenes. It is the theme of Davos' entrance monologue, and it recurs both in the discussions of Demipho's greed (67-70) and attitude to his son's marriage (119-21) and in the description of the poverty of the orphan girl ('the sheer misery and burden of poverty' 94, 'honest daughter of honest parents' 115). It is notable that the sympathy is on the side of the poor. This is not due simply to the fact that this is a dialogue between slaves, or to any antagonism on Terence's part towards the rich (if we can believe the traditional biography, he was himself a slave befriended by a noble patron: see the Penguin introduction, pp. 12-13); rather, sympathy for the poor is part of the general 'humanity' of Terence's outlook (Introd. §15).

[7] The language is lively and colloquial, as befits a conversation between slaves. Apart from the humour of Davos' interjections, the most notable features are the striking imagery (40 n., 47 n., 72 n., 76 n., 79 n., 85 n., 144 n.) and the use of colloquial and proverbial expressions (59 n., 68 n., 77-8 n., 83 n.).

[8] These scenes, like the prologue, are in spoken verse (ia⁶); Terence never uses recitative for his opening scenes (Introd. §27-8).

40 scraping up something: This familiar metaphor would have sounded more original in Terence's day. It occurs three times in Terence, but is otherwise very rare in Greek and Roman comedy.

43 rations: According to Donatus, a slave's rations were four measures of grain a month. Presumably these could be commuted to the monetary equivalent, or bartered.

47 stung: Lit. 'struck', which is probably a metaphor from gladiatiorial combat.

48 birthdays: Roman comedy provides the earliest reference in the classical world to the giving of gifts for birthdays, a custom which we take for granted in modern times. Apart from this passage, there are two allusions in Plautus (*Epid.* 639-40, *Pseud.* 179-81): the *Epidicus* passage, like the *Phormio* one, refers to the birthday of a child, and only the *Pseudolus* passage, where a pimp demands birthday gifts, refers to the birthday of an adult. If these references are taken over from the corresponding Greek comedies, they would be evidence for the custom in fourth and third century Greece, where otherwise we hear only of birthday gifts for kings.

49 an initiation ceremony: Donatus implies that in Apollodorus there was a specific reference to initiation in the Samothracian mysteries, which was the Athenian custom for children of a certain age. It is typical of Terence to omit minor details of the Greek context where these would have puzzled the Roman audience.

50 here *is* Geta: Davos terminates his own monologue with an 'introduction formula' (Introd. §29), which serves as a stage direction.

51 If a red-head comes asking for me: By a common convention Geta emerges from Demipho's house speaking 'over the shoulder' to someone inside (Introd. §20).

red-head: Red hair is particularly associated with slaves in comedy, reflecting no doubt the northern european origin of many of them: Pseudolus is described as red-headed at Plaut. *Pseud.* 1218, as is Leonida at Plaut. *Asin.* 400. It does not follow that all slaves in comedy had red hair, but a significant proportion probably did; the ancient encyclopaedist Pollux ascribes red hair to five of the eight types of slave masks which he lists.

52 I was just going to look for you: This is a variation on the common 'response formula' ('I was looking for you') used by characters who have just been accosted (Introd. §30).

p.230 **59 Go on, you idiot:** This is one of the many colloquial phrases which enliven the scene.

66 Lemnos...Cilicia: Lemnos is an island in the north-east of the Aegean sea which had long-standing connections with Athens. Cilicia, which is on the southern coast of what is now Turkey, appears in Plautus as a place for mercenary service (*Trin.* 599, *Mil.* 42); it does not occur elsewhere in Terence, and it is not clear why it is chosen here for Demipho's journey.

68 mountains of gold: According to Donatus, this is a proverbial exaggeration: Plautus has the similar phrase 'mountains of silver' (*Mil.* 1065).

70 a rich patron: The Latin simply says 'a king' (*rex*), a word which in comedy is often metaphorical, meaning 'rich', 'powerful'.

72 guardian: The allusion is to the the slave's role as pedagogue or tutor to the sons of the family, a practice which was common in Athens but relatively new at Rome in Terence's day (Introd. §8). The Roman comic dramatists tend to substitute the nearest Latin equivalent *magister* ('schoolmaster'), which is the word used by Terence here: the Greek word *paedagogus* is found only once in Terence (144 n.).

job: Lit. 'province'. Again the terminology is interesting. The Latin word *provincia* means 'sphere of duty', and it then comes to be applied especially to a conquered territory which is the 'province' of a particular governor. Its application to the 'job' of a slave is thus deliberately pretentious: Terence is following several examples of the humorous use of the word in Plautus.

76 broke my back: Lit. 'destroyed my shoulder blades', a reference to being whipped, which the translation does not capture.

77-8 It's folly to kick against the pricks: This is an old Greek proverb, going back at least as far as Aeschylus in the fifth century B.C., which is much quoted in later antiquity (and in the account of St Paul's conversion in *The Acts of the Apostles*). This is its first and only occurrence in classical Latin.

79 work the market: i.e. adapt to the situation as you find it. Donatus explains that this is a reference to the practice of those merchants who do not decide their prices beforehand but adapt them, or even withdraw their goods, according to the state of the market.

82 lute-player: Terence uses the Greek word *citharistria*, of which 'lute-player' is a better translation than the traditional 'lyre-player'; the cithara was a smaller guitar-like instrument which sat on the knee, whereas the lyre sat on the floor like a harp. Both were stringed instruments, and were usually played with a plectrum; they were not used for solo performance but to accompany singing. In the context of a girl working for a pimp, it is worth noting that the girl is envisaged as an entertainer, who is even sent to music school to improve her skills, not simply as a purveyor of sexual favours.

83 that dirty pimp: Lit. 'foul', 'unclean' (Lat. *inpurus*). This is a strong term of abuse, used in comedy mainly by slaves and usually directed at pimps and other despised characters. The word 'that' is not in the Latin, so that there is no explicit suggestion that Dorio's house is visible on stage, despite the Penguin stage direction.

231   **85 feast his eyes:** This is another familiar metaphor, which appears here for the first time in Latin literature.

86 music school: The Latin says simply 'school' (*ludus*), even though a music school is clearly meant; there were no music schools in the Roman educational system (*Eun.* 476-7 n.).

89 barber's shop: Barber's shops were evidently good places to pass the time and catch up with the gossip, both in Greece and Rome. Donatus tersely comments 'a fit place for the idle'.

92 a young man...in tears: There is another interesting point of difference here between Greek and Roman culture. According to Donatus, in Apollodorus' play it was the barber himself who told the story of the orphan girl, having just cut her hair as a token of mourning; and Terence made the change in order not to puzzle the Roman audience with the 'foreign custom' (cf. 49 n.): the Greeks cut the hair in mourning, whereas the Roman custom was to loosen it At the same time Terence's addition of the weeping young man with his graphic description of the scene enhances the pathos of the story.

97 laid out facing the door: in preparation for the funeral.

106 hair loose: 92 n.

109 his own girl: Lit. 'the music-girl': Terence here uses the Latin *fidicina* (*Eun.* 457 n.) rather than the Greek equivalent (82 n.).

114 it wouldn't be right: Lat. *aequom*, one of Terence's favourite ethical terms and part of his general concept of 'humanity' (Introd. §16).

an Attic citizen: The girl's citizen status is made clear from the outset, in contrast to Pamphila's in *Eunuchus*, which is only conjectured. There is no hint of the girl's parentage, but granted the conventions of the genre (Introd. §1), the audience might well suspect that she will turn out to be the long-lost daughter of one of the characters of the play.

p.232   **120 a girl with no dowry and no family:** These are the usual objections of fathers in comedy to their sons' marriage proposals (cf. Men. *Dysk.* 794-6, Ter. *Ad.* 728-9, p. 373).

122 a real adventurer: Lat. *parasitus*, sometimes translated 'hanger-on', 'sponger' (*Eun.* 228 n.). The translation 'adventurer' underlines the fact that Phormio is not another Gnatho but a different type of parasite altogether, the practical helper and schemer (Introd. §12); Donatus several times calls him a *sycophanta* ('trickster', 'swindler'), which is a much better description of his role. It is interesing that Terence himself, in listing some of the stock characters of comedy (*Heaut.* 38, p. 102), distinguishes between the 'greedy sponger' (*parasitus*) and the 'shameless impostor' (*sycophanta*).

125-6 The law says...: This is an Athenian law, which would have been familiar to the Athenian audience: Terence has no doubt introduced this summary himself for the benefit of the Roman spectator. It is a law which is several times invoked in comedy, notably at Men. *Asp.* 184-7 and Ter. *Ad.* 650-2 (p. 369). Since its purpose was to safeguard the property of the family, it applied not to all orphan girls but to those who in the absence of any brothers stood to inherit the family property from their dead fathers. Since women could not in strict law own the property, the object of these enforced marriages was to produce a son, who would legally inherit it and thus keep it in the family.

138-9 I shall meet my fate with equanimity..: As Donatus notes, this heroic philosophising by a slave is intended to be amusing.

141-2 Let him off just this once...: This is the standard plea on behalf of the erring slave (*Eun.* 852-3 n.).

233   **144 playing escort:** The Latin is *paedagogus* (72 n.). Davos is speaking metaphorically: it was one of the duties of the pedagogue to escort his charges to school and back. Terence evidently expects his Roman audience to appreciate the point, which suggests that the pedagogue was now becoming a familiar figure at Rome.

145 He hasn't much...?: Davos has already been told (84) that the fathers had ensured that there wasn't a penny to offer for the girl. The repetition serves to underline Phaedria's problem to the audience.

147 Is his father back?: Again, the question is for the sake of the audience. The return of Phaedria's father is foreshadowed, but not until after the return of Antipho's: it is the Antipho half of the dual plot which will be developed first.

150 customs office: The customs officers, who collected harbour taxes, evidently had the right to hold and examine letters arriving from overseas; there are references to their unsealing and inspection of letters at Plaut. *Trin.* 793-5, 809-10.

151 Nothing else I can do...?: This is the standard 'leave-taking formula', which here receives a conventional reply 'look after yourself' (Introd. §29). The exchange serves as a stage direction: Davos now departs and does not appear again in the play. It suits the staging best if he and Geta leave in opposite directions, and, since Geta is going to the harbour (i.e. to the audience's left: Introd. §19), we can suppose Davos to leave in the direction of the forum (i.e. to the right).

152 Here, boy! Is no one coming?: This is another implicit stage direction (Introd. §29): Geta knocks at the door of his house and a slave emerges.

give it to my wife: Lit. 'to Dorcium'. Slaves could not legally marry, so that strictly Dorcium is Geta's concubine. We have to infer that this is an exit line; after handing over the bag of money to the slave, Davos goes off to the harbour to collect the letter, leaving the stage momentarily empty.

I. iii: ANTIPHO, PHAEDRIA (153-78, pp. 233-4)

[1] Antipho and Phaedria enter in conversation. Antipho, terrified at the prospect of his father's return, wishes that he had never married the orphan girl. Phaedria assures him that he is much worse off himself, having to deal with a pimp.

[2] There is no indication in the text of the direction from which Antipho and Phaedria enter, which could in theory be from either of their houses or from either of the wings. But the most likely is from Chremes' house, since all the other possibilities have just been in use, the two wings for Davos' and Geta's departures and Demipho's house for the slave to receive Geta's money.

[3] The scene continues the exposition. Its function is to develop

the characterisation of Antipho and Phaedria (35ff n. 4). Both belong to the type 'young man' (Lat. *adulescens*: Introd. §1). Phaedria belongs to the sub-type who fall madly in love with a *meretrix*; here, though still 'glad to die' if he could enjoy his love (165-6), he emerges at the more level-headed and philosophical of the two (172 n.). Antipho belongs to the sub-type who fall in love with poor citizen girls; his situation is unusual in that, rather than having to work towards a marriage in face of his father's disapproval, he is already married at the beginning of the play, and regrets it. His first words show him 'in terror of [his] father's return' (154), confirming Geta's previous statement (118, p. 231); he looks like being the less attractive character, regretting what he has done ('if only I hadn't been so thoughtless' 155), ungrateful to Phormio ('I wish Phormio'd never thought of suggesting it' 157), and generally gloomy, helpless, and pessimistic ('I'm sadly afraid he's bringing me bad news' 178). The names 'Antipho' and 'Phaedria' both occur as young men's names in *Eunuchus*, but are otherwise very rare in comedy: on the literal meanings see *Eun.* 46ff n. 4, 539ff n. 2.

[4] This scene is in recitative, reflecting its higher emotional level. Mixed metres are used for Antipho's complaints and a single metre (ia^8) for Phaedria's counterarguments (from 'anyone would beg and pray' 164). On the metres see Introd. §27-8.

153-5 best interests at heart... in the right spirit: These lines suggest that the underlying father-son relationship is more positive than has so far been implied.

159 it would have been hell, but only for a few days: The point is presumably that it would have been easier for Antipho to give up the girl before they were married than to face the continual threat of separation now that they are living together.

p.234 **168 free and well-born:** According to Donatus, 'well-born' (Lat. *ingenuus*) refers to character and 'free' (Lat. *liberalis*) to birth. But in the context the main point is that the girl is free-born and therefore marriageable. Phaedria conveniently overlooks the fact that her family is too poor to provide a dowry (120 n.).

172 each one discontented with his own lot: There seems to be no ancient proverb equivalent to our 'The grass is always greener on the other side of the fence', but the thought was commonplace. Menander's tutor Theophrastus included 'The man who blames his fate' among his *Characters*, and Horace based his first *Satire* (1. 1) on discussions of the theme by the Hellenistic philosophers.

177-8 isn't that Geta I see...? Yes it is: The transition to the next scene is effected by an introduction formula, which simultaneously acts as a stage direction (50 n.).

running this way: As the audience will recognise, this heralds the use by Terence of the 'running slave' convention (*Eun.* 4 n.).

178 bad news: i.e. not merely a letter but the return of Antipho's father, as again the audience will guess: Mercury at Plaut. *Amph.* 986-8 sums up the function of the running slave as to report 'the ship safe and the arrival of the angry old man'. Geta has been off-stage for only twenty-six lines (153-78), during which time he has been to the harbour and back. This is not particularly significant for Roman comedy, where compression of off-stage time is relatively common, but it does provide a clue to the act-division of the Greek original, since the Greek convention seems to have been that characters could only go to the harbour and back (or to the forum and back) over a choral interlude (Introd. §23). But in fact this is relatively early in the play for the end of the Greek first act, and there is the other possibility that there was a postponed divine prologue at this point, which could similarly have 'covered' Geta's movements.

I. iv: GETA, ANTIPHO, PHAEDRIA (179-230, pp. 234-7)

[1] Geta arrives from the harbour (left) with news of Demipho's return. Antipho's courage fails him, and he runs off (right), leaving Phaedria and Geta to face Demipho.

[2] This scene leads directly to Demipho's return, with which the development of the plot begins. Its main point is its humour, particularly in the parody of the running slave convention and in the panic-stricken behaviour of Antipho. At the same time it provides further characterisation of Geta and the two young men.

[3] Geta here begins to display some of the attributes of the 'tricky slave' character (Intr. §7). In particular, (i) he utters a 'panic monologue' ('You're done for...It'll make things worse...Oh misery' 179-90; (ii) he takes charge of the situation, with Phaedria accepting his orders ('just tell me what to do' 223); (iii) he indulges in military terminology with himself in the role of commander (229-30 n.). At the same time his loyalty to his younger master is emphasised ('I'm worried to death for Antipho...But for him I'd have...done a bolt' 187-90).

[4] Of the other characters, the characterisation of Antipho as feeble and frightened is confirmed ('I can't change' 206, 'he's hopeless' 208); indeed, he is almost a caricature as he tries to compose his face (210-14) and then runs away at Demipho's approach (216-18). Phaedria continues to be more level-headed; and two new features of his character are introduced, namely loyalty to his brother ('I'll do my best' 228) and subservience to his slave (219 n.). There is also a new angle on the character of Demipho, with references to his 'temper' (189) and 'savage bursts of fury' (213), which appear to put him into the class of the 'angry old man' (*senex iratus*: Introd. §3).

[5] The scene falls into three parts metrically: (i) mixed-metre recitative for the running slave passage (to 215); (ii) tr^7 (the standard recitative metre) for the delivery of Geta's news (from 'Pretty free with your orders' 196); and (iii) ia^6 (spoken verse) from the point

where Demipho is seen approaching (from 'I can't stay' 216). For the various metres and their effect see Introd. §27-8.

179-96 You're done for...the very man I wanted: This is the first of ten occurrences in the play of Terence's favourite scene-opening pattern, the 'overheard entrance monologue' (Introd. §19) accompanied by asides and terminated formulaically (Introd. §30). In this case, as already foreshadowed (177-8 n.), Terence is using a particularly elaborate and unrealistic form of this, the 'running slave' monologue (Lat. *servus currens*). This was so well established as a convention that Terence twice refers to the *servus currens* as one of the stock characters of comedy (*Heaut.* 37, p. 102; *Eun.* 36, p. 166), and Plautus actually makes characters in his plays refer to the stage routine (*Amph.* 987, *Capt.* 778). In the fullest form of the convention, as developed by Plautus, the running slave arrives breathless with important news, having searched the whole city for his master, pushing bystanders out of his way in his haste; he fails to see his master, who is in fact on stage and who comments aside (often to a friend) on the slave's behaviour; when the master does accost him, the slave abusively rejects his approach before realising that it is in fact his master; and he then finally delivers his message, often interrupted by anxious questioning. Plautus uses the convention in eight plays, and can stretch the routine to over sixty lines; Terence has four examples, all much briefer, two of which are in *Phormio*. It is interesting that Terence uses the routine as much as he does, granted its unrealistic nature; it provides not only comedy, but dramatic irony (since the audience already knows, or can guess, the slave's news), and it highlights a dramatic point in the development of the plot. The convention presumably derives from Greek New Comedy, though no fully fledged examples have yet been discovered: the nearest parallel is the breathless entry of Pyrrhias at Men. *Dysk.* 81-97.

184 master's here: i.e. Demipho is back (178 n.).

What's his trouble?: Antipho evidently is not close enough to catch what Geta says.

p.235   **186 Labour wasted:** Lit. 'I should be washing bricks', a colourful proverbial expression taken over from the Greeks.

195 Let's call him back: This is one of the standard formulae for interrupting a running slave monologue.

196 Pretty free with your orders...whoever you are: The running slave typically refuses to recognise his master.

198 All right...I say: These seven speeches all fit into one line of Latin verse, which is good example of the rapidity which Terence's dialogue can achieve (*Eun.* 697 n.).

p.236   **201 Phanium:** This is the first of seven occurrences in the play of the name of Antipho's bride, who was referred to in the opening scenes simply as 'the girl' (Lat. *virgo*: lit. 'maiden'). Like most young girls in comedy, Phanium does not appear as a character in the play. The name 'Phanium' is rare but occurs as a courtesan's name in Menander and in the Greek Anthology; its literal meaning is 'little torch'. On young girls in comedy see Introd. §2 (cf. *Eun.* 440 n.).

203 Fortune favours the brave: This is a common proverb, found here for the first time in Latin, but already known in one form or another to the Greeks (with examples in Menander and Sophocles). On the personification of Fortune see *Eun.* 1046 n.

210-11 Look at my face...That'll do: Antipho's comic attempt to compose his face raises the question of masks in the Roman theatre. Greek New Comedy, like all Greek drama, had masks, and the natural assumption would be that Roman comedy took over the masks of Greek comedy as it took over the costumes. This assumption is supported by the continuous tradition of representations of comic masks in art from Greek to Roman times; but it is contradicted by some writers of later antiquity who imply that masks were not introduced at Rome until after the days of Terence. Despite this conflict of evidence, it seems highly probable that Roman comedy was masked from the beginning. In a mask, Antipho's attempts to put on a brave face would have to be imagined by the audience, but this does not provide evidence that masks were not worn. The same is true of the blushes of Aeschinus at *Ad.* 643 (p. 369): even without a mask an actor would have difficulty in feigning a blush. There are similar instances in Greek Comedy, where masks certainly were worn; the lead character in Aristophanes' *Lysistrata* (7-8) is told to stop scowling because it spoils her appearance. On masks in Roman comedy see Beare 303-9, Duckworth 92-4, Gratwick 83-4, Sandbach 111-12

Is that all right...That'll do: These six utterances occupy one line of Latin verse (cf. 198 n.)

213 bowl you over: The Latin image is of being trampled or driven off by a team of oxen.

215 Who's that old man...? Yes, it's the master: The introduction formulae mark the transition to the the following scene (177-8 n.), though Demipho does not actually appear for another sixteen lines (Introd. §19).

).237 **216-18 Where are you going? Stop, sir:** These are effectively stage directions written into the text (Introd. §29), from which we infer Antipho's headlong exit from the stage. Since Demipho is approaching from the harbour (left: Introd. §19), the obvious staging is for Antipho to run off right.

219 What'll happen now, Geta?: This marks the surrender of the initiative by Phaedria: Geta can now adopt the 'tricky slave' role.

222 our duty: Note that both slave and cousin have a 'duty' (Lat. *oportet*: Introd. §16) to support Antipho against his father. This is very much a reversal of the real-life situation in Rome, where the father (*paterfamilias*) had absolute rights not only over his slaves but over his sons: on the other hand, the 'duty' of helping one's friends is very much part of Terence's 'humanity' (Introd. §15).

229-30   attack...ambush...reserve...give ground: In theory, these four terms could have been translated from their Greek equivalents. But the third is a clearly a Roman term (*succenturiatus* = 'a man brought into a century to fill a gap', the century being a unit of Roman army organisation but not of Greek), and the more likely view is that Terence is here reproducing in a mild form the exuberant Roman military imagery employed by the tricky slaves of Plautus.

The renaissance editors somewhat inappropriately placed the end of Terence's first act after 230: the stage is not empty and this scene clearly leads straight into the next one.

II. i: DEMIPHO, PHAEDRIA, GETA (231-314, pp. 237-41)

[1] Demipho arrives from the harbour (left), furious at the news of Antipho's marriage and his failure to resist the case in court. Phaedria explains that Antipho was too shy to do himself justice, and Geta excuses himself on the grounds that slaves are not permitted to give evidence; nor could they take the option of marrying the girl to someone else because they did not have money for a dowry. Demipho sends them to fetch Phormio and Antipho.

[2] Demipho's arrival thus sets up prospects of two confrontations (Demipho-Phormio and Demipho-Antipho), and the developnic.it of the plot begins in earnest. The initial emphasis is all on the Demipho-Antipho-Phanium half of the double plot; but, by making Phaedria face Demipho on Antipho's behalf, Terence involves one young man in the affair of the other, thus linking the two halves (Introd. §17).

[3] The characterisation of Demipho has to be seen against the background of two stock types of father, the *senex durus* and *senex lenis* (Introd. §3). In previous scenes we have noted wealth (35ff n. 4) and anger (179ff n. 4) as two of Demipho's characteristics. Here there are several more references to his anger ('I'm so angry' 240, 'you're angry with him' 259), but Terence is careful to distinguish him from the exaggerated *senex iratus* of Plautus. Demipho himself claims that he is by nature an 'indulgent father' (*lenis* 262), whose temper has been changed by his son's behaviour. He is also willing to recognise points which can be made in Antipho's defence ('I grant that' 236, 294); and he appreciates that he will need skilled advice, not merely bluster, to confront Phormio (313 n.). 'Demipho', which recurs as an old man's name in Plaut. *Cist.* and *Merc.*), literally means 'voice of the people', rather suggesting a person with some authority.

[4] Of the other characters Geta continues to show some of the attributes of the tricky slave, with his assertion that he can deal with the situation ('I'll find one, don't worry' 235, 'Leave it to me, I'll solve it' 238), his asides and repartee (esp. his parody of Demipho's philosophising: 251 n.), his reference to slave punishments (249-50 n.),

and his spirited response to Demipho's accusations (290 n.). Phaedria's main characteristic is the loyalty with which he defends Antipho; he also puts on a good show of injured innocence ('He's doing well' 285).

[5] The scene begins in recitative (mainly ia⁸), reflecting the emotional state of Demipho's monologue, but reverts to spoken verse at the point where he is greeted by Phaedria ('Good morning, uncle' 254).

231-53 So that's it...coming to meet me: This is another overheard entrance monologue, accompanied by asides and terminated formulaically (179-96 n.). Demipho has somehow heard all about the court-case and Antipho's marriage, even though he has only just returned to Athens. This may not be realistic writing by Terence, but it is economic, in that it enables the plot to proceed without any delay.

232 authority: The Roman audience would no doubt see this as an allusion to the Roman father's absolute power (*patria potestas*) over his family, which meant that the son needed his father's permission before he could marry. In Athens the father did not have such an absolute legal right, but it is nonetheless generally assumed in Greek comedy (e.g. Men. *Dysk.*) that the son will seek his father's consent.

233 impudence: The son should show proper respect for his father's authority: the Latin concept is *pudor* (Introd. §16).

234 guardian: Terence again avoids the word *paedagogus* (72 n.), subsitituting the the non-technical term *monitor*.

238 **239 Now what am I to do?:** Donatus, who is at some pains to trace the gradual softening of Demipho's anger as the scene progresses, suggests that his indignation is already weakening.

241-6 It just shows...pure gain: This passage is quoted by Cicero (*Tusculan Disputations* 3. 30) in the course of a discussion of mental distress. The advice 'expect the worst and you will be grateful if it doesn't happen' was no doubt something of a commonplace, but Cicero associates it especially with the Cyrenaic school of philosophy, one of those which flourished at Athens at the time of New Comedy. Terence presumably took the passage directly from Apollodorus, who will have been reflecting the philosophical discussions of his own day.

249-50 flogging, fetters, grinding at the mill...toiling on the farm: These are the traditional punishments feared by the tricky slave of comedy. Plautine tricky slaves are full of graphic descriptions of the punishments which they face (e.g. *As.* 31-9), but this is the most extensive list in Terence (cf. *Andr.* 199-200, p. 47).

251 None of this...pure gain: Geta parodies Demipho's philosophising by transferring it to his own less exalted experience. The same device is used at *Ad.* 413-31 (pp. 358-9) by the slave Syrus.

252 why don't you approach him...?: Lit. 'why do you delay to approach him?', a combination of 'action formula' and 'approach formula' (Introd. §29).

254-6 Good morning...all right with you: This interchange provides a good example of Terence's manipulation of the conventions of the 'homecoming scene' (Introd. §30). After a brief exchange of greetings ('Good morning', Lat. *salve*) the angry Demipho cuts short the formalities; he does not allow Phaedria to complete the formulaic pleasantry 'I'm delighted to see you [safely back]', but buts in with the response formula 'I don't doubt it' (= 'I'm sure you are'). Then instead of enquiring about Antipho's health, Demipho brusquely asks *where* he is; Phaedria nonetheless responds with the conventional 'he's well'.

p.239   **265 Know one, you know the lot:** The expression is proverbial.

267 It's a mutual benefit society: Demipho obviously disapproves in the context of people conspiring together to save each other's skins. But in more general terms helping one's fellow men is a positive aspect of Terence's philosophy (Introd. §15).

271 property and reputation: The objection to young men's love affairs in Roman comedy regularly involves the financial aspect as well as the moral (*Eun.* 79 n.).

276-7 take from the rich...and give to the poor: This recalls the emphasis in the opening scene on rich-poor relationships (35ff n. 6), though here, since the argument is meant to appeal to the wealthy Demipho, the sympathy is on the side of the rich. The idea of courts favouring the poor will derive from the democratic Athens of the Greek original; it was hardly the case in Terence's Rome, where the courts were in the hands of the upper classes.

p.240   **281-2 well-brought-up :** Lat. *liberalis*, one of the key words of Terentian ethics, implying behaviour worthy of a free man (Introd. §15).

284 embarrassment: The Latin is *pudor* again (233 n.), here implying a proper sense of modesty.

285 This is where I come in: Lit 'do I delay to approach' (252 n.). After an unusually long passage of eavesdropping and asides, Geta finally discloses himself to Demipho.

286-7 Good morning...I'm glad to see you safely back: Terence again briefly deploys the homecoming formulae (254-6 n.).

287 guardian: This time the Latin is *custos* ('guard') (234 n.).

prop and mainstay: Demipho is of course being ironic. The same metaphor occurs twice in Plautus: the reference seems originally to have been to the ridge-pole of the house.

290 deserves them least of anybody: Lit. 'unjustestly' (Lat. *inmeritissimo*), a word coined by Geta for the occasion; the translation rather conceals the exuberance of Geta's language.

292-3 The law doesn't permit...: Neither in Athens nor in Rome could a slave appear in a court of law, though statements made by slaves under torture could be produced in court as evidence.

297 dowry...another husband: Demipho is making a valid point, which has so far been ignored. The law gave the nearest male relative this option if he did not want to marry the heiress himself.

302 Who'd give him credit while you're alive?: Young men in comedy do contract loans (e.g. Philolaches in Plaut. *Most.*); they also complain about the difficulty of obtaining them. Plautus twice refers (*Pseud.* 303-4, *Rud.* 1381-2) to the specifically Roman law (the Lex Plaetoria of about 200 B.C., designed to protect minors against fraud) which allowed contracts made with those under twenty-five to be rescinded; one result of this must have been that money-lenders were chary of making loans to minors. But here the following 'while you're alive' suggests that a different point is being made: the creditor was more likely to be able to recover his money when the son was financially and legally independent than when he relied on his father's wealth and willingness to repay. In strictly legal terms, at Athens the son became independent at the age of eighteen (whereas at Rome he remained under the power of his father so long as the latter was alive: cf. 232 n.), but young men in comedy are always presented as being financially dependent on their fathers.

303 I won't have it: As Donatus points out, Demipho has now lost the argument, and is reduced to 'irrational exclamation'.

241   **307 the man who acted for the girl:** Lit. 'patron'; the Latin *patronus* is here equivalent to the Greek *prostates* (*Eun.* 1039 n.).

310 straight - there: As Geta's aside makes clear, Phaedria does not in fact go to find Antipho but to join his girl-friend at the pimp's house. The staging here is debatable. If Dorio's house is not on stage (83 n.), the most convenient staging is for Phaedria to exit left (i.e. Dorio's house is notionally towards the harbour) and Geta to exit right (i.e Phormio's house is notionally towards the town centre). Since Antipho in fact ran off right (216-18 n.), the audience will appreciate that Phaedria has gone in the wrong direction to find him.

to Pamphila: This is the first of three occasions in the play that Phaedria's girl-friend is named; she has so far been referred to as 'the lute-player' or 'the music-girl'. Like Phanium (201 n.), Pamphila does not actually appear on stage. On the name see *Eun.* 440 n.

311-14 I'm going in...: Demipho is left on stage to utter a brief 'exit monologue', one of only two in the play (Introd. §22).

give thanks to the gods...Then...go into town: There is an interesting difference between Greek and Roman custom here, which has led to a problem of staging in Terence's play. The Latin makes it clear that Demipho is referring to the Roman gods of the store-cupboard (*Penates*), who were worshipped inside the Roman house. The Greek returning traveller would on the other hand pay his respects to the altar of Apollo which stood outside the Greek house. In Terence therefore Demipho has to go inside at this point, and we never actually see him depart for the town, though he is returning from there when he next appears (348, p. 243); this contra-venes the normal rule of staging by which characters reappear from the direction in which the audience last saw them disappear. In Apollodorus' play the Demipho character would have greeted the altar of Apollo and gone straight off to the town at this point without entering his house, and the staging problem would not have arisen (see the Penguin footnote, p. 243).

313 friends to support me: *Eun.* 340 n.

314 ready for Phormio: There are two reasons for supposing a Greek act-break at this point : (i) a choral interlude is needed before 348 to cover Demipho's journey into town to fetch his advisers; (ii) time is needed here for Geta to go and find Phormio, an errand for which Terence allows only four lines (311-14). The latter is a very un-realistic compression of off-stage time in the Latin play (Introd. §23).

II. ii: PHORMIO, GETA (315-47, pp. 241-3)

[1] Geta returns (from the right: 310 n.) in conversation with Phormio, who promises to save the situation.

[2] The scene itself adds nothing to the plot, though it does lead directly into the Demipho-Phormio confrontation of the following scene. Its main function is to bring Phormio on stage at last. He was described in the opening scenes as a *parasitus* (122 n.) and as an 'impudent rascal', and the audience will have been waiting with some anticipation to see him in action. Here his confidence in his own trickery is reaffirmed ('Bring on the old man. Now all my plans are laid' 321) and his willingness to suffer the consequences ('the full flood of the old man's wrath to be diverted on to me' 323). Terence also goes to some length to portray him as the traditional parasite, exalting in the free meals that he is able to extract from his patron; there are reasons for thinking that this aspect of his characterisation is an addition by Terence to the Greek original (334 n., 338 n., 339 n., 342-3 n.). The colourfulness of Phormio's character is underlined by the liveliness of his language, which is full of metaphors (318 n., 321 n., 323 n., 326 n., 330-1 n., 333 n., 341 n.), and includes such other devices as self-address (317 n.), conundrum (342-3 n.), and hyperbole (327 n., 345 n.). The name 'Phormio', as Donatus tells us, was taken over from Apollodorus, but it is not clear why Apollodorus chose it. It is not otherwise found in comedy, but was a common real-life Greek name; it may be relevant that the contemporary Syrian king Seleucus had a famous parasite called Phormio. The literal meaning of the name is debated, possibly 'little mat', with reference to the parasite's traditional poverty.

[3] The arrival of Phormio immediately puts Geta in the shade. Phormio has usurped the function of the 'tricky slave', and Geta's utterances in the scene, including a series of pleas for help which Phormio arrogantly ignores (319-20), are brief and insignificant.

[4] The metre changes from spoken verse to recitative (tr⁷), with the clear intention of heightening the presentation of Phormio.

317 it all devolves on you, Phormio: The self-address,

which adds a mock heroic note, is a not uncommon device in 'deliberative' monologues in comedy (Introd. §22).

318 It's your cooking, you must eat it: This is a proverbial expression, which is particularly appropriate for a parasite.

Prepare for action: Lit. 'gird yourself'; it is debatable whether this is intended as a military image.

321 all my plans are laid: Lit. 'drawn up' (Lat. *instructa*), which immediately suggests the drawing up of forces for battle. This time the miltary reference is unmistakable: Phormio is using the kind of imagery favoured by tricky slaves (cf. 229-30 n.).

323 full flood to be diverted: The image changes to the world of natural disasters.

326 tested the path...put my feet: This looks like a metaphor from making one's way down a dangerous path (e.g. one covered with brambles or infested with snakes).

327 beaten up...nearly to death: This is not to be taken literally; it is typical of the 'buffoonish talk of shady characters', as Donatus says.

330-1 The net isn't spread...: The metaphor now changes to the realm of fowling (*Eun.* 247 n.).

333 fleeced: Lit. 'from whom something can be scraped off' (cf. 40 n.), so that this is not the common image from shearing sheep.

334 get me convicted and take me off home: The implication is that Phormio, as a penniless trickster, would be unable to pay any fine that was imposed on him for assault, and could then as a debtor be made over to his creditor as a bondsman. There is a clear allusion here to Roman law (at Athens enslavement for debt was forbidden), and the alliterative language used by Terence is also distinctively Roman (*ducent damnatum domum*). This is the first sign of Terentian adaptation in the scene, and it occurs precisely at the point where Phormio begins to talk of himself as the conventional parasite.

338 its a man's patron: The Latin for 'patron' is *rex* (70 n.). There is no sign in the rest of the play of a patron who provides Phormio with free meals: in fact the whole passage 338-345 is quite detached from the plot of Phormio.

339 contribute nothing: The Latin is *asymbolum* (*Eun.* 540 n.). Donatus expressly says that 'this passage' (meaning apparently from '*You* contribute' to 'first drink') does not come from Apollodorus but from an unnamed Latin author whom he quotes: the sense of the quoted passage is similar but the only words which the two passages have in common are 'washed' and 'smiles'.

341 grin and bear it: Lit. 'bare his teeth'; Donatus implies that this is a metaphor from snarling dogs.

342-3 difficult sort of dinner...what you'll take first: This whole joke, and the 'conundrum' form in which it is expressed (unlikely statement, followed by 'how do you mean?', followed by ingenious explanation), is more typical of Plautus than of Terence or of Greek New Comedy. This again looks like an addition by Terence.

345 guardian god: Phormio ends with a resounding hyperbole.

346-7 clash...hold your ground: Geta responds with some military metaphors of his own, though now it is Phormio, not himself, who is cast in the role of military commander (cf. 321 n.).

play with him: *Eun.* 55 n.

II. iii: DEMIPHO, PHORMIO, GETA (348-440, pp. 243-7)

[1] Demipho returns from the forum (311-14 n.) with his three advisers, and is accused by Phormio of deliberately denying knowledge of his poor relative Stilpo, the father of Phanium. Demipho offers to provide a dowry if Phormio will take the girl away, and, when this is refused, threatens to expel her. Phormio threatens to take Demipho to court if he does, and returns to his house.

[2] The Demipho-Phormio confrontation provides the first climax of the play. Though Phormio has the upper hand, the confrontation is not decisive (it ends with threats on both sides), and so the momentum of this half of the dual plot is maintained. The Chremes-Phaedria half still remains very much in the background.

[3] The confrontation is described with some skill. Phormio, as befits the clever trickster, wins the argument, but Demipho is no fool and is not easily defeated. Phormio in general lacks the colourful language of the preceding scene, though he does have a couple of vivid metaphors (382 n., 439 n). His skill lies here in his choice of tactics, which are to provoke Demipho to anger by a variety of means (351 n., 358 n., 392 n., 411 n., 420 n., 422-3 n., 431 n., 435 n.); he also shows his resourcefulness in setting up the charade with Geta (350-73), in deploying his knowledge of the law (404 n.), and in his ability to think on his feet (388 n.). At the same time he does have a moment of human fallibility, when he forgets the name Stilpo (386). Demipho, angry as he is, maintains an icy politeness at first ('By your leave...' 378, 'please refresh my memory' 383), presses home the question of his precise relationship to Phanium ('how did he say I was related to him?' 381, 'come on, how is she my relative?' 398, 'But where do *we* come in?' 418), shows *his* knowlege of the law and suggests a reasonable compromise (409-10 n.), and only in the end loses his temper and resorts to threats (425 n., 436-7 n.). Geta plays up well with Phormio in the opening charade, where he exhibits a colourful line in abuse (372 n., 373 n., 374 n.), but is otherwise reduced to a minor role in which he merely makes asides.

[4] The fates of Antipho and Phanium are at stake, but the real interest of the scene is in the cut and thrust of the confrontation. It is often the case in Roman comedy that the love affair which is nominally at the centre of the plot takes second place to the intrigues which

develop around it. This is particularly true of the Plautine plays which are based upon the plotting of a tricky slave; it looks like being true also of *Phormio*, where Phormio plays a similar trickster's role.

[5] The metre reverts to spoken verse (ia^6).

350 Stand by me please: These words are addressed to Demipho's three advisers, who are mute characters in this scene. Their presence adds to the visual effect of the confrontation, with on one side the respectable older citizen flanked by his peers and on the other the disreputable parasite supported by a slave.

350-73 Now play up...jail-bird?: The technique of this 'faked dialogue', with Geta and Phormio intending to be overheard by Demipho, is analogous to the 'faked monologue' technique used by Pythias to deceive Parmeno in *Eunuchus* (*Eun.* 943 n.). Terence has another faked dialogue at *Andr.* 722-95 (pp. 74-8), where one of the intended fakers amusingly fails to understand what is going on. The technique is probably derived from Greek New Comedy, though there are no faked dialogues in surviving Menander or in Plautus.

351 I'm going to tease him: Lit. 'stir him up': Terence makes Phormio's tactics explicit from the beginning.

352 Does Demipho deny...?: Phormio seizes the initiative.

356 Stilpo: The Roman audience has no means of knowing whether the name is fictitious or not and cannot appreciate the irony of the situation. The Athenian audience, on the other hand, may have been told Stilpo's identity from the beginning, if we accept the conjecture that Apollodorus' play had an expository divine prologue (35ff n. 3).

358 See what avarice does: Phormio takes the initiative by putting Demipho morally in the wrong.

.244 361-2 I've nothing against young Antipho...: Phormio is maintaining the fiction that he and Antipho are adversaries.

367 One of the best I ever set eyes on: The picture of Stilpo as an honest poor toiling countryman represents a further (in this case oblique) attack on Demipho's avarice. It also recalls the rich-poor theme of the opening of the play (35ff n. 6).

368 go to hell: Lit. 'to an evil cross', i.e. 'may you be crucified'. This vulgar expression is common in the racy language of Plautus but occurs only here in Terence.

371 in this shabby fashion: Lat. *inliberaliter*, lit. 'unworthily of a free man' (281-2 n.). Phormio is in effect accusing Demipho of betraying the moral standards of his class (Introd. §16).

372 you foul-mouthed brute: Geta responds with another vulgar term of abuse (Lat. *inpurus*: 83 n.): Terence is here abandoning his usual linguistic refinement in order to highlight the supposed indignation of Geta on Demipho's behalf.

373 jail-bird: Lit. 'you prison', an insult which does not occur in Plautus or elsewhere in Terence.

374 Extortioner! Twister!: Lit.' extortioner of goods, contortioner of laws'. Geta is now coining abusive phrases of his own.

375 Who's that? Oh it's you, sir: The recognition formulae, as often in Terence, have a particular point (Introd. §30). Geta is making a great pretence of not having known that Demipho is present.

378 young man: Lat. *adulescens*. This is our only indication of Phormio's age, though Demipho may simply be condescending in calling him this. The term is not restricted to teenagers: Cicero once refers to himself at the age of over forty as an *adulescens* (*Philippics* 2. 118).

p.245   **382 Fishing for information:** The metaphor is more familiar to us than it would have been to Terence's audience; it does not occur anywhere else in Latin until the time of Cicero.

388 You're up to some trick: Phormio neatly covers his lapse of memory.

390 Who did you say?: Demipho presumably overheard the name Stilpo during the faked dialogue (356) and there is no reason why he should not catch it again now; Terence is fixing the name in the audience's mind by the repetition.

392 You ought to be ashamed of yourself: i. e. for telling a bare-faced lie. Phormio now invokes the concept of decency (Lat. *pudor*: 233 n., 284 n.), again implying that Demipho is not living up to the standards of his class (371 n.).

393 a few thousands: Lit. 'ten talents', i.e. sixty thousand drachmas. Phormio now returns to the charge of avarice (358 n.).

p.246   **398 our side**: i.e. Demipho.

404 ask for a new trial: It was specifically laid down in Athenian law that, once an action had been decided in court, it could not be heard again. In this case, Phormio implies that Demipho might be able to use his influence with the magistrates to reopen the matter, but he is clearly being ironic; the phrase translated 'top dog' (405) literally means 'sole ruler', which is an absurd suggestion in democratic Athens. It is true that there was a provision for a case concerning an orphan heiress to be reopened if a new claimant appeared with a stronger claim, but this is not the situation here.

408 sooner than have to go to law: Demipho's unwillingness to go to law may be regarded as a virtual acknowledgement that the case cannot be reopened; he has (or thinks he has) the facts on his side, but the court has already decided otherwise.

409-10 the dowry the law prescribes: Demipho has already shown himself aware of this alternative (297 n.). He now shows knowledge of the detailed provisions of the law: the five hundred drachmas which he here offers is exactly the sum which is laid down in cases of this kind. It is not a princely sum. Wealthy fathers in comedy regularly give two talents (i.e. twelve thousand drachmas) as dowries for their daughters (*Heaut.* 838, p. 141), and some go as high as ten talents (sixty thousand drachmas: *Andr.* 951, p. 87) or even twenty.

Clearly we have to make allowances for comic exaggeration, but, even if in real life dowries rarely exceeded one talent, this is still twelve times the amount that is laid down for the orphan heiress.

get her out of my house: It is sometimes objected that Demipho says nothing of the divorce from Antipho which will have to be arranged before Phanium can be married to somebody else. But a wife's father (or other guardian) could set up a divorce by removing her from her marital home, and this is effectively what Demipho is inviting Phormio to do.

411 Very nice of you: The laugh of the Penguin stage direction is actually written into the Latin text (*hahahae*: cf. *Eun.* 497 n.). This is another device designed to annoy Demipho; Phormio is adopting an air of superiority by refusing to take seriously what is in fact a reasonable offer on Demipho's part.

413-17: Do you really mean to tell me...: This is not a serious answer to Demipho's offer either. Phormio claims that, whereas the purpose of the law is to enable the orphan to contract a respectable marriage rather than be forced by poverty into a life of prostitution, Demipho is employing it to treat Phanium like a prostitute who can be used and then paid off. This is a slanted view both of the purpose of the law (125-6 n.) and of Demipho's behaviour; Phormio is again seizing the moral high ground.

417 live with him alone: i.e. as a respectable married woman.

419 what's done can't be undone: This is a proverbial phrase which Phormio is here using in its original legal sense (lit. 'don't reopen a case which has already been decided').

420 nonsense: Phormio now resorts to plain abuse.

.247 **422-3 You're past the age of marrying:** This is not a relevant point, but another insult, with the implication that Demipho is a doddering old man.

425 I shall forbid him the house: This is an extreme threat; by mentioning 'your son' (422) Phormio has succeeded in reawakening Demipho's anger against Antipho (239 n.).

430 Do what's worthy of you: Lat. *dignum* (Introd. §16): this is a return to the charge of betraying the standards of his class.

431 let us be friends: This is a patronising offer, coming from a parasite to a man of standing, and is of course the last thing that Demipho wants.

434 amuse you in your declining years: cf. 422-3 n.

435 Temper, temper: Lit. 'diminish your anger', a remark calculated to increase it.

436-7 If you don't...I shall throw her out: Demipho has now withdrawn his threat against Antipho (425 n.), and is restricting his action to Phanium. Again, there is no explicit mention of a divorce, but this would be a formality if the husband expelled his wife.

438 She's a free citizen: 114 n.

439 I'll bring an action: Lit. 'I will impinge an action':

Phormio uses a colourful word usually associated with physical violence (fists or cudgels).

that's *my* last word: Phormio successfully caps Demipho's last utterance (437), and strides off home (right: 310 n.) in triumph. He has made an unforgettable impression.

II. iv: DEMIPHO, GETA, HEGIO, CRATINUS, CRITO
(441-64, pp. 247-9)

[1] Demipho sends Geta into the house to see if Antipho has returned home, and consults his three advisers on his best course of action. They give him conflicting advice, which leaves him none the wiser. Geta reports that Antipho is not yet back, and Demipho goes off to the harbour for news of Chremes, whom he wants to consult.

[2] The point of the scene is the comic skit on Demipho's advisers (called *advocati* in the scene-headings of the MSS), which is beautifully handled (447 n., 454 n., 457 n.). The scene does not advance the plot: the activities of Geta on its fringes fail to bring the foreshadowed Demipho-Antipho confrontation any nearer (445 n., 459-60 n.).

[3] There are a number of indications that this scene may be Terence's invention rather than taken over from Apollodorus, notably (i) that it involves five speaking actors as against Greek New Comedy's normal limitation to three (Introd. §24), and (ii) that it appears to involve questions of Roman law as well as Greek (449-51 n.). It is interesting to compare the other appearance of *advocati* in Roman comedy (Plaut. *Poen.* 504-816), where the 'advocates' are of a rather different type, grumbling poor men summoned to act as witnesses for a young noble. In both cases a Roman note can be detected: in *Poenulus* the poor are doing their duty to the rich as in the Roman patron-client relationship, and in *Phormio* the wealthy are helping each other in terms of the *amicitia* between leading Roman families (Introd. §16) and their shared rhetorical-legal education.

[4] Strictly speaking this should not be regarded as a new scene, since no new character enters (35ff n. 2), and the Bembine MS, which is the oldest MS of Terence, does not mark it as such. But the departure of a major character (as of Phormio at 440) is also sometimes taken as indicating a scene-division, and the discussion between Demipho and his advisers clearly is a separate entity.

[5] The spoken verse (ia^6) continues.

441-4 Oh the trouble...: Demipho's anger at Antipho's behaviour (425 n.) is now replaced by worry and a desire to hear Antipho's view of the situation. He is thus behaving more reasonably towards his son than the average *senex iratus* (153-5 n.).

p.248   **445 go and see if he has come home:** Apart from removing Geta from the stage while Demipho consults his advisers, this renews expectations of the Demipho-Antipho confrontation which has already been foreshadowed as the second major confrontation of the play (231ff n. 2). Demipho had previously sent Phaedria to find Antipho (line 309, p. 241), but he has not returned.

447 Hegio: Hegio's unwillingness to take the responsibility of speaking first is the first comic touch in the scene. The name 'Hegio', which recurs in Plautus' *Captivi* and Terence's *Adelphoe* as the name of a respected elderly gentleman, suggests 'leader', which is ironic in view of Hegio's failure to display any leadership here.

448 Cratinus: There are no other characters named 'Cratinus' in Roman comedy or in surviving Greek New Comedy, though there are passing references to a Cratinus at Plaut. *As*. 866 and Ter. *Ad*. 581; it was a common real-life Greek name suggesting 'power'.

449-51 act in your best interests...rightly and properly: There is an echo here of Greek philosophical discussions (developed especially in the fifth and fourth centuries B.C.) on whether one should prefer the expedient to the just. Cratinus wants to have it both ways: in 'rightly and properly' there is an allusion to one of Terence's favourite ethical concepts (Lat. *aequom*: 114 n.).

rendered null and void: Terence here uses Roman legal terminology (Lat. *restitui in integrum*), which raises the suspicion that he has Roman legal practice in mind rather than Athenian. As already pointed out (404 n.), Demipho could not have had the same case retried in Athenian law, whereas at Rome the so-called 'praetorian edict' (the edict reissued annually by the praetor) did allow for the annulment of a court decision. Under the Lex Plaetoria (302 n.), this was especially the case where minors under the age of twenty-five were concerned and where there was proof of fraud.

454 there are as many opinions as there are men to give them: The Latin is much pithier (*quot homines tot sententiae*: lit. 'as many men, so many opinions'). The thought itself is proverbial, but Terence's formulation of it has been much admired and quoted down the ages. Hegio is treating Cratinus' opinion with elaborate politeness before contradicting it.

456 discreditable to attempt it: Hegio implicitly condemns Cratinus' equation of the expedient with the right (449-51 n.).

Crito: 'Crito' is another common real-life name; it is used for an elderly man also in Terence's *Andria*. The literal meaning is 'judge' or 'decider', another ironic touch in that Crito fails to come down on either side of the case.

457 I must have further time...: Crito's failure to support the view of either of his colleagues means that the whole exercise has been a waste of time.

459-60 They say he's not back...wait for my brother: The foreshadowed Demipho-Antipho confrontation is postponed, and the audience's expectations are directed towards the return of Chremes.

p.249   **464 Good, here he is on his way back...:** Before Geta can leave the stage, Antipho conveniently arrives; he is coming from the right (216-18 n.), and thus avoids Demipho, who is going off to the harbour (left). The renaissance editors put the end of Terence's second act here, even though the stage is not empty. It is difficult to establish where the act-breaks fell in the Greek original.

III. i: ANTIPHO, GETA (465-84, pp. 249-50)

[1] Antipho returns (right), full of remorse at his flight, and Geta assures him that they have stood up for him against Demipho. But his panic returns at the news that Demipho is awaiting Chremes' advice.

[2] The scene maintains the momentum of the Demipho-Antipho side of the plot towards its next significant point, which is going to be the discussion between Demipho and Chremes (459-60 n.). Apart from this, it adds some touches of characterisation. Antipho, who so far has not been a very attractive character (153ff n. 3), partially redeems himself by his remorse for his cowardice ('you've...your lack of spirit to blame' 465), his concern for Phanium ('You're her only hope now, poor girl' 470), and his gratitude to his helpers ('dear man, thank you all' 478). Geta, while giving full credit to Phaedria and Phormio, permits himself a little self-congratulation (*'I*'ve done all I can too, sir' 478); he also indulges in some striking metaphors (477 n., 484 n.).

[3] The scene also highlights several aspects of Terence's humanity (Introd. §15), with its emphasis on Antipho's duty to Phanium (469 n.) and on the loyalty to Antipho of Phaedria, Phormio and Geta (222 n.).

[4] The metre changes back to recitative, with metrical variations dividing the scene into three sections: (i) mixed recitative for Antipho's monologue, (ii) ia^8 for Geta's reassurances (from 'Just what we've been saying' 471), and (iii) mixed recitative again for the renewal of Antipho's panic (from 'The first round's over' 479).

465-70 In fact...for everything: This is another overheard entrance monologue (231-53 n.), but a reasonably realistic one, in that it is essentially reflective (Introd. §22), it is not punctuated by asides, and it is terminated with a simple formula (472 n.).

465 In fact, Antipho: On the self-address see 317 n.

466 leaving your life in other folks' hands: There is a deliberate echo in Antipho's opening words here of his parting words at 218 (p. 237: 'I'm leaving Phanium in your hands - and my life'). Similar verbal linking devices can be found in Menander.

469 through her misplaced trust: This is overt moralising; the Latin concept here is *fides* (Introd. §16).

472 I was looking for you: On the formula see *Eun.* 743 n.

474 suspected anything: Lit. 'scented', 'caught a whiff of', a colloquialism which is common in comedy.

p.250   **477 calming him down:** This is scarcely a fair description of

Phormio's effect on Demipho. The original meaning of the Latin verb (*confutare*) was 'prevent from boiling over', but Terence may be using it here rather in its later sense of 'confound', 'refute'.

482 how I dread seeing my uncle safe home again: Donatus seems to imply that in the Greek original the Antipho character expressed the hope that his uncle would not return safe; if so, Terence has toned this hope down in keeping with Roman feelings of deference towards elder members of the family (cf. *Ad.* 519 n.).

484 Coming away from his private wrestling-ground: i.e. from the pimp's house. The image of the pimp's house as a wrestling-ground (the same image is used of a courtesan's house at Plaut. *Bacch.* 66) must be a Greek one; the wrestling-ground itself belongs to Greek society rather than Roman, and there is no native Latin word for it (both Plautus and Terence use the Greek word *palaestra*). The Latin actually says 'coming *out* from', which is the one hint in the text that the pimp's house is on stage (cf. 83 n., 310 n.).

III. ii: PHAEDRIA, DORIO, ANTIPHO, GETA
(485-533, pp. 250-3)

[1] Phaedria returns, arguing with the pimp Dorio, who is proposing to sell Pamphila to a soldier. Antipho and Geta take Phaedria's side, and Dorio eventually agrees to sell Pamphila to Phaedria, if he brings the money the following morning.

[2] The focus of the plot now suddenly changes: the Antipho problem, which has been steadily developed since the end of the first act, is now dropped, and Phaedria's affair is brought back into the foreground. But, as before, Terence has taken trouble to link the two halves of the plot by involving one young man in the affair of the other (231ff n. 2): now it is Antipho's turn to stand up for Phaedria. And the involvement of Geta in both halves of the plot creates a further link.

[3] The scene requires four speaking actors, which raises the interesting question which of the four characters did not take part in the corresponding scene in Apollodorus (441ff n. 3). It is Geta who has the least to say, but he is required in the preceding and succeeding scenes, and it is difficult to see how he could plausibly have been removed from the stage before this scene and brought back after it. The most likely omission from Apollodorus is therefore Antipho, and it has been argued that Antipho did not appear at all in the central part of the Greek original (i.e. in the scenes corresponding to Terence's III. i-iii and IV. iii-iv). This theory, if true, has interesting implications for Terence's originality; it would be Terence who has given the more responsible turn to Antipho's character and who has highlighted the theme of mutual help which is prominent in this part of the play.

[4] Dorio belongs to the stock type 'pimp' (Lat. *leno*: Introd. §11). He is typically heartless ('stubborn and hard-hearted' 497), and

unscrupulous ('Aren't you ashamed? / Not in the least' 525-6). He enunciates the pimp's position very clearly: he is in the business of selling girls whom he has legitimately bought (511 n.), he is not interested in 'promises and tears' but in ready cash (520-2), he will disregard prior agreements (525 n.) in favour of a 'first pay first served' policy (533). He is not meant to be a sympathetic character; on the other hand he is not (like some of Plautus' pimps) cheated or made to look a fool, and he does display a certain ingenuity and verbal skill in the course of the argument (492-4 n., 499 n., 500 n., 508 n., 519 n., 525 n., 528 n., 531 n.). Dorio appears only in this scene and thus has a relatively minor part in the play. The name 'Dorio' does not otherwise occur in comedy, though it is attested as a real-life Greek name; it is etymologically connected with the word for 'gift', and is thus suitable for a character preoccupied with money.

[5] Of the other characters, there is something of a reversal in the portrayal of the two young men (153ff n. 3). Antipho, who has so far appeared as the more feeble of the two, speaks up strongly against Dorio on Phaedria's behalf; it is he who raises the point about the day fixed for Phaedria to pay ('Surely, if I remember rightly...' 523-4); and it is he who has the more colourful language (491 n., 506 n.). Conversely Phaedria, who has been portrayed as the stronger and more philosophical, loses his argument with the pimp and is reduced to envy of Antipho ('you lucky, lucky man' 504) and abuse of Dorio (509 n.). Geta does little more than offer witty asides and one virulent term of abuse (526 n.).

[6] The recitative continues, with mixed metres at first and tr⁷ from the point where Antipho intervenes (from 'Oh Antipho' 504).

485-503 Dorio, do listen...*his* bit of trouble: The scene opens with an overheard dialogue, with Antipho and Geta commenting aside on the conversation between Phaedria and Dorio. On this staging see *Eun.* 771-91 n.

489 where are you going?: This is a stage-direction written into the text: Dorio pretends to depart.

p.251 **491 I'm afraid this man is / Asking for trouble?:** Lit. 'I'm afraid that the pimp is / sewing something for his own head', a colourful phrase which combines the metaphorical 'stitch together trouble for someone' and the proverbial 'bring something on one's own head'. With this division of the line Antipho's confident start is undercut by Geta's heavily ironic reply. But the MSS actually give the whole sentence to Antipho.

492-4 However did you guess that? / Nonsense / Rubbish / Moonshine: Dorio offers an amusing series of pithy rejoinders, all consisting of a single word in the Latin: 'However did you guess that?' is a translation of the one word *hariolare* (lit. 'you are a diviner'). The word for 'Rubbish' is *logi* (lit. tales'), a Greek word taken over into Latin; since this occurs several times in Plautus also, it was presumably part of the Greek-based slang current in Rome at the time.

493 a good investment: The implication is that Phaedria will continue to be a regular customer of Dorio's.

496 one of the family, a father, a real friend: Phaedria is reduced to a desperately unlikely declaration, which would appear even more extreme to the Roman audience than to the Greek, granted the Roman emphasis on the family and the dignity of the *paterfamilias*.

499 How can *you* be..?: Dorio neatly caps Phaedria's question, using the same sentence structure.

500 fancy words: This is a colourful metaphor: the Latin word literally means 'decorated', and is often applied to the adornments of horses or to military medals. There is also an elaborate assonance in the Latin in this line between the words for 'move' (*ducas*), 'words' (*dictis*), and 'make off with' (*ductes*).

501 the pair of them run true to type: It is tempting to see this as a reference to the stock types of the *leno* and *adulescens* as they appear in comedy; such 'metatheatrical' references are very rare in Terence, though common in Plautus (*Eun.* 354 n.).

502 *his* bit of trouble: Lit. 'another anxiety'. The point of this remark has puzzled commentators from Donatus onwards. The Latin text has been variously interpreted and emended, but none of the solutions proposed is very convincing.

504-7 Oh Antipho...can't hold on: This exchange recalls the similar conversation at lines 153-76 (pp. 233-4), but with the roles reversed: there it was Antipho who called Phaedria 'fortunate'.

p.252   **506 I've the proverbial wolf by the ears:** This was a well-known proverb in antiquity, occurring several times in Latin literature and with a Greek equivalent quoted by Donatus (cf. *Eun.* 832 n.).

508 That's exactly how.../...know your job: This is another cryptic interchange. Dorio must mean that he is similarly at a loss with Phaedria, and Antipho retorts that, as a pimp, he should know how to deal with impecunious young men.

509 This beastly brute: Phaedria uses the word 'inhuman' (Lat. *inhumanus*), humanity being a quality in which pimps are conspicuously lacking.

511 What's wrong in that?: The Latin is *indignum* (Introd. §16). Dorio expresses the simple businessman's ethic of the pimp. He has the law on his side, but the audience is unlikely to sympathise.

512 cancel his bargain: Phaedria relies on the typical faithlessness of the pimp, to which he evidently has no objection when it is exercised in his own favour.

513 the next three days...promised by my friends: This looks like a desperate invention by Phaedria; Dorio refuses to take it seriously.

516 he'll repay it twice over: 493 n.

519 neither of us can: Dorio is being ironic.

p.253 **525 Is it past the date? /...the new one's come first:** Dorio's reply rests on a neat verbal antithesis ('go past' / 'precede').

Aren't you ashamed?: Aeschinus appeals in vain to the concept of *pudor*.

526 you muck-heap: Geta suddenly bursts in with a piece of vivid abuse, more typical of Plautus' language than of Terence's (cf. 372 n.). The term 'muck-heap' occurs also at Plaut. *Pers.* 407, where it is similarly addressed by a slave to a pimp.

527 ought you to behave like this?: Antipho now appeals to Dorio's sense of duty (Lat. *oportet*: 222 n.).

528 Actually it's he who's cheating *me*: This is another ingenious but specious argument on Dorio's part.

531 However...This is what I'll do: Dorio speaks as if he is offering a concession to Phaedria, but in fact he is simply following his usual preference for ready cash over prior agreements.

532 the Captain: The mercenary soldier is the traditional rival of the young man of comedy (Introd. §13).

533 Good-bye: There is nothing in the text about entering the house or slamming the door, as in the Penguin stage direction. If his house is not on stage, Dorio will exit left (310 n.).

III. iii: PHAEDRIA, ANTIPHO, GETA (534-66, pp. 253-5)

[1] As Phaedria laments his situation, Antipho calls on Geta to find the money for him, and Geta proposes to seek Phormio's help.

[2] The scene advances the Phaedria affair, with Antipho's affair now relegated to the background. It also foreshadows the return of Phormio, whose involvement in both affairs provides another link between the two halves of the double plot (485ff n. 2).

[3] In terms of character the portrayal of Geta is the most interesting. Antipho treats him as a typical tricky slave, declaring Phaedria's dependence on him ('you're the only one who can save him' 539) and asking him to find the necessary money (540). But Geta is bereft of ideas ('What can *I* do?' 540, 'just you show me where' 540, 'What help?' 553) and not at all eager to get himself into more trouble after his involvement with Antipho's affair ('Isn't it triumph enough...to have escaped...?' 543-4, 'the old man's mad enough...' 546-7). In the end Geta does think of a plan ('He'll be all right' 555), and confidently promises to find the money ('You *shall* have it at once' 559), but it immediately transpires that he is relying on Phormio to help. So Terence is playing off his characterisation of Geta against the tricky slave type; in the end, of course, Geta cannot play the role of supreme trickster in the play because that role has been usurped by Phormio. Of the young men, Antipho continues to act strongly on Phaedria's behalf, in contrast to his previous feebleness in his own affair, even urging Geta to cheat his father (541 n.); and Phaedria's behaviour becomes

still more emotional with his dramatic threat to follow Pamphila to the end of the world or die (551-2 n.).

[4] This is marked as a new scene in all the MSS, even though no new character enters (cf. 441ff n. 4): it is again the departure of one of the characters (Dorio) which has led to the scene-division .

[5] The recitative continues: the whole scene is in tr⁷.

534 what shall I do?: The question recalls the opening words of Phaedria at *Eun.* 46 (p. 167): it is typical of the *adulescens* in comedy that he cannot solve his own problems.

536 I had it promised: The details remain vague; it is evidently out of the question that the 'friends' concerned could produce the money any earlier than the three days mentioned before (513 n.).

538 repay his kindness: The Latin is *beneficium*, which recalls the concept of friendship based on the exchange of mutual favours (Introd. §16). But Antipho's motives are more altruistic, and the whole speech is better taken as an expression of the ideal of helping each other, which part of Terence's concept of humanity and is very prominent in this part of the play (465ff n. 3).

539 the right thing to do: Lat. *aequom* (449-51 n.).

.254   541 A word's enough for the wise: The expression is proverbial (cf. Plaut. *Pers.* 729). Antipho is hinting that Geta should trick his father out of the money. This is the stock device of the tricky slave in comedy (*Eun.* 386 n.), but the suggestion is not quite in keeping with Antipho's expressed terror of Demipho (154, p. 233).

543 triumph: i.e. significant achievement; the image is military (*Eun.* 393-4 n.).

544 stick my neck out: The Latin has a different idiom, lit. 'ask for crucifixion'.

551-2 follow her or die: Charinus at Plaut. *Merc.* 857-63 makes an identical threat: reactions of this kind are typical of the *adulescens* in comedy when crossed in love. Other Terentian examples are Clinia at *Heaut.* 117 (p. 105), who serves overseas as a mercenary soldier, and Ctesipho at *Ad.* 275 (p. 351), who threatens to go into exile. No young man in comedy ever commits suicide, though several hint at it, including Charinus at *Andr.* 322 (p. 53) and Antipho at *Phorm.* 686 (p. 260).

552 but not too quickly: i.e. 'but don't act too hastily'; the remark would be funnier if it referred to the speed of the divine help, but this is not really the implication of the Latin.

.255   556 We're all in this together: This is a reversal of the normal tricky slave situation, where it is the slave who reassures his young master. Antipho again gives explicit expresssion to the philosophy of mutual help (538 n.).

557 three thousand drachmas: As the following lines suggest, whether this is expensive or not depends on one's point of view. Three thousand drachmas is in fact an average sum in comedy for the purchase of a girl from a pimp: the range extends from two thousand (Plaut. *Pseud.* 51-2; cf. Ter. *Ad.* 191) to four thousand (Plaut. *Epid.* 51-2). Sums of two and three thousand drachmas are attested for the purchase of expensive courtesans in real life; for comparison, the average daily wage for a skilled craftsman in Menander's Athens was only two drachmas. On monetary values see also 409-10 n. (dowries), 789 n. (value of estates), *Eun.* 169 n. (price of slaves).

560 I must have Phormio to help me: We are now more than half way through the play, and Phormio has been on stage for only two scenes (II. ii-iii). Geta here foreshadows his reappearance and reinforces his characterisation: Terence is careful to keep Phormio in the audience's mind through such references.

562 a friend to his friends: A proverbial turn of phrase, which, as Donatus makes clear, Terence has taken over from Apollodorus. This is yet another reference to the theme of mutual help.

563 Is there anything I can do for you?: 151 n.

564 comfort your poor Phanium: This was one of the objects of Antipho's return at 465 (p. 249), which was interrupted by Phaedria's appearance with the pimp; Antipho's departure here is thus neatly linked with his arrival (cf. 466 n.).

566 I'll tell you on the way: This is a device for keeping the audience in suspense; at the same time it is economic of stage time, since it is repetitive for the audience to have the plan outlined first and then to see it put into operation. But there must also be some suspicion that Geta does not yet have a plan worked out. There is an interesting parallel at Plaut. *Pseud.* 380-408, where Pseudolus, who is a true tricky slave, refuses to divulge his plan to his master ('No point in going over it twice - plays are long enough as it is' 388), and then confesses to the audience that he does not have 'a ghost of a plan' (397-8).

Geta and Phaedria now depart to look for Phormio, who had said that he would be available at home (440, p. 247). Since they do not meet Demipho and Chremes arriving from the harbour (left), it is more convenient for the staging if they exit right, which confirms that Phormio's house should be notionally situated in this direction (310 n.). The stage is empty, and the renaissance editors put the end of Terence's third act at this point.

IV. i: DEMIPHO, CHREMES (567-90, pp. 255-6)

[1] Demipho returns from the harbour (left) with Chremes. It transpires that Chremes has been to Lemnos to look for a daughter which he has had by a Lemnian woman, but the girl and her mother have meanwhile moved to Athens to look for him. The news that Antipho has married Phanium is a blow to Chremes, since the two fathers have agreed that Antipho shall marry Chremes' daughter in order to keep the circumstances of her birth secret.

[2] Though Chremes is Phaedria's father, his arrival in fact interrupts the development of the Phaedria side of the plot, to which the two preceding scenes have been devoted, and throws the focus back on Antipho's affair. The revelations of this scene come as an enormous surprise to the audience. We were told in the first act that Chremes had gone to Lemnos (66, p. 230), but no reason was given for his journey; and there has been no hint anywhere in the play of his extramarital affair. However that may be, granted the conventions of the genre (114 n.), the audience will have no difficulty in recognising that Chremes' Lemnian daughter and Phanium must be one and the same person; and, if they have time to collect their wits, they will now realise that the plot is centred on a number of ironies which they have so far missed. Antipho *is* after all related to Phanium (they are first cousins), so that Phormio's fiction turns out to be fact. Demipho is furious at Antipho's marriage, but he has in fact married the girl whom Demipho himself wants him to marry. And the real reasons for Demipho's opposition to Antipho's marriage and his eagerness to consult Chremes now become apparent; it is not just that Phanium has 'no dowry and no family' (120 n.) but that he and Chremes have other plans for his son. The fact that there are no parallels in Menander or Plautus for the withholding of crucial information to this late stage lends strong support to the view that the exploitation of surprise is Terence's own innovation: Apollodorus' play would have had an expository prologue putting the Athenian audience in possession of all the facts from the beginning (Introd. §33, cf. 35ff n. 3)

[3] We might have been expecting Chremes to be portrayed as the 'lenient father' (*senex lenis*) as a foil to Demipho who has many of the traits of the 'stern father' (*senex durus*) (231ff n. 3). But it turns out that with Chremes the emphasis is not on the father-son relationship but on his own sexual affairs, which brings him rather into the category of 'lecherous old man' (*senex amator*), though he does not quite fit this category either (Introd. §3). He shares with the type the desire to keep his affair secret from his wife ('I'm terrified...of my wife's getting to hear about this' 585); but his lechery is not to the fore, and he deserves some credit for trying to arrange a settled future for his daughter. And there is just a hint of sympathy in the suggestion that his wife belongs to the domineering dowried type who are often satirised in comedy (587 n.). Chremes also displays a certain verbal wit (575 n., 587 n.). Demipho's role in the scene is largely to elicit responses from Chremes. There is no sign here of his quickness to anger or his greed for money; he accepts without question that he should help his brother out of his difficulty ('the whole thing is a great worry to me. I shan't give up trying...' 588-9). The theme of loyalty and mutual help, which has so far been centred on the sons, is thus extended to the fathers.

[4] The scene reverts to spoken verse (ia⁶), marking a change of tone after three scenes of recitative.

567 Lemnos: 66 n.

571 with all her household: This suggests a number of slaves accompanying the mother and daughter, but, when they arrived in Athens, there was only 'one old woman' to help with the mother's funeral (98-9, p. 231). The discrepancy is not an important one.

572-3 why did you stay there so long...?: Chremes' sickness is simply a device used by Terence to add some verisimilitude to the story. Chremes has to be kept away from Athens long enough for Antipho's affair with Phanium to develop.

575 it's illness enough to be old: It is clear from Donatus that this piece of wit was taken over from the Greek original; the thought is proverbial.

576 the sailor who brought them: This is another circumstantial detail to make the story convincing.

586 throw everything up: Lit. 'shake myself out'. This is a colourful phrase; it is not clear precisely what metaphor is intended. .

587 my person is the only thing...I can call my own: The Latin is rather neater, lit. 'of my possessions I only am mine'. There are two implications:

(i) Chremes is relatively poor, whereas Demipho is rich (69, p. 230), which is a common contrast in comedies featuring two old men (e.g. Men. *Sam.* and Ter. *Ad.*);

(ii) Chremes' possessions consist largely of his wife's dowry, and dowried wives are generally represented in comedy as domineering and unpleasant (Introd. §5).

590 our previous arrangement: Namely, that Antipho should marry Chremes' daughter.

IV. ii: GETA, DEMIPHO, CHREMES (591-605, pp. 256-7)

[1] Geta returns (right), full of praise for Phormio, who has expressed himself delighted to help. Geta is taken aback when he finds Chremes back home as well as Demipho, but consoles himself that he now has two possible sources of money.

[2] We now return to Phaedria's affair, after the interruption of the previous scene. Phormio's readiness to help sets up expectations of a Phormio-Demipho confrontation on behalf of Phaedria, to match the first Phormio-Demipho confrontation on behalf of Antipho, a parallelism which further helps to bind the two halves of the plot together .

[3] Geta's moment of panic on seeing Chremes (600 n.) is reminiscent of the panic of some of Plautus' tricky slaves (179ff n. 3). He also talks of 'tackling' the two old men (604-5 n.) as if he was going to handle the situation in person. But his loss of the chief trickster's role in the play is underlined by his opening line (591), where he applies to Phormio the adjective *callidus* (here translated' quick-witted') which is traditionally applied to the tricky slave (cf. *Eun.* 1009-11 n.). There

is also no sign of the plan which Geta previously claimed to have in mind (566 n.): by his own account he had to ask Phormio to suggest how they could get the money ('I came to...find out how' 592-3).

[4] The scene provides another instance of Phormio's being char-acterised in his absence (560 n.). Here Geta brings out his quickness to grasp the situation ('I'd scarcely said half before he'd got the point' 594), his positive delight in helping ('He was delighted...He thanked heaven' 595-6), and his eagerness to 'show himself...the friend' of the two young men (597-8, cf. 562 n.).

[5] There is a minor awkwardness of staging here. Geta's speech is technically an entrance monologue on an occupied stage, since Demi-pho and Chremes have not departed, but the two old men show no signs of hearing or seeing him until they are accosted in the following scene (609). There are other similar cases in Terence (*Eun.* 507-31 n., 629ff n. 4) and even more extreme ones in Plautus (e.g. at *Most.* 903-33), but nothing really comparable in Menander. It is tempting to explain these awkwardnesses in terms of Roman adaptation of the Greek originals; here Terence may have complicated the staging by bringing back Antipho at the beginning of the next scene (485ff n. 3).

[6] The spoken verse (ia⁶) continues.

).257 **600 But there he is:** The recognition formula (177-8 n.) im-plies that the monologue is about to be terminated, but Geta continues for another five lines.

My God: Lat. *attat,* expressing sudden alarm (*Eun.* 757 n.).

603 two strings to one's bow: The Latin is plainer, lit. 'to enjoy a double hope'.

604-5 aim at...tackle: There is a hint of the tricky slave's military imagery here (179ff n. 3), in that both the Latin words are often found in military contexts.

IV. iii: ANTIPHO, GETA, CHREMES, DEMIPHO
(606-81, pp. 257-60)

[1] As Antipho emerges from his house, Geta tells the old men a prepared story: he has negotiated with Phormio, who is willing to marry Phanium himself if Demipho provides a dowry of three thousand drachmas. Demipho regards this as exorbitant, but Chremes urges him to agree and offers to pay. They withdraw to Chremes' house.

[2] This is the point where the two halves of the plot become firmly interlinked. Geta and Phormio are pursuing a solution for Phaedria's problem (cf. 667 n.), but their plan has major consequences for Antipho. If this latest plan is carried through, Phaedria's problem will be solved, but only at the cost of destroying Antipho's marriage and landing Phormio with a marriage which he does not want. It is

evident that Phormio does not intend to honour his agreement to marry Phanium, but how then will he retain the old men's money?

[3] The scene has interesting implications for the division of the trickster's role in the play (534ff n. 3). Instead of the expected second direct confrontation betweeen Phormio and Demipho, we have a 'confrontation by proxy' with Geta as the intermediary. On the one hand, the new plan has clearly been devised by Phormio, and it is every bit as ingenious and impudent as his original one: Phormio's character comes over very strongly, even though he is not himself present on stage (591ff n. 4). On the other hand, Geta is more than a mere narrator of Phormio's words: he pretends to be taking the old men's side, and he maintains his story successfully against Demipho's objections.

[4] The characters of the two old men are nicely contrasted. Demipho, who previously offered five hundred drachmas as a dowry for Phanium (409-10 n.), is now willing to pay a thousand, but becomes furious at the impudence of Phormio's demands and at the thought that he is being tricked ('What impudence!' 644, 'No, no. That's too much' 664, 'Does the scoundrel think he can fool me?' 669). This is the reaction of the hard-headed businessman. Chremes, on the other hand, in his desperate eagerness to hide his guilty secret, approves of Geta's negotiations from the outset ('No, no, he's right...' 640-1) and has none of Demipho's reservations about the amount being demanded, which he is willing to pay himself if Demipho refuses ('You can have that thousand from me' 664, 'Calm yourself, please; I'll pay' 670, 'He shall have it at once' 677).

[5] Antipho's overhearing of the conversation and his ever more despairing asides ('What's he up to?' 626, 'Has he gone off his head? 636', 'Is this malice or sheer stupidity?' 659, 'your tricks have been the death of me' 671-2) add an extra dimension to the dramatic effect of the scene. As Donatus points out, the introduction of Antipho adds to the confusion, and his fear of losing his wife here adds to his eventual happiness when his problem is solved. It seems probable that it is Terence who deserves the credit for introducing Antipho here; the scene requires four actors and none of the others could be dispensed with in the three-actor Greek original (cf. 485ff n. 3).

[6] It is interesting that we have now lost sight of the father-son relationship as one of the themes of the play. Chremes' relations with Phaedria have never received any emphasis; and, though there was originally some exploration of Demipho's attitude to Antipho (231ff n. 3), it is his conflict with Phormio which has now become the focus.

[7] The is a very complex scene. Basically, it is a narrative by Geta of a fictitious off-stage conversation with Phormio, which is interrupted by questions and comments by Demipho and Chremes and punctuated with asides by Antipho: there are thus five speakers involved if Phormio is included. There are parallels elsewhere in comedy for narrative speeches including off-stage conversation (e.g.

Men. *Sam.* 206-82, *Sik.* 176-271; Ter. *Hec.* 361-414, pp. 307-9); but the conversations in these cases are not fictitious, nor is the narrative interrupted by other speakers. There is also a parallel for a fictitious narrative drawing comments and questions from an interlocutor (Plaut. *Bacch.* 251-348), but this is a narrative of events not of a conversation. So the *Phormio* scene seems to be unique in its complexity.

[8] The spoken verse (ia⁶) continues for the third successive scene.

606 I'll just wait for Geta: Antipho emerges from Demipho's house, where he has been comforting Phanium (565, p. 255). The comforting has been relatively brief: Antipho is evidently more intent on the progress of Geta's consultation with Phormio on Phaedria's behalf. But his eyes light not on Geta but on Demipho and Chremes, and this reawakens his fears for himself ('I dread to think...' 608). He stands by to listen, presumably just outside his own door.

609-10 Now for it...How are things with you, sir?: This interchange consists of entirely of the conventional homecoming formulae, though some are disguised by the translation ('Now for it' is literally 'I will approach'; 'Well' is 'Greetings'). This time Terence keeps the formulae very brief, rather than manipulating them for special effect (254-6 n.).

613 Was it you...? Shocking, isn't it..?: The first half of this line is addressed to Demipho, the second to Chremes. 'Shocking' is *indignum* in the Latin (511 n.).

.258   **623 generous:** Better 'a gentleman' (Lat. *liberalis* : 281-2 n.).

624-5 all his friends without exception: This does not accurately represent the advice of Demipho's *advocati* (441-59, p. 248), but there is no reason why it should.

626-7 he'll have the law after him: This is an allusion to Phormio's parting threat to take Demipho to court if he ejected Phanium (438-9, p. 247).

628 *You*'ll be...in trouble: Geta uses the colourful metaphor 'you will sweat', and precedes it by an exclamation (Lat. *heia*).

631 it isn't his life and liberty at stake: The immediate point is that, if Phormio brought and won a case against Demipho, Demipho, being a rich man, could easily pay whatever fine was imposed. But Geta is also reminding Phormio, that the situation would be different if he himself were prosecuted and condemned: as an impoverished trickster he would not be able to pay a fine, and would thus be in the position of a debtor, liable (in Roman law) to bondage (334 n.).

634 drop his present suit: In fact Demipho has rejected the idea of reopening the original case (408 n.) and has not threatened any other legal action.

637 fair: Lat. *aequom*.

.259   **644 a good six thousand /...something not so good:** The word-play in the Latin is slightly different. Phormio asks for *talentum magnum* ('a large talent', where the 'large' identifies the Attic talent as against other currencies), and Demipho threatens to give him not *magnum* but *malum* ('trouble'), which often implies a thrashing. The talent is equivalent to six thousand drachmas.

What impudence!: Demipho here invokes against Phormio the concept of *pudor* which Phormio had invoked against him (392 n.).

646-7 He's not gained much...a dowry like that: Donatus tellus that in the Greek play it was the old man who said 'What do I gain by not having brought up a daughter, if a dowry is to be given for someone else's?' By transferring the remark to Geta Terence has 'improved' the slave's story.

by not bringing up a daughter: The translation reproduces the ambiguity of the Latin (*suscipere* = 'taking up'), which could be interpreted to imply that Demipho did in fact have a daughter born to him but chose to expose her as a baby. Exposure of unwanted children is a common feature of comedy (e.g. *Heaut.* 615, p. 129; *Hec.* 400, p. 308), and was a real-life practice in the Graeco-Roman world. If Demipho had exposed a daughter, this would add to his portrayal as niggardly over money and expense. But the Latin is capable of a more general interpretation (= 'by not having a daughter'), and we cannot insist on its more limited meaning here.

651 the right thing: Lat. *aequom* again (cf. 637 n.); there is a certain irony in putting this ethical principle in a trickster's mouth.

653 if she had to slave for a rich husband: The Latin neatly substitutes 'to be given into servitude' for the usual 'to be given into matrimony'. Phormio typically takes the side of the poor (367 n.).

654 to be quite frank with you: This heralds a tissue of lies.

655 a bit: This (Lat. *aliquantulum*) is the first of a series of 'diminutive' forms in the Latin, designed to make Phormio's demands sound small; the others are 'small house' (*aediculae*) 663, 'litttle maid' (*ancillula*) 665, 'few sticks (*pluscula*) of furniture' 665.

657 the girl who's now engaged to me: This is a new element in the situation dreamed up by Phormio.

661 What if he's up to the eyes in debt?: Lit. 'owes his soul'. Demipho is quick to pick up the potential implications of Phormio's reference to debt, despite the diminutives.

663 No, no: The Latin has the colourful exclamation *oiei*.

666 the expense of the wedding: The implication is that this falls on the bridegroom, not on the bride or her family. This seems to have been the general practice in real-life Athens and Rome, though the evidence is self-contradictory and there may have been no fixed custom. In Plautus' *Aulularia* the bridegroom Megadorus pays for the wedding feast, but at the same time the bride's miserly father Euclio is criticised for not paying for it (*Aul.* 294-5). In Plautus' *Curculio* the wedding feast takes place at the bridegroom's house (*Curc.* 728) and thus presumably at his expense.

667 You can reckon all this as another thousand: This makes three thousand altogether. As the audience will recognise, this is exactly the sum needed to buy Pamphila from the pimp (557).

.260   **669 I'm not paying a penny:** Demipho withdraws his original offer to pay one thousand drachmas for the mortgaged land (662).

scoundrel: The Latin has the strong word *inpuratus* (a form of *inpurus*: 83 n.), lit. 'foul', 'filthy', 'unclean'.

fool: The word also implies 'mock', 'jeer at'.

673 only right: Lat. *aequom*, this time in Chremes' mouth.

674 as soon as possible: The money is needed by 'tomorrow morning' (531, p. 253), if the pimp is to be paid before the soldier arrives to claim Phanium

678 much good may it do him: Demipho actually says 'much bad', reversing the usual good wishes to the about-to-be married.

679-80: I've got money...my wife's property in Lemnos: Chremes has as little compunction about using his wife's money for his own purposes as he had in involving himself with the Lemnian woman in the first place. These two lines have a significance beyond their immediate context (cf. *Eun.* 143-4 n.). They not only (i) provide a plausible source of money for Chremes to give to Demipho to pay off Phormio, but (ii) explain why Chremes has been journeying to Lemnos and how he came to be involved with a Lemnian woman, and also (iii) confirm the picture of a poor husband with a dowried wife (587 n.).

681 I'll take it from that and tell her you needed it: This is evidently an exit line: Chremes goes into his house with Demipho to hand over his wife's income from her Lemnian estates and to tell her that he is subtracting three thousand drachmas to give to Demipho. But this motivation is rather weak. The old men do not need to go into the house to fetch the money, since Chremes already has it with him (679), and there is no sign when they come out that they have had any contact with his wife. All this increases the suspicion that Terence has adapted Apollodorus' play in this section: he has had to find a way of removing the old men from the stage to make way for the following Geta-Antipho scene, which is his own invention (682ff n. 4).

IV. iv: ANTIPHO, GETA (682-712, pp. 260-1)

[1] Antipho comes forward and expresses his anger at what appears to be his betrayal by Geta. Geta explains that Phormio will not actually marry Phanium but find an excuse. As the old men reappear, Geta sends Antipho to tell Phaedria that money has been found.

[2] The scene serves to clarify the working of Phormio's plan and thus answer the questions which the previous scene raised. Phormio will use the old men's money to pay the pimp, invent excuses for postponing the wedding (701-10), and finally back out of the marriage, repaying the old men with the money that Phaedria's friends will by

then have raised (703-4).

[3] The credit for the plan obviously goes to Phormio, so that the process of characterisation in absence continues (591ff n. 4). At same time, it is Geta who dominates on stage, brushing aside Antipho's objections with a mixture of insolence (683 n.), comic invention (705-10 n.), and self-confidence ('He will, trust me' 711). Antipho reacts with bitter irony ('Do you think you've done enough?' 683, 'just give it to him if you want a proper job made of it' 689, 'I suppose he'll choose to go to jail on our behalf' 695-6), abuse (684 n.), imprecation ('may all the powers of heaven and hell condemn you...' 687-8), and in the end resignation ('Oh if only he will' 711).

[4] The whole scene may be Terence's addition to the play; it presupposes that Antipho was eavesdropping in the preceding scene, which falls foul of the Greek three-actor rule (606ff n. 5), and it creates difficulties with the movements of the two old men (681 n.). There is also a distinctly Plautine ring about some of the language (682 n., 684 n.) and a Roman preoccupation with portents (705-10 n.).

[5] The spoken verse continues for the fourth successive scene.

682 Diddling the old men: Lit. 'wiping the old men's noses', a Greek idiom common in Plautus but used only here by Terence.

683 It's all I was told to do: cf. 541 n. As Antipho's response shows, Geta has deliberately misunderstood the question. Antipho actually means 'Don't you think you've done far too much?' but Geta takes him to mean that he has done too little.

684 you wretch: Lit. 'you whip-dog' (Lat. *verbero*), a form of abuse commonly directed at slaves; it is very common in Plautus, but occurs only twice in Terence. The Greek equivalent *mastigia* is also found in Roman comedy (*Ad.* 782 n.).

686 the rope's round my neck: Lit. 'the matter has come to a rope', i.e. 'I might as well hang myself' (cf. 551-2 n.).

688 anything you want done: The 'you' is singular: Antipho is not so much addressing the audience (which is not Terence's manner) as speaking aside to himself.

p.261 **690 touch on that sore spot:** Lit. 'touch this wound', a relatively unfamiliar metaphor in Terence's time.

696 go to jail: i.e. as an insolvent debtor. The reference is to private bondage rather than public imprisonment (334 n.).

705-10 I've had so many warnings...shortest day: This list of 'warnings' (Lat. *monstra*: i.e. portents or prodigies) includes some Roman touches (707 n., 708-9 n.), and may well be Terence's own invention; the Romans regarded portents very seriously (there are regular lists in the historian Livy) and took great care to expiate them. On the other hand, the Greeks also were superstitious; and Menander's tutor Theophrastus gives a long list of omens in his sketch of 'The superstitious man' (*Characters* 16). Donatus suggests that Terence is here satirising the superstitious; in the immediate context Geta is also teasing Antipho by responding humorously to an earnest question.

706 a strange black dog: Animals feature regularly in portents and omens, including dogs (Horace lists a pregnant bitch at *Odes* 3. 27. 2 as a portent deterring intending travellers), but this particular one seems to be unparalleled in Greek and Latin literature.

707 a snake fell...through the skylight: A snake in the house is one of the omens heeded by Theophrastus' 'superstitious man'; but the detail of the 'skylight' (Lat. *impluvium*) suggests a Roman house rather than a Greek one (*Eun.* 589 n.).

708 hen crowed: According to Donatus, midwives believed this to be an omen that the wife would outlive the husband.

708-9 soothsayer...diviner: Terence uses the Latin terms *hariolus* (a general word for a soothsayer, prophet, diviner: cf. 492-4 n.) and *haruspex* (a specific word for an interpreter of the entrails of sacrificial animals). This latter science was highly developed by the Etruscans and handed down from them to the Romans; there is no direct Greek equivalent to the *haruspex*.

709 before the shortest day: i.e. before the winter solstice on 21 December: it was evidently considered unlucky to conduct business as the days shortened. It may or may not be relevant that January was the favourite month for weddings in Athens, so much so that the name of the Athenian month corresponding to January (Gamelion) literally means 'Wedding Month'.

712 run along and tell Phaedria: When we last saw Phaedria, he was leaving with Geta by the right-hand exit to look for Phormio (566 n.). Antipho therefore must exit to the right. Since the old men, who are already emerging from Chremes' house, do not see him, it would suit the staging here better if Chremes' house were on the left side of the stage, so that he did not pass through their line of sight.

IV. v: DEMIPHO, CHREMES, GETA (713-27, pp. 261-2)

[1] Demipho reappears with Chremes from the latter's house, ready to hand over the cash to Phormio before witnesses. Chremes is anxious that the news shall be broken gently to Phanium, and suggests that his wife should explain the situation to her. Demipho goes off (right) with Geta to pay Phormio the money.

[2] The plot moves another step towards the solution of Phaedria's problem, though he will still need his friends to come up with the money to repay to Demipho and he will still need to secure Chremes' consent to his affair. The scene also sets up the possibility of a showdown between Chremes and his wife; the plan to involve the wife with Phanium seems harmless enough in itself, but the more perceptive of the audience will realise its potential implications.

[3] The characterisation of the old men continues to be sketched in by small touches. Demipho, as befits the money-conscious businessman,

is determined to hand over the money before witnesses ('I'll see he doesn't cheat us' 713); he is still very unhappy about the transaction and unimpressed with Chremes' concern for duty ('What the hell does this matter to you?' 723). Chremes, as befits a man with a guilty secret, is very anxious that their plan should be carried out securely and speedily, so that there can be no hitch or change of mind ('do hurry up before his mood changes' 716). He is also at some pains to justify their treatment of the unknown orphan girl; for him this is a matter of appearances ('Doing your duty isn't enough unless people know and approve' 724) and of what the girl might say (725). It is also a sign of Chremes' fear of his wife that he asks Demipho to approach her to speak to the girl rather than doing this himself.

[4] The metre changes back to recitative (ia⁸).

p.262   **718 How right you are:**   Geta is being ironic: Phormio will in the end turn them down, but not for the reasons suggested.

719 ask her to see the girl: Demipho's wife would have been the obvious person to comfort Phanium, as being her mother-in-law: we have to assume that she is dead.

721 more her sort and a better match: Lit. 'more suitable in that he is more one of her family'. Phormio has claimed to be a friend of the family (Stilpo was given some land by Phormio's father to farm: 364-5, p. 244), whereas Antipho has had no previous dealings with them.

722 done our duty: Lat. *officium*, another common ethical term in Terence, often used as here with reference to the behaviour of the fortunate towards the less fortunate (Introd. §15-16).

726 Women are better at handling women: This is a proverbial idea, found also in Greek tragedy (Euripides, *Helen* 830).

727 I'll ask her: But first Demipho goes off (right) to pay off Phormio, taking Geta with him and leaving Chremes alone on stage. The renaissance editors for some reason ended Terence's fourth act at this point, even though the stage is not empty, rather than after the next scene (765), where there *is* an empty stage.

V. i: SOPHRONA, CHREMES (728-65, pp. 262-5)

[1] Sophrona, Phanium's nurse, emerges from Demipho's house lamenting Phanium's fate, and recognises Chremes as Stilpo. Chremes confesses that this was an assumed name, and is overjoyed to discover that Antipho's wife is none other than his own daughter. They go into Demipho's house.

[2] The scene finally confirms that Phanium is Chremes' daughter, and thus brings Antipho's problem close to solution. All that is needed now is for Demipho to approve of his marriage, which is a foregone conclusion, and for Phormio to wriggle out of his own entanglement

with Phanium. There is also another hint that the plot may be moving towards a confrontation between Chremes and his wife (744 n.).

[3] Chremes is vividly characterised as the man with a guilty secret ('Come...further from the door' 741, 'Don't ever call me by that name again' 742), who is more than a little afraid of his wife ('I've a wife behind it - a dangerous one' 744, 'in case...somehow my wife found out' 746). Sophrona is the typical nurse of comedy (Lat. *nutrix*), being in fact drawn rather more fully than most (Introd. §14). She is rather helpless ('What shall I do?' 722), self-critical (730 n.), and prone to lamentation ('my mistress will be cruelly wronged' 730, 'we poor women' 747, 'The mother, poor soul' 750), but she is intensely loyal to the family, even to Chremes ('No one shall hear it from *me*' 765).

[4] The recitative continues. Sophrona's lament and the recognition are in mixed metres; the furtive conversation about Chremes' wife is in ia^8 (from 'Don't ever call me...' 742); and the rest (from 'Now please tell me' 748) is in ia^7.

263   **730 all through taking my advice:** It was Sophrona who had insisted at 112-16 (p. 231) that Antipho must marry Phanium 'all proper and legal'.

733 It was our poverty which drove me to it: Sophrona's self-justification serves to recall the theme of wealth and poverty which was prominent at the beginning of the play (35ff n. 6).

this marriage wasn't secure: The youth's father's consent was all important (232 n.).

735-40 Unless my eyes deceive me...Did you say No?: This exchange is based on the conventional recognition and approach formulae ('Is it *x*? Yes it is. I'll go up. I'll speak to him': Introd. §29-30), but is unusually elaborate in that neither party is expecting to see the other. Moreover in the circumstances Chremes has to think twice before revealing himself, and ends by *denying* the recognition.

740 Stilpo: The significance of this name now becomes clear (356 n.). It was not an invention by Phormio for the court case, but the actual name by which Phanium knew her father, which Phormio must have learned from Antipho. Terence has laid his clues carefully.

744 I've a wife behind it - a dangerous one: Lit. 'I have a savage wife enclosed here'. The metaphor seems to be that of the wild-beast pen ('enclosed' = 'caged'): at Plaut. *Men.* 159 the husband refers to his house as 'the lioness's den'. The imagery confirms that Chremes' wife is the domineering dowried wife of the comic tradition (587 n.), thus whetting the audience's appetite for a showdown between them.

264   **751 That's bad...:** Chremes is given no chance to express his remorse for Phanium's mother's fate at any length. It is not clear whether Terence is deliberately characterising Chremes as unfeeling or is simply pressing on to the immediate point of Phanium's marriage.

754 Has he two wives?: In view of his own behaviour, it is more than a little ironic that Chremes leaps to this conclusion about Antipho.

756-7 could marry her without a dowry: This was the crucial point from Phanium's point of view, since undowried girls (in comedy and presumably in real life) have difficulty in finding husbands of good family. Megadorus at Plaut. *Aul.* 238-9, who actually prefers an undowried wife, is something of an exception.

757-8 chance brings about more than we dare to hope: This is another piece of philosophising which Terence presumably took over from Apollodorus (cf. 241-6 n.). The idea that things often turn out better than we hope is a commonplace one, going back to the Greek poet Theognis (sixth century B.C.) and occurring twice in Plautus. In Terence's ascription of this to 'chance' there is a hint of the personification of Fortune which became popular in the the time of Greek New Comedy (*Eun.* 1046 n.), though the word 'fortune' is not in fact used here.

762 Now think what we must do, sir: Sophrona prefers action to philosophising.

p.265 **765 I'll tell you the rest of the story indoors:** With his usual economy (231-53 n.), Terence moves off-stage a conversation which would only tell the audience what they know already. By 'indoors' Chremes must mean Demipho's house, where he will be reunited with his daughter. The stage is now empty (727 n.).

V. ii: DEMIPHO, GETA (766-83, pp. 265-6)

[1] Demipho and Geta return (right) after handing over the money to Phormio. Demipho is none too happy at having encouraged Phormio's villainy, especially when Geta expresses doubts whether Phormio will actually marry Phanium. Demipho goes into Chremes' house to fetch his wife, leaving Geta to reflect that, though their trick has succeeded for the moment, they are only putting off the evil day. He goes into Demipho's house to warn Phanium what is happening.

[2] This is a transitional scene which (i) emphasises the problems inherent in Phormio's trick and (ii) brings the confrontation between Chremes and his wife one step nearer.

[3] The scene confirms the characterisation of Demipho as tight-fisted, begrudging the money he has handed over to Phormio ('It was bad enough...' 769-70) and regretting that he went along with Chremes' suggestion (767 n.). He also shows the tendency to philosophise which we have seen before (766-72 n.). Geta, in Phormio's continued absence from the stage, plays the tricky slave role, risking remarks which might have given the game away ('Let's hope the plan comes off...he might change his mind' 773-4), and uttering a typically despairing monologue after Chremes' departure (778-83 n.).

[4] The recitative continues (now in ia[7]).

766-72 Well we've only ourselves...handled this affair: Demipho indulges in some general reflections, which recall his earlier bout of philosophising (241-6 n.). Though Demipho enters in conversation with Geta (Introd. §19), the passage is essentially a monologue: Geta's responses ('Quite so' 771, 'Too true' 772) are scarcely noticed.

767 preserve our own reputation: This is a reference to Chremes' scruples (713ff n. 3) rather than to Demipho's own.

768 We shouldn't overshoot the mark: Lit.: 'Flee in such a way as not to pass the house'. The phrase is evidently proverbial, but it is not found elsewhere in Latin and its precise reference is not clear. Donatus paraphrases 'Flee in such a way that you do not pass your house, which is your safest refuge', and offers two further explanations involving thieves and guards, but none of this seems to fit Demipho's case.

777 tell her that Nausistrata is coming: It is not strictly necessary for Geta to warn Phanium of Chremes' wife's visit (Nausistrata is not actually named in the text until the next scene). In fact, Geta's presence in the house will have unexpected consequences.

778-83 We've got the cash...anything he says: As Demipho goes into Chremes' house, Geta is left on stage to deliver what turns out to be an exit monologue, one of only two in the whole play (311-14 n.). In content it resembles the monologues of Plautine tricky slaves who foresee the failure of their plans and anticipate dire punishments (e.g. Plaut. *Bacch.* 358-65); Geta's language is much less extravagant, but it does include self-address and a colourful mixed metaphor (780 n.)

778 an action against us: The reference is presumably to the possibility that Demipho will sue Phormio to recover his money when it becomes clear that Phormio is not going to marry Phanium.

.266 **780 You're stuck in the same mud, Geta; you'll have to repay a new loan:** i.e. 'you have not solved the problem: you are exchanging one difficulty for another'. This line was famous enough in antiquity to be quoted by the fourth century Christian writer Lactantius. Terence has combined the common metaphor of being stuck in the mud (i.e. in a difficult situation) with the idea of raising a second loan to repay the first; the latter is almost literal here in that Phormio has 'borrowed' the money from the old men to purchase Pamphila but is going to have to repay them. On the self-address ('Geta') cf. 317 n.

782-3 Well, I'm off home to tell Phanium...: The stage is empty again, for the second time in twenty lines (765 n.).

V. iii: DEMIPHO, NAUSISTRATA, CHREMES
(784-819, pp. 266-9)

[1] Demipho emerges from Chremes' house with Nausistrata, who agrees to persuade Phanium to accept the plan for her new marriage to

Phormio. Chremes' rushes out of Demipho's house with the news that the new marriage is off, but has some difficulty in explaining why to Demipho in Nausistrata's presence. After Nausistrata has gone back into Chremes' house, Chremes reveals that Phanium turns out to be his own daughter, and Demipho invites him indoors to hear the full story.

[2] The plot advances the plot on two fronts. The revelation of Phanium's identity to Demipho is a necessary step towards the happy outcome for Antipho, and the bringing of Chremes and Nausistrata together on stage provides a foretaste of thir anticipated showdown.

[3] Nausistrata belongs to the type 'married woman' (Lat. *matrona*) and, it seems, to the sub-type of the 'dowried wife', who is generally represented in comedy as being domineering and unpleasant (587 n.). In this scene it is clear that Nausistrata is the dominating type ('I wish I'd been born a man' 792); her contempt for her husband is very evident ('What a difference there is between one man and another!' 790), as is its basis in the wealth inherited from her father. But there are signs also of a more sympathetic side to her nature: she is willing to help Demipho ('You're welcome' 787) and concerned for Phanium's welfare ('Now don't you be wronging a relative' 803, 'I'm sure it's best for everyone that she should stay' 814-15). It is interesting that she is named 'Nausistrata' rather than Terence's usual 'Sostrata' (*Ad.* 285ff n. 5). 'Nausistrata' literally means 'ship-host', which has masculine connotations (cf. 'Battleship'), and in real life its male equivalent Nausistratos is much more common.

[4] This is one of the more amusing scenes in the play, with Chremes trying to convey his news to Demipho without betraying his guilty secret to Nausistrata. The essence of the humour is dramatic irony, with the audience and one of the characters 'in the know' and the other two characters unaware of the true situation. There are several 'crossed-purposes' scenes of this kind in Roman comedy, notably at Plaut. *Capt.* 533-658, where the slave Tyndarus vainly tries to prevent his fellow captive Aristophontes giving away his real identity to their captor Hegio, and at Ter. *Andr.* 716-95 (pp. 74-8), where the maid Mysis takes part in the slave Davos' scheme to deceive the old man Chremes without really understanding what is going on.

[5] The recitative continues, with a change from ia^7 to ia^8 at Chremes' entry (795), where some MSS in fact mark a new scene.

786 as your money did before: This must be a reference to the story concocted by Chremes (680-1, p. 260) that the three thousand drachmas taken from Nausistrata's estate to pay Phormio were in fact needed by Demipho. Demipho is loyally maintaining this pretence: the cross-reference shows Terence's usual care for small details (466 n.).

789 twelve thousand drachmas: Lit. 'two talents of silver'. As Demipho's cry of astonishment (Lat. *hui*) suggests, this is meant to seem a very large amount; if the annual income was two talents, the value of the property may have been perhaps five times as much; and if, as we may suppose, Nausistrata's father also owned property in Attica, he will have been a very wealthy man. The actual sum is hard to evaluate. As far as comedy is concerned, one comparison is with Menedemus at *Heaut.* 145-6 (p. 106), who seems to have bought his estate for fifteen talents (ninety thousand drachmas). But this is a very large sum in comparison to real-life figures in fourth-century Athens, where, so far as our evidence goes, only the very wealthy had estates worth five talents or more. Clearly we have to allow for the general tendency of comedy to exaggerate monetary amounts; by contrast, the farm of the misanthrope Knemon at Men. *Dysk.* 327-8 is worth only two talents, which seems a much more realistic figure.

793-4 save your strength for the girl: This has two implications, both of which are somewhat unexpected, (i) that Nausistrata is in fact elderly, and (ii) that Phanium, who has so far been simply a pawn in the machinations of the two fathers, is a girl of some spirit.

.267 **795 I say, Demipho:** Chremes reappears from Demipho's house, where he went to explain the situation to Sophrona. This looked as if it was simply a device to remove the Chremes-Sophrona conversation off-stage (765 n.). But it has led to a further dramatic discovery: Terence is plotting the movements of his characters with some skill.

801 she is related to me: Lit. 'she is related to us', which would be a better translation (cf. 'there's no one so nearly related to her as we two are' 808).

.268 **814-15 I'm sure it is best for everyone that she should stay:** Nausistrata speaks more truly than she knows.

a very ladylike girl: Lat. *perliberalis* (Introd. §15). Nausistrata now returns to her house in obedience to Demipho's suggestion ('we needn't keep you' 813). It is a little surprising that the 'dominating' Nausistrata here meekly withdraws rather than demanding to know more of Chremes' newly found relative, but Terence has good dramatic reasons for saving this revelation till later. Some scholars, who believe that Nausistrata is Terence's addition to the play, have seen this awkwardness, such as it is, as a sign that Terence inserted her into here into what was originally a scene between the two fathers, in which case it is he who is responsible for the delightful irony of the scene.

.269 **818 It isn't safe to tell you out here:** Terence amusingly underlines Chremes' nervousness about his guilty secret, while at the same time contriving once more to move a 'superfluous' conversation off-stage (765 n.). As the two fathers go indoors, the stage is left empty yet again (782-3 n.); this is an unusual sequence of empty stages.

V. iv-v: ANTIPHO, PHORMIO (820-40, pp. 269-70)

[1] Antipho returns from the town (right) after his meeting with Phaedria, glad that his cousin's problem has been solved but seeing no solution to his own. Phormio also returns from the town, with the

news that Dorio has been paid and the girl delivered to Phaedria; he proposes now to take a few days rest himself, and asks Antipho to plead Phaedria's case to Chremes.

[2] The plot marks time during these two brief scenes (which are here taken together for sake of convenience). Terence is positioning his characters for the next stage in the action, which will presumably be the divulging of Phanium's identity to Antipho and Phormio.

[3] Antipho here is very reminiscent of the Antipho of the first act, envying Phaedria his situation and needing Geta's support to face his father (153ff n. 3). In fact this speech would fit much better if this was Antipho's first return to the stage after running away in a panic (218, p. 237): the references to keeping the secret (825-7 n.), to 'going home now' (826), and to 'the best moment to approach my father' (828) seem to ignore the new plan to marry off Phanium to Phormio. This lends some support to the theory that in Apollodorus Antipho took no part in the middle section of the play (485 ff n. 3).

[4] Phormio returns to the stage for the first time since 440 (p. 247). It is a relatively low-key return, but we may note the satisfaction with which he reports the success of his plan for Phaedria (829-30) and the impudence with which he now plans to take several days off (832), even though neither of the young men's problems is finally solved.

[5] The recitative continues, with ia^7 for Antipho's monologue and ia^8 for the Phormio scene.

820-8 No matter...my father: This speech is the only example in the play of an entrance monologue delivered on an empty stage; all the other entrance monologues are of the overheard type (Introd. §22).

821-2 How sensible people are...: Thus is a further addition to the general philosophical element of the play: cf. the philosophising of Davos (55-6, p. 229), Phaedria (162-72, p. 234), and Demipho (241-6, p. 238; 776-70, p. 265)

825-7 If the secret...some hope I can keep my wife: In the context these remarks can only refer to the 'secret' that Phormio has no intention of marrying Phanium and to Geta's reassurances that Phormio will find excuses to back out (696-712, p. 261). But the whole passage is much better suited to the original situation where Antipho was hoping to keep the circumstances of his own marriage to Phanium secret (cf. 'Has my father suspected anything?...Is there any hope then?' 474, p. 249).

829 removed the girl: This seem to prove that the pimp's house was not one of the three stage houses (cf. 484 n.), since, if it was, the removal of the girl would have had to be enacted on stage. The idea that she might have been removed by a back gate out of sight of the audience is not really tenable. The back gate is rarely used in comedy; when it is, its use is made explicit, as e.g. at Plaut. *As.* 741-4, where the old man is anxious not to be seen returning by his slaves.

832 have some peace for a drink: This idea seems to have been transferred from the traditional tricky slave character, who similarly takes time off for a drink after carrying out a successful deception (e.g. Syrus at *Ad.* 590-1, p. 366, cf. Plaut. *Pseud.* 1051).

833 Why, it's Phormio: Phormio's overheard entrance monologue is swiftly terminated by a simple 'recognition formula' (Introd. §30). Pace is important at this stage of the play (cf. 179-96 n.).

835-6 take a turn in your part /...you to take over his: Antipho had hidden from his father at 218 (p. 237); Phaedria had pleaded Antipho's case at 254-84 (pp. 238-40). The exchange of roles underlines the ethic of mutual help, and provides a neat structural correspondence. But in fact Antipho does not plead Phaedria's case to Chremes; he disappears from the play at this point, leaving something of a loose end. On the theatrical metaphor ('part') see *Eun.* 354 n.

837 while he comes over to my house for a drink: There is something ironic in a parasite offering entertainment at home instead of seeking it abroad, but Phormio is not an ordinary parasite.

Sunium: *Eun.* 115 n.

838 the maid: for Phormio's 'wife' (665, p. 259).

839 if they don't see me around...: Phormio should be spending the money on preparations for his wedding, and the old men might become suspicious if he were not seen to be doing so.

270 **840 That sounded like your door:** Lit. 'your door creaked': Introd. §20.

V. vi-vii: GETA, ANTIPHO, PHORMIO (841-93, pp. 270-2)

[1] Geta emerges from Demipho's house in great excitement, and reports to Antipho and Phormio that he has discovered that Phanium is Chremes' daughter; moreover, both the fathers have agreed to her marriage with Antipho. After Antipho has followed Geta back inside the house, Phormio perceives a new opportunity to swindle the old men out of their money, and slips into a side-street to lie in wait.

[2] Antipho's problem is now solved, and a final piece of trickery is foreshadowed to solve Phaedria's. Suspense is thus maintained right into the final scenes. The audience can scarcely foresee exactly what Phormio's new plan entails, though they may guess that it involves some exploitation of Chremes' guilty secret. Terence is leading up to a finale in which Phormio will hold centre stage and prove himself the trickster supreme. But for the most of this scene it is Geta who dominates the attention, with his 'running slave' antics (841-53 n.), his animated narrative of his discovery, and his generally heightened diction (842-3 n., 844 n., 849 n., 850 n., 856 n.). Geta is thus allowed one final flourish before he disappears from the play (cf. 534ff n. 3).

[3] The passage is here treated as a single scene for the sake of convenience. No new character enters to mark the beginning of v. vii (i.e. Phormio's monologue), but Terence does make a metrical

distinction. The recitative continues (now in tr⁷) for the Geta-Antipho
Phormio dialogue, but Phormio's monologue is in spoken verse (ia⁶),
which is the first spoken verse for seven scenes.

841-53 O Fortune...come here, sir: This is Geta's second
'running slave' monologue in the play (cf. 179-96 n.); this time he is
bringing Antipho good news, which makes a neat contrast with the
first, in which the news was bad. Many of the traditional features of
the running slave scene are deployed, including the failure to see the
master for whom the message is intended, the puzzled aside comments
of the master to a friend ('Do you understand what he's saying?' 846),
the abusive rejection by the slave of the master's approach (849 n., 850
n.), the elaborate recognition formula ('Can it be the man...? I do
believe it is' 852), and the anxious questioning of the slave's message
('What was it?','I've no idea', 'I don't believe you' 871-3).

841 O Fortune, lucky Fortune: In the Latin Geta appeals to
Fortuna and Fors Fortuna, two distinct divinities which had their
separate temples at Rome. Donatus explains that Fortuna was the
goddess of uncertainty, Fors Fortuna the goddess of good luck. The
distinction is Roman, though the personification of Fortune is Greek
and is already common in Greek New Comedy (757-8 n.).

842-3 heaped.../...rid: The Latin has the neat word-play
'burdened...unburdened'.

844 Quick, make ready: Lit. 'I am delaying myself, in that I
do not burden my shoulder with this cloak'. The translation loses (i)
the action formula 'I am delaying' (252 n.), (ii) the further word-play
on 'burden' (842-3 n.), and (iii) the allusion to the comic slave's practice of throwing his outer garment (Lat. *pallium*) over his shoulder in
order to speed his progress. The best commentary on this practice is
Plaut. *Capt.* 778-9, where the parasite Ergasilus, similarly bearing
good news to his patron, says: 'Now I've decided to imitate the slaves
of comedy: I will throw my *pallium* round my neck, so that he shall
hear this news from me first'.

847 I'll try Dorio's: The language (lit. 'I will go from here to
the pimp') rather suggests that Dorio's house is off-stage (829 n.).

849 A proper nuisance...: Lit. 'you'll never overcome me
with your odiousness'.

850 Go hang yourself!: Lit. 'get yourself thrashed' (Lat.
vapula), a colloquialism found only here in Terence, though it occurs
several times in Plautus. The ancient lexicographer Festus tells us that
it was particularly used to respond to threats.

you rascal: Lat. *verbero* (684 n.).

p.271   **856 soak you...in delight:** This is a bold metaphor which has
no direct parallel in Plautus or in Greek New Comedy. Donatus explains that the reference is to soaking with oil or perfume.

857 Never mind about promises: Phormio finally brings the running slave to order, Antipho having failed to make much progress.

861 I'm not going into that, sir: The audience is again spared unnecessary repetition (818 n.).

862 the women's quarters: The reference is to the typical Greek house, where the women had separate quarters at the back. Terence actually uses the Greek word *gynaeceum* here (as does Plautus at *Most.* 755), since there was no Roman equivalent; Roman houses were constructed on a different principle which did not involve the segregation of the women.

869 like this: This is a stage direction written into the text (152 n.): Geta cups his ear with his hand

873 had a secret affair: The Latin word (*consuescere*) can cover anything from a single night of intimacy (as of Jupiter with Alcumena at Plaut. *Amph.* 1122) to an affair of many years (as of Pamphilus with Bacchis at *Hec.* 555, p. 315).

875 There's a reason: Phanium had known her father by the name Stilpo, as Phormio knows well enough (390, p. 245).

877 I've heard something about that story: It seems strange that Antipho should only now recall a story about Phanium's father; it also seems unnecessary for Terence to manufacture a corroborative detail at this point. The object presumably is to make it more plausible that Antipho should believe the good news; there is a similar case at Plaut. *Capt.* 1023-4, where the slave Tyndarus, who has throughout the play been the captive of a gentleman named Hegio, dimly remembers in the last scene that his father was called Hegio.

890 play a new part: Lit. 'assume a new gesture and expression', a vivid version of the common theatrical metaphor (835-6 n.).

891 side-street: The whole point of Phormio's manoeuvre is to convince the old men that he is just returning from the town, i.e. that he has not been concocting further schemes with the sons. It follows that the side-street (Lat. *angiportum*) mentioned here is a notional off-stage side-street in the direction of the town (right). So the passage lends no support to the idea of an *angiportum* between the stage houses which actors could use as a hiding-place (*Eun.* 845-6 n.); it might serve to arouse the old men's suspicions if Phormio suddenly emerged from such a place.

892 appear when they come out: Since Phormio is lurking rather than departing and will reappear almost immediately, this speech should be classed as a 'link monologue' (the only one in the whole play) rather than an exit monologue (Introd. §22).

893 give up the idea of pretending to go to Sunium: As planned at 837-8 (p. 269). The abandoned scheme is part of the characterisation of the tricky slave, and here of Phormio as the supreme trickster: at *Heaut.* 608-9 (p. 129), Syrus has a plan to get money from Menedemus which he never puts into operation.

V. viii: DEMIPHO, CHREMES, PHORMIO
(894-989, pp. 272-7)

[1] Demipho and Chremes emerge from Demipho's house and are accosted by Phormio, who expresses his readiness to receive his bride. Demipho tries to back out of the agreement, and refuses to allow Phormio to keep the dowry, threatening to take him to court. Phormio now reveals that he knows Chremes' secret, and Chremes immediately agrees to let him keep the money. But Demipho argues that Chremes should tell Nausistrata the secret himself to forestall Phormio's blackmail, and in response to further threats by Phormio repeats his suggestion that they should take him to court. The old men now try to seize Phormio, who shouts to Nausistrata to come out.

[2] The interest of the scene lies in the battle of wits between Phormio and the two fathers; as the play moves towards its ending, the two sons (neither of whom reappears in the play) are very much in the background. In terms of the plot, Phormio has achieved his object by the point at which the old men give up their claim to the money ('And I'll accept your offer' 947), and it is sometimes argued that Apollodorus' play might have ended at this point (951 n.). But, with the renewed objections by Demipho which follow, the scene gathers new momentum, and sets up the final confrontation between Chremes and Nausistrata, which has been in prospect ever since Chremes decided to involve Nausistrata with Phanium (713ff n. 2).

[3] This Phormio-Demipho confrontation mirrors the earlier one in the second act (348-440, pp. 243-7), which gives a certain structural symmetry to the play. A comparison between the two reveals both variations and similarities. In the first Phormio was acting on Antipho's behalf, here he is acting on Phaedria's; in the first he was refusing to take a dowry, here he is refusing to give it back; in the first Phormio confronted Demipho alone, here he faces Chremes as well. In both Phormio remains cool and in control; in both Demipho shows himself a spirited opponent; both end with Demipho reduced to anger but refusing to admit defeat.

[4] Phormio's principal tactic here is to claim for himself the traditional virtues (904 n., 908 n.), while putting the old men in the wrong (915 n., 927-8 n., 948-9 n., 951 n.), thus occupying the moral high ground as he had in the first confrontation. As before, he shows himself a master of instant repartee (932-3 n., 935-6 n.); he displays great skill in playing his trump card, revealing his knowledge of Chremes' secret bit by bit and leaving Chremes to identify himself as the guilty husband (937-47); and, when momentarily taken aback by Demipho's renewed objections, he recovers and reasserts himself with great vigour (968-75 n.). With his domination assured, his language takes on something of the exuberance of his opening scene (946 n., 954 n., 963 n., 964 n., 968-75 n.); and he responds with nonchalance both

to threats of being sued ('Certainly' 981) and to actual physical violence ('Knock an eye out if you like' 989). Demipho makes some good points, turning back Phormio's own previous arguments on himself (914 n.), threatening to call his bluff (932-3 n.), and sensibly advising Chremes to forestall the blackmail by confessing the truth (958-61); but he loses his temper sooner than in the earlier confrontation, resorting to abuse (930-1 n., 962 n.), imprecations ('May all the powers... see him damned' 976), threats (981 n.), and eventually violence (988 n.). As in their previous scene with Geta (606ff n. 4), the two old men are clearly contrasted: Demipho's main motivation is a determination not to be mocked or cheated of his money ('is this man to have the laugh on us...?' 955-6), whereas Chremes is ready to surrender instantly to preserve his secret ('What do you want for yourself?...' 946-7).

[5] The spoken verse (ia⁶) continues.

895 things have turned out well for us: The scene begins on an ironic note: Demipho is blissfully ignorant of Geta's eavesdropping and the use to which Phormio will put it.

897 squanders: The Latin is more colourful (*dilapidare*: lit. 'dismantle stone by stone').

.273   **900-2 On the same old errand.../...what I'd undertaken?:** The drift of this interchange seems to be: PH. About the marriage again? DE. Yes, indeed. PH. I knew it: what did you want this time? DE. Don't adopt such a sneering attitude. PH. I suppose you didn't trust me to keep my word.

904 to be a man of my word: Phormio begins by claiming for himself the traditional virtue of *fides* (469 n.).

905 the perfect gentleman: Lat. *liberalis*: Chremes recognises Phormio's tactics.

906 I am on my way now...to tell you: Phormio seizes the initiative, before Demipho can deliver his message (cf. 352 n.).

908 as was only proper: Phormio's second claim is to 'proper' behaviour'; the Latin here is *par* (lit. 'equal'), which is virtually a synonym of *aequom*.

910-13 my brother here has persuaded me...a scandal: Demipho counters Phormio's moral stance by assuming a moral position himself. But the alleged persuasion by Chremes is an invention: Demipho cannot give Phormio the real reason for his change of heart since their previous confrontation.

914 the ones you used against me: This is a reference to 413-17 (p. 246).

915 make a fool of me in this high-handed way: Rather than answering Demipho's arguments, Phormio immediately counterattacks with a charge of arrogance (358 n.).

.274   **922-3 transferred back.../...drawn:** Our impression has been that Demipho paid Phormio in cash with money that Chremes had acquired in Lemnos (679-80, p. 260), and that Phormio paid Dorio also in cash (829, p. 269). But here the Latin uses the technical terms of banking (*rescribere* and *discribere*): Demipho demands to be repaid throught the banking system, and Phormio implies that he banked the money and then withdrew it to pay off his creditors. This raises interesting questions about banking in Greece and Rome. Athens had sophisticated financial systems by the period of New Comedy, whereas banking was relatively new at Rome in the time of Plautus and Terence. In fact there are no direct references to bankers in Terence, but Plautus alludes to them in eleven of his plays, using the Greek word (*trapezita*) as well as its Latin equivalent (*argentarius*); the picture in Plautus is of one-man operators with a base in the forum, who both receive money on deposit and lend it out at interest.

927-8 not right that I should be cheated: Phormio now accuses the old men of failing to observe proper behaviour (cf. 908 n.: the Latin here for 'right' is *aequom*) as well as of bad faith.

930-1 Go to hell...you miserable creature: Lit. 'Go to trouble (= 'get thrashed': 644 n.), you runaway' (*Eun.* 668-70 n.). Demipho has already lost his temper. The virulence of his abuse here is striking: both of these phrases are rare in Terence, and both are more properly addressed to slaves.

932-3 Would you marry her.../ Try me: There is a moment of suspense here, as Demipho hits on what is in fact Phormio's weak point, but Phormio response is instant and effective.

935-6 hand over my money / hand over my wife: Phormio neatly caps Demipho's phrase, as he had previously (439 n.).

940 women of property: Lit. 'dowried women'. The allusion is of course to Nausistrata (587 n.); it introduces a new phase of the scene, in which Phormio takes the offensive and Chremes replaces Demipho as his main adversary.

p.275 **942 another wife in Lemnos:** Phormio has turned the 'secret affair' reported by Geta (873 n.) into bigamy.

943 had a daughter: Lat. *suscipere*, in its more general sense (cf. 646-7 n.).

It's the end of me: Lit. 'I am buried'.

946 Rubbish: Lit. 'fables' (492-4 n.).

948-9 putting me off...like a pair of stupid children: Phormio repeats his allegation that the old men are mocking him (915 n.), but now, with victory in his grasp, he is more contemptuous than indignant.

951 cancel what was just agreed: This repeats the accusation of bad faith (927-8 n.). There is a pause here as Chremes and Demipho confer out of Phormio's hearing. Scholars have noted various oddities about the rest of the scene, which have led them to suggest that what follows is an addition by Terence to the Greek original: (i) Demipho's renewed objections (954-63) look like an afterthought: they would have fitted better *before* Chremes agreed to let Phormio keep the money and Phormio accepted the offer (947); (ii) Phormio's response (968-75) does not in fact invalidate Demipho's suggestion that the old men should tell Nausistrata the truth themselves; and (iii) the physical violence at the end of the scene (982-9 n.) is 'Plautine' in tone. These points are interesting but not in the end decisive: if they were, it would follow that Terence has altered the whole ending of the play.

954 That's stung them: Lit. 'I have thrown in a small stone' (Lat. *scrupulus*). The expression, which is proverbial, apparently refers to a stone in the shoe which makes walking uncomfortable.

958 misdeeds: The Latin is *peccatum*, which, though it can refer to a mere slip or blunder, frequently denotes a moral offence. The same word is translated 'sins' at 973.

962 this filthy brute: Lat. *inpuratus* (669 n.): Demipho is echoing his previous violent reaction to Phormio's effrontery.

963 I'm caught: Phormio's sudden loss of confidence (emphasised in the Latin by the exclamation *attat*: 600 n.) creates another moment of suspense (cf. 932-3 n.). Like many other aspects of Phormio's characterisation, this is derived from the traditional Plautine tricky slave, who has similar moments of panic when things begin to go wrong (179ff n. 3).

964 in desperation: Lit. 'in gladiatiorial spirit', i.e. determined to conquer or die. Since gladiatorial shows were not a Greek custom, this is a rare example of a Roman allusion by Terence, who generally preserves the Greek context of his plays intact (229-30 n.).

968-75 Is this how...dissolve into tears: Phormio rebounds to the attack with a speech full of vivid imagery, notably 'trying my patience' (969: lit 'goading'), 'wash away your sins' (973), 'blaze of fury' (974), 'dissolve into tears' (975).

978-9 deported...a desert island: This suggestion, like the similar jocular reference to the confinement of the wicked at Plaut. *Trin.* 547-52, should be regarded as the product of a comic imagination rather than as an allusion either by Terence or by Apollodorus to contemporary legal practice. Exile was generally available in both Athens and Rome as a means of avoiding the death penalty and as a penalty for some major offences, but deportation to a specific place becomes common only in the much later time of the Roman emperors.

981 let's take him to court: Demipho reverts to his previous proposal (936), from which he had been diverted by Phormio's revelation that he knew Chremes' secret.

982-9 After him...both of you: The scene concludes with some knockabout farce, as Phormio moves towards Nausistrata's house and the two old men attempt to seize him. Visual humour of this type is more in Plautus' manner than Terence's, though there are slapstick scenes elsewhere in Terence (e.g. the Sannio scene at *Ad.* 155-75, pp. 345-6). And there are also examples of slapstick in Menander (e.g. the teasing of Knemon at *Dysk.* 910-64), so that we cannot deny the possibility of a similar scene in Apollodorus at this point. In Terence's scene the action is not easy to interpret, especially as the MSS are in some confusion as to which speech belongs to which old man. It seems likely that Demipho is trying to seize Phormio to take him to court, whereas Chremes is more intent on preventing him from going in to see Nausistrata, but this distinction is obscured in the Penguin assignation of the speeches (985 n., 986 n.).

983-4 I'll have the law on you for assault: It was illegal in both Athens and Rome to lay violent hands on a citizen. At Athens there were crimes (such as theft and adultery) for which one citizen could arrest another, but Phormio has not committed any of these, and the proper procedure, if Demipho wanted to prosecute Phormio for breach of contract, would have been for him to issue a summons before witnesses. At Rome the ancient law of the Twelve Tables did allow for the arrest of a defendant who refused to come to court, though the normal procedure was again to issue a summons before witnesses and to take sureties for attendance on the appointed day.

985 Take him off: This is in fact the technical word (Lat. *rapere*) for haling a defendant off to court, and as such might be more appropriate to Demipho.

p.277   **986 Shut your dirty mouth:** The word 'dirty' (Lat. *inpurus*) echoes Demipho's previous abuse of Phormio (962 n.), so that this speech also might be assigned to Demipho.

988 punch him in the belly: Instructions of this kind are in comedy generally given to thug-slaves rather than old men (cf. *Ad.* 171, p. 346: 'plant your fist straight in his jaw'), so that we are perhaps to imagine that Demipho is not addressing Chremes but a slave of his who has come out of the house in response to his master's call (982). There are no more examples of this kind of violence in Terence, but several in Plautus (the most extreme example is at *Men.* 990-1020).

989 Knock an eye out: Threats to gouge people's eyes out are also common in Plautus but absent from Terence, though there are two references to eye-scratching in *Eunuchus* (*Eun.* 740 n.).

V. ix: NAUSISTRATA, CHREMES, DEMIPHO, PHORMIO (990-1055, pp. 277-81)

[1] Amidst protests from Chremes, Phormio tells Nausistrata about his Lemnian wife and daughter. Nausistrata is indignant, but begins to relent as Demipho pleads Chremes' case. Phormio now reveals how he has tricked the old men into providing the money for Phaedria's affair. Nausistrata takes Phaedria's side against Chremes, and resolves to take her son's advice on whether to forgive her husband. Meanwhile she offers her services to Phormio, who suggests an invitation to dinner.

[2] The final scene creates a neat conclusion to the play. Phormio achieves his final triumph, Chremes is unmasked in front of his wife,

the old men are defrauded of their money, and Phaedria is assured of his father's consent to his affair. With Antipho's marriage to Phanium already agreed, all the lines of the plot are brought to a satisfactory conclusion; we can infer that Nausistrata will in fact forgive Chremes, and that the two will live unhappily together ever after (1030 n.).

[3] The ending also fits the characterisation that has been built up for the various characters. Phormio, the supreme trickster, plays his final card with his usual panache, humbling the guilty Chremes and ensuring not only the retention of the old men's money but Chremes' consent to Phaedria's affair; it is a fitting touch that, in his role of parasite, he ends by gaining himself an invitation to dinner (1053 n.). His language is predictably colourful in his hour of triumph (994 n., 997 n., 1015 n., 1028 n., 1053 n.). Chremes, who has spent most of the time since his return desperately trying to conceal his secret, is dumbfounded before his wife ('Struck dumb' 991, 'frozen stiff' 994) and, after some feeble protests, is reduced to silent acceptance of his fate; in the end he comes off more lightly than he had feared (1047-8 n.), but we can feel that he has been suitably punished for his misbehaviour. Demipho, who resists Phormio on Chremes' behalf and pleads Chremes' case with his wife with some tact (1020 n., 1032-3 n.), ends on a sympathetic note; he has been sufficiently punished already for his bluster by the indignity of being tricked by Phormio. Nausistrata, who has been portrayed as a domineering wife, is given the last word over her husband, as expected; but the wife's viewpoint is realistic expressed (1024 n.), and any thought that as the traditional 'dowried wife' Nausistrata might forfeit our sympathy is dispelled.

[4] So there are no surprises or discrepancies in the finale to raised the suspicion that Terence has altered the ending of his Greek original, as seems to be the case in both *Eunuchus* and *Adelphoe* (Introd. §34). Chremes' fear of being found out is such an essential part of the plot that his final exposure before Nausistrata on stage constitutes the obvious ending. Nevertheless, some scholars have argued that the last scene and a half of *Phormio* are Terence's own creation (cf. 951 n.). The most convincing argument is the technical one. Terence's last scene is a four-actor scene, which cannot have stood in Apollodorus in that form; moreover Terence's scene cannot easily be reduced to three actors, in that all four characters seem to be indispensable. It would be quite possible to construct an alternative ending for Apollodorus in which Nausistrata did not appear (814-15 n.) and even one in which Chremes' guilty secret was never divulged. Chremes' consent to Phaedria's affair could have been extorted by Phormio as part of the blackmail of the penultimate scene and the play could have ended there; alternatively, it might have been secured in a final scene by the return of Antipho, who is specifically asked to plead Phaedria's case in Terence but in the end does not do so (835-6 n.). In the end, all this is interesting speculation but nothing can be proved.

The fact that two of Plautus' plays (*As.* and *Cas.*) end with wives on stage triumphant over their erring husbands does not help to solve the problem. On the one hand, the Plautine examples suggest that this was a recurrent ending in Greek New Comedy and thus quite possible for Apollodorus; on the other, they might have served as a model for a change by Terence to the ending of *Phormio*.

[5] To return to Terence's version, if the play has an obvious moral, it lies in the fate of Chremes, who is forced to submit to the judgement of his wife and son; the father of the family has by his errant behaviour forfeited his dignity and his position of authority. We have also noted the stress placed on the ethic of helping one's friends and the general expectation that people should behave according to a code of decency. It is probably a mistake to look for anything deeper than this; the audience is likely to be more involved in the success or failure of Phormio's schemes than in any great moral issue. For readings of the play see Forehand 90-2, Goldberg 75-90, Konstan (1983) 115-29 (a study in 'citizen disorder').

[6] The scene begins with spoken verse (ia⁶) as in the two preceding scenes, but there is a change at 1011 ('Demipho, I appeal to you') to recitative (tr⁷), which is the traditional metre for the finale (*Eun.* 1049ff n. 7).

993 D-don't you b-believe: There is no suggestion of stuttering in the Latin either here or in Chremes' next speech.

994 Strike me dead...frozen stiff: Phormio's language is striking; these particular phrases are relatively familiar in English but do not occur anywhere else in Plautus or Terence.

997 crazed: Lit. 'delirious', another vivid term.

p.278   **1005 he married a wife:**   Phormio repeats his assertion that Chremes had committed bigamy (942 n.). This is contradicted later in the scene by Demipho ('seduced this woman...never touched her after that' 1018), but taken up again by Nausistrata ('you have two wives' 1041). The strongest reason for believing Phormio's version is that Chremes never attempts to contradict it. However Terence intended us to interpret the situation, it is striking that he has totally ignored the relevance of the question to Phanium's citizen status. It was taken for granted at the beginning of the the play (114, p. 231), when the facts about her father were not known, that Phanium was an Athenian citizen, and, as such, could be given to Antipho in a regular citizen marriage. But the discovery of these facts has altered the situation, in that the daughter of a bigamous union (or of casual affair) between an Athenian male and a Lemnian woman would not have full Athenian citizen rights. There may be a hidden assumption, with which Terence has not troubled his Roman audience, that Phanium's mother was actually an Athenian citizen (this is historically plausible in that there was an Athenian settlement on the island of Lemnos in which the settlers retained their Athenian citizenship); but this goes only part of the way to removing the problem, since any marriage between her and Chremes would still have been bigamous. In the end, since Terence ignores the whole question, we can only conclude that he has deliberately kept it out of focus. For Chremes the whole point of marrying Phanium to Antipho was to keep the true facts of her birth within the family (579-80, p. 256); and this will presumably still be done, though Nausistrata's concurrence will now be required.

1007 had a daughter: The Latin is *suscipere* again (943 n.).

1009: cruelly unfair: Lat. *indignum* (511 n.).

1010 It's only when they're with their wives...: There is an amusing hint here of the decline of sexual relations between Chremes and Nausistrata. A similar complaint is made of the lecherous old man Demaenetus at Plaut. *As.* 812-13.

1011 Demipho, I appeal to you: At this point Demipho takes over the pleading of Chremes' case, and the scene goes into recitative to heighten the atmosphere of the finale.

1012-13 journeys...long visits...low prices: This expands Nausistrata's earlier complaint about Chremes' mishandling of her father's properties on Lemnos (788-90, p. 266).

1015 that's the last word on him: Lit. 'words are being spoken to the dead'. Phormio uses a proverbial phrase which elsewhere means 'words are being wasted on someone who is not listening', so that the implication here would be that Demipho has no hope of persuading Nausistrata. But the Penguin translator prefers the alternative interpretation 'a funeral oration is being pronounced' (i.e. Chremes is as good as dead), which picks up Chremes' own 'I am buried' (943 n.) and is repeated in Phormio's announcement of Chremes' funeral (1026).

p.279 **1017-19 about fifteen years ago...after that:** The details of Chremes' Lemnian affair are still being filled in (cf. 1012-13 n.). It follows that Phanium is only fourteen or fifteen years old; there are only three girls loved by *adulescentes* whose ages are specified in Roman comedy (*Eun.* 318 n.), and Phanium is the youngest.

when he was drunk: This is one of the defences commonly offered in comedy for the sexual misbehaviour of the *adulescens* (*Ad.* 469-71 n.). With the young, it is generally regarded as an acceptable excuse, but it is presumably intended to seem a lame one in the case of Chremes.

1020 to show your usual good sense: Demipho is using the technique of flattery.

1024 Am I younger now and more attractive...?: The importance of physical attractiveness is often stressed in comedy by courtesans, who rely on their beauty to attract men ('It's only our looks which attract lovers to wait on us, and when these fade they take their attentions elsewhere' *Heaut.* 389-90, p. 118). Here it is part of a realistic, and sympathetic, analysis of the prospects of an ageing wife when faced with an unfaithful husband.

1028 I'll see he suffers the same misfortune as this man:
The sentence has an archaic ring in the Latin, which suggests that it
may be a quotation from Roman tragedy or epic. This whole pro-
clamation marks the climax of Phormio's triumph; he has proved his
ability to inflict misfortune on anyone who dares oppose him.

1030 something to whine about: The implication is that the
marriage will continue its unharmonious path. The word 'whine' (Lat.
ogganire) is a colloquialism which occurs in Terence only twice (cf.
Ad. 556 n.); the ancient scholiast tells us that the word is properly
applied to a dog (i.e. 'whine', 'snarl', 'yap', 'growl').

1032-3 I know it all as well as you do. / Certainly not:
Demipho tactfully accepts Nausistrata's viewpoint.

p.280 **1042 you're shameless:** Nausistrata invokes the concept of
pudor against Chremes, just as Phormio had against Demipho (392
n.).

1047-8 getting off lightly, much better than I expected:
Lit. 'I am coming off fine and well and beyond expectation'. The MSS
unanimously assign these lines to Phormio, though some scholars have
felt that they would more appropriately be given to Chremes. With the
translation 'getting off lightly' they do seem to suit Chremes better, but
with the literal translation Phormio could be saying 'things have turned
out splendidly, even better than I expected; not only is Antipho safely
married but I have enjoyed exposing the misdeeds of Chremes'.

1048 Please tell me your name: Nausistrata is making a
gesture of friendship by addressing a social inferior by name; the same
technique is used by Demea to the slave Geta at *Ad.* 891 (p. 381).

1053 a slap in the eye: Lit. 'to make his eyes smart', a final
piece of vivid imagery from Phormio.

invite me to dinner: Phormio assumes the role of hungry
parasite, as at 326-45 (pp. 242-3), where it was noted that this aspect of
his characterisation was probably a Terentian addition (315ff n. 2).

p.281 **1055 Farewell, and give us your applause:** It is uncertain
who delivered these lines, whether Phormio as the final speaker or the
whole cast (*Eun.* 1094 n.). The following stage direction is the invention of the Penguin translator; in practical terms, it is more likely that
the Phormio actor entered the stage building along with the rest.

The Brothers

PRODUCTION NOTICE (p. 335)

See the notes on the Production Notice of *Eunuchus*.

funeral games for Lucius Aemilius Paulus: This is our one clear example of dramatic performances at games outside the regular calendar of public festivals, but there may well have been others. The second performance of Terence's unsuccessful *Hecyra* took place at the same games (see the Production Notices to *Hec.*: pp. 287-8). The choice of plays by Terence for this funeral celebration establishes a clear link between Terence and Aemilius Paullus, who had won the Third Macedonian War for Rome in 168 B.C. and was one of the leading political figures of the day. In an era when Roman statesmen were divided in their attitudes to the importation of Greek civilisation to Rome, Aemilius was one of those who who sought to combine the best of Greek culture with Roman.

Quintus Fabius Maximus and Publius Cornelius Africanus: The games were put on by Aemilius' two elder sons, who, as their names indicate, had been adopted into two of the other leading Roman families. The latter, who is commonly known as Scipio Aemilianus, gathered round him a circle of literary and philosophical friends, with which Terence was in some way connected (on the so-called Scipionic Circle see the Penguin introduction, pp. 13-15).

Lucius Ambivius Turpio and Lucius Hatilius: Introd. §25.

Music composed by Flaccus: Introd. §26.

Sarranian pipes: As the Penguin note says, Sarranian pipes were equal ones. Equal pipes were also used for *Andria* and *Hecyra*. It is a plausible conjecture that they were played in unison, but their effect on the mood of the play is very difficult to gauge.

The author's sixth play: *Adelphoe* was Terence's sixth and last play, performed in 160 B.C. Terence died soon afterwards: see the Penguin introduction (p. 12) and appendix (p. 392).

SYNOPSIS (p. 336)

See the note on the Synopsis of *Eunuchus*.

CHARACTERS (p. 337)

See the note on the Characters of *Eunuchus*.

Of the fifteen parts listed here for *Adelphoe*, ten are speaking parts, but only five of these are of any size. The two leading roles are those of the old man Demea, who is on stage for fifteen scenes, and the slave Syrus, who is on stage for twelve, and one could imagine the two leading actors of the Roman troupe playing these two parts. Another possibility mentioned by the ancient commentator Donatus (*Preface* 1. 4) is to regard Demea's brother Micio as one of the leading roles: though Micio is on stage for only eight scenes, the essence of the play is the clash between the two brothers. If we look behind the Roman play to the three-actor Greek original, the interesting prospect emerges that in Menander's play the leading actor played both Syrus and Micio, and the second actor combined Demea and his son Ctesipho, who never meet on stage in Terence's version.

Scene

See the note on the Scene of *Eunuchus*.

Adelphoe requires only two stage houses, those of Micio and Sostrata. There is just a hint that of the two Micio's is to be placed on the left (543 n.). The Penguin edition again assigns the harbour to the right-hand entrance along with the forum, but for no compelling reason. This commentary follows the conventional staging with the forum on the right and the harbour (and the country) on the left.

PROLOGUE (1-25, p. 339)

See the introductory notes to the Prologue of *Eunuchus*.

1 The poet: Terence.

2 unfair critics...his enemies: Notably Luscius of Lanuvium (Introd. §31).

6-7 *Joined in Death*...same name: Plautus in fact translated Diphilus' Greek title (*Synapothescontes*) into Latin (*Commorientes*).

Diphilus: None of Diphilus' plays remains, but from the fragments which have and from Plautus' surviving adaptations (*Cas.* and *Rud.*) we can deduce that Diphilus went in for lively scenes and bold contrasted characters. It thus seems that he was a less sensitive and sophisticated writer than Menander.

9 girl: The Latin is *meretrix* (Introd. §9).

11 word for word: This should probably not be taken at face value; it may well be a sop to Luscius' demand for literal translation.

13 plagiarism: As in *Eunuchus* Terence implicitly admits to *contaminatio* while actually defending himself against the charge of *furtum* (Introd. §32). Here he is careful to establish that, though Plautus had used Diphilus' play, he had not used the particular scene.

15-21 As to the spiteful accusation...each one of you: This paragraph engendered much speculation in antiquity, as can be seen from the biography of Terence by Suetonius (see the Penguin appendix, pp. 389-93). The basic problem is that the description of the 'eminent persons' who allegedly assisted Terence as 'men who...find favour with you all and with the general public' and 'whose services in war, in peace, and in your private affairs, are...available for each one of you' hardly fits Terence's circle of young friends in the 'Scipionic Circle'. It could in fact be applied much better to the older generation, that is, the contemporaries of Aemilius Paullus, at whose funeral games *Adelphoe* was performed. It is notable that Terence does not actually deny the charge but turns it into a compliment by referring to these elder statesmen as his patrons. He may in fact be setting up a smoke-screen to cover assistance from his younger friends, but the extent of any collaboration can hardly be determined.

22 an outline of the plot: *Eun.* 45 n.

24-5 your good will...fresh enthusiasm: *Eun.* 44 n.

I. i: MICIO (26-81, pp. 341-2)

[1] The old man Micio emerges from his house, worried that his son Aeschinus is not yet home from a party. He explains that he himself is an easy-going town-dwelling bachelor, who has adopted the elder son of his strict married country-dwelling brother, and is bringing him up on the basis of lenience and affection rather than by firm discipline, much to the brother's annoyance.

[2] This is the only one of Terence's plays which begins with a monologue rather than a dialogue. Micio's speech fulfils the functions of an expository prologue, in that it sets the basic scene (with the two brothers bringing up the two sons on different educational principles) and introduces the two contrasted main characters of the title. The expository technique is very similar to that of Menander's *Samia*, which opens with a monologue by the young man Moschion, and there is no immediate reason to suppose that Menander's *Adelphoi* did not begin with a similar speech by the Micio character. This is in fact the longest monologue in the whole of Terence, who generally avoids long monologues as being too artificial a device (Introd. §22): within the conventions of the genre it is a reasonably realistic soliloquy, with Micio expressing his feelings as to an unseen audience

[3] Micio belongs to the type of the 'lenient old man' (*senex lenis*: Introd. §3), and may indeed be regarded as the best example of this type in surviving Greek and Roman comedy. Interesting comparisons can be made with his counterparts in other plays of Terence, notably the repentant Menedemus in *Heauton*, who swings from an extreme of harshness to an extreme of leniency. But Micio is not just a type. Interesting aspects of his character which emerge in this opening scene are his capacity for ironic self-criticism ('Why on earth should a man take it into his head...?' 38-9), his admission of the importance to him of his son's affection ('I do all I can to ensure that he returns my affection' 50), and his firm conviction of the philosophical rightness

of his educational methods ('A father's duty then is...If he fails to do this, he should admit he doesn't know how to manage his children' 74-7). There is also the fact that he is a bachelor with an adopted son, unlike the usual lenient father: it remains to be seen to what extent Terence will exploit this distinction. The name 'Micio', which is attested in real life at Athens and elsewhere but not otherwise in comedy, seems to mean 'small', here perhaps suggesting a neat dapper figure. The fact that the 'Paullus' of Aemilius Paullus also means 'small' has suggested to some scholars that Terence meant by his choice of name to allude to his patron and even to his patron's ideals; but this is unlikely, when the dénouement of the play is considered.

[4] Micio's monologue also foreshadows the prominence of the theme of education in the play (Introd. §4). This is going to be not simply a clash of characters but a clash of rival educational methods. For the moment we must suspend judgment on where Terence's sympathies lie; Micio's arguments here seem sensible and plausible, especially to the modern liberal mind, but we have so far seen only one side of the question.

[5] The scene, like the prologue, is in spoken verse (ia⁶): Terence never uses recitative for his opening scenes (Introd. §27).

26 Boy!: The play opens dramatically with Micio emerging from his house and calling in vain to one of the slaves who should have escorted Aeschinus home from last night's party. This sets the time of the scene as sometime after dawn. The Latin actually names the slave as 'Storax', a rare name with connotations of 'fragrance'.

30-1 angry wife: The audience might be forgiven for supposing that Micio speaks as a married man rather than a bachelor. The satirical tone of these remarks, and the attitude to marriage which they imply, is typical of the older male characters of comedy, whether bachelors (e.g. Periplectomenus at Plaut. *Mil.* 679-700) or married men (e.g. Menaechmus at Plaut. *Men.* 110-22).

36-8 The boy may have caught a chill...: Similar anxieties are cited by the bachelor Periplectomenus at Plaut. *Mil.* 719-22 as a reason for not wanting to have children.

41 quite different tastes: These are expressed here in terms of life-style, the town against the country and the easy life against the hard and thrifty one; this is an important background to the different educational principles of the two brothers.

43-4 count me lucky never to have taken a wife: This remark is likely to be in a similar vein to Micio's previous one on wives (30-1 n.), in which case he is quoting the view of his friends in order to endorse it. But it should be noted that the literal translation of the Latin is 'and, a thing which others count lucky, I have never taken a wife': Terence does not specify who the 'others' are, and in the end Micio's own feelings are left open.

47 adopted: Terence does not explain why Micio's brother gave his elder son away for adoption; the audience will probably infer that Demea was too poor to bring him up himself.

52 exercise my authority: This is a point to which Terence's audience may well have reacted differently from Menander's. In the Greek original Menander may have been consciously echoing a dictum of the Peripatetic school, as preserved at Aristotle *Ethics* 5. 10. 8, that the 'equitable man' is one who 'does not insist upon his rights'. The Romans on the other hand were used to the concept of 'paternal authority' (*patria potestas*), which gave the father absolute rights over his children, even of life and death, and the traditional Roman view would be that the father had a duty to exercise his authority.

.342   **57 treated honorably and like gentlemen:** Lit. 'restrained by a sense of decency and gentlemanliness'. Terence here introduces two of the moral concepts (Lat. *pudor* and *liberalitas*: Introd. §15-16) which are going to be prominent in the play (*pudor* occurs eleven times and *liberalitas* seven). The frequent occurrence of these and similar concepts (cf. 64 n., 69 n.) helps to underline the serious moral tone of *Adelphoe*.

64 has no feeling: Lit. 'is too hard' (Lat. *durus*); Demea is thus labelled as the *senex durus* (81ff n. 4).

right and reason: The concept of 'right' (Lat. *aequom*: Introd. §16) is even more prominent in *Adelphoe* than *pudor* and *liberalitas*, occurring sixteen times.

67 affection: The Latin is *amicitia* ('friendship'): see 72 n.

69 do his duty: This is a fourth recurrent moral concept of the play (Lat. *officium*: Introd. §16).

72 kindness: The concept of 'kindness' or 'favour' (Lat. *beneficium*) is often linked with that of 'friendship' (Lat. *amicitia*: 67 n.), with the implication that the friendship is not disinterested but implies mutual obligations (Introd. §16). Micio certainly seems to be taking this attitude here: cf. 'I do all I can to ensure that he returns my affection' (50) and '[he is] eager to make you a return' (73). The same idea of a son repaying his father's kindness by being well behaved is found at Men. *Sam.* 17-18.

74-5 a father's duty is to train his son...: This seems at first sight an exemplary theory, but two passages of Aristotle's *Ethics* offer an interesting commentary. Aristotle too believed in the importance of training or 'habituation' to virtuous acts, though without the emphasis on free will (*Ethics* 2. 1); he also believed that 'gentlemen' can be inspired to virtuous acts by reason, but that the mass of the population respond only to fear of punishment (*Ethics* 10. 9. 3-4).

78 that's the man...Yes it is: As Demea approaches Micio terminates his own monologue with a standard 'introduction formula' (Introd. §29), which marks the transition to the next scene.

80-1 Glad to see you well: Lit. '...safely arrived': Micio uses the polite formula for greeting those returning to the city from overseas or (as in Demea's case) from the country (Introd. §30).

I. ii: MICIO, DEMEA (81-154, pp. 342-5)

[1] Demea appears on stage, furious at reports that Aeschinus has broken into a house and abducted a girl, and blaming Micio for letting him go astray. Micio argues that young men should be allowed to have their fling, and urges Demea to concentrate on the upbringing of his other son. Demea reluctantly agrees, and departs. Micio, left alone, voices his own disquiet at Aeschinus' behaviour.

[2] Demea is probably to be envisaged as entering from the forum (i.e. right). Micio greets him as if he is arriving from the country (80-1 n.), but Demea has already heard reports of Aeschinus' activities, which implies that he has already been into town.

[3] The scene is still basically expository, extending the characterisation of Micio, introducing Demea on stage, offering a glimpse of Aeschinus in action, and providing our first account of the character of Demea's other son. With two contrasted fathers and two contrasted sons the scene is set for a typical Terentian double plot (Introd. §17).

[4] The clash between the two old men is revealing for the characterisation of both and for their respective philosophies of education. Demea belongs to the type of the 'stern old man' (*senex durus*) and, it seems, to the sub-type of the 'angry old man' (*senex iratus*: Introd. §3): he is described as 'cross' (79) and 'put out' (82), and takes the offensive in blaming Micio for Aeschinus' behaviour. We may suspect that his account of Aeschinus' doings is meant to look wildly exaggerated (120-1 n.): he chooses to ignore the fact that the abducted girl is a *meretrix* (90 n.), and it can scarcely be true that Aeschinus '[beat] the master and the whole household pretty well to death' (89-90) or that 'the scandal's all over the town' (91-2). Demea is confident that his own system of education is the right one ('if he needs an example, why on earth can't he look at his brother...?' 94-5, 'learn how to be a father from others who really know' 125), but he makes no attempt to argue his case: it is taken as axiomatic that 'thrifty, sober' living is the proper behaviour for young men (95). This is not to say that Demea's characterisation is totally unsympathetic. His outburst against Micio's treatment of Aeschinus is at least based on genuinely held moral principles; and, though in the end he seems to wash his hands of Aeschinus ('Let him...ruin... himself; it's no concern of mine' 134), it is clear that he has a deep concern for his own 'flesh and blood' (137). The name 'Demea', common in Athens in real life, occurs in several plays of Menander's as an old man's name; it suggests 'man of the people' or possibly 'countryman'. If Micio is to be in some sense to be equated with Aemilius Paullus (26ff n. 3), the obvious equation for Demea would be with Cato, leader of the conservative faction at Rome and one of Paullus' major political

opponents, but, for the reason already given, it is unlikely that Terence intended these equations to be pressed.

[5] Micio reacts impatiently and even arrogantly to Demea's complaints ('Is anything as unjust as a narrow-minded man!' 98, 'you are all wrong, Demea' 100, 'Now listen to me' 113, 'either shut up or...' 123); but it is clear that he is provoked by Demea's attitude (I'm in for a scolding as usual' 79-80) and that his dogmatic response is a calculated tactic ('I wasn't going to show him I was upset' 142-3). Micio is as confident as Demea that his own system of education is the correct one, but he does produce supporting arguments; it is 'no crime...for a young man to enjoy wine and women' (101-2) in that this is the natural behaviour of young men, and, if they are not permitted to have their fling when they are young, they will do so when they are 'past the right age' (110). This being so, Micio sees the consequences of Aeschinus' reported behaviour in purely financial terms, and for him this is no problem ('Thank God I have the means' 121-2). At the same time Terence makes clear that Micio's permissiveness is not total. He tells Demea that he is only going to pay 'as long as it suits me' (118), and he admits at the end of the scene that he is in fact worried at Aeschinus' behaviour ('I don't really like it' 142, 'Aeschinus has treated me pretty badly...' 147-8).

[6] For the moment at least, Terence is allowing Micio to present the more convincing case; but it should be noted (i) that he wins the immediate argument only on the different point that each should look after his own son, and (ii) that the reported behaviour of Aeschinus casts some doubt on the practical success of Micio's methods.

[7] The spoken verse (ia⁶) of the preceding monologue continues.

81 Good, I was looking for you: Micio's 'I'm glad to see you safely back' (80-1 n.) would normally have evoked the polite response 'I'm sure you are', but Demea substitutes a rather more abrupt formula (Introd. §30: cf. *Eun.* 776 n.). Donatus implies that in Menander's version Demea did respond appropriately to Micio's greeting, so that this is a subtle change introduced by Terence to emphasise Demea's gruffness. In the Latin Demea even interrupts Micio half way through a line. It is comparatively rare for Terence to begin a new scene in mid-line; three of his eight examples are in *Adelphoe*.

343   **83 I told you so:** This is an example of the typical 'aside in conversation' where one character turns away to make a remark not intended to be heard by the other (Introd. §21). This is a common feature of comedy, which Terence generally uses in a reasonably natural way: Micio is here uttering an exclamation, rather than overtly addressing the audience.

84 shame: The Latin concept is *pudor* (57 n.).

85 fear: Demea unintentionally recalls Micio's objections to morality enforced by fear (58, p. 342).

90 girl: Demea uses the neutral word 'woman' (Lat. *mulier*), even though the girl is in fact a *meretrix* belonging to a pimp.

101 It's no crime: Micio here uses the strong Latin word *flagitium*, which suggest moral outrage (*Eun.* 382 n.). The word occurs fourteen times in the six plays of Terence; six of these occurrences are in *Adelphoe*, and all are spoken by or to Demea.

103-5 If you and I didn't do these things...: This argument is a variation of the reflection offered by several of Plautus' 'lenient old men' (e.g. Callicles at *Pseud.* 436-42) that 'after all, we behaved like this when we were young'. Micio is contriving to imply that Demea's morality is merely a product of circumstances.

106 If we had had the means: The clear implication is that both Micio and Demea were poor when they were young. Terence nowhere in the play explains how Micio came to be wealthy.

107 humanity: This is perhaps the most important of Terence's ethical concepts (Introd. §15); the ideal of sympathetic human understanding and a concern for others forms the moral basis of Terence's plays, as it does of Menander's.

108 as a young man should: Lat. *decet* (lit. 'it is fitting': Introd. §16); this word occurs seven times in the play.

112 crime: Lat. *flagitium* (101 n.).

p.344 **120-1 broken a door-lock...torn someone's clothes:** Micio reduces Demea's allegation that Aeschinus had beaten the master and the household pretty well to death (89-90) to something that can be remedied financially without too much trouble. Some of the audience will have seen Micio's attitude as irresponsible, but it is more likely that Terence intended to underline Demea's exaggeration.

123 name anyone you like to judge between us: The phrase has a legal ring. Both Greek and Roman law provided for civil disputes to be settled by an 'arbitrator' acceptable to both sides; Menander's *Epitrepontes* takes its name (*The Arbitration*) from just such a scene (*Epitr.* 218-375).

p.345 **140 I won't be too hard on him:** With these words Demea leaves the stage. It is a feature of Roman comedy that departing characters usually indicate where they are going, but this is not so here. It is a reasonable assumption that, unless otherwise stated, characters depart from the same direction from which they came. Demea probably arrives from the forum (above, n. 2) and departs again in that direction; when we next see him (355, p. 356), he has heard more about the circumstances of the girl's abduction.

141-54 There's something...still in town: Micio is left on stage to utter an 'exit monologue', one of five exit monologues in the play. In general, Terence makes sparing use of exit monologues, which by definition lead to an empty stage and thus break up the continuity of the action (Introd. §22). But there are more empty stages (in fact nine) in *Adelphoe* than in Terence's other plays.

145 being unreasonable: Lit. ' scarcely behaving with

humanity' (107 n.).

149 whores: Latin *meretrices*.

151 announced his intention of marrying: Granted the conventions of comedy (Introd. §1), the audience may interpret this remark as deliberate foreshadowing on Terence's part, and suspect that the *meretrix* whom Aeschinus has just abducted may turn out to be in fact an innocent citizen girl whom he can in the end marry. There is a parallel case in Plautus' *Rudens*, where the girl Palaestra, who is in the possession of a pimp, turns out to be the long-lost daughter of the old man, who duly marries her to her lover.

152 he was growing up and settling down: The Latin (*defervescere*) is more vivid, lit. 'his youth had gone off the boil' or 'had ceased fermenting'.

154 if he's still in town: The renaissance editors put the end of Terence's first act at this point on the basis of the empty stage. As far as Terence is concerned, this is an academic point, since Roman plays were performed continuously (Introd. §23). As for the Greek original, it is unlikely that the first act was as short as this: we also have to reckon with the possibility that it included a delayed divine prologue, but this is a question best postponed for the moment.

II. i. SANNIO, AESCHINUS, PARMENO
(155-208, pp. 345-8)

[1] Aeschinus enters with the abducted girl, pursued by the pimp Sannio. With the help of the slave Parmeno, the girl is ushered safely into Micio's house. Aeschinus rejects Sannio's protests, and follows into the house, having offered to pay the cost price of the girl and no more. Sannio decides to accept the offer, though without much expectation of prompt payment.

[2] The direction from which Aeschinus and the other characters appear is not defined, but, since they have not met Micio who has just left for the town (right), it will suit the staging best if they enter on the opposite side (left). In this case Sannio's house is notionally situated towards the harbour; it must also be some distance away if the portrayal of the abduction as still in progress is to have any plausibility.

[3] This is the scene which we are told in the prologue was borrowed from Diphilus' *Joined in Death* (6-11, p. 339). The borrowing extends to the point where Aeschinus goes into Micio's house (196); we can deduce from Donatus that the following monologue by Sannio was part of Menander's original *Adelphoi* (198-200 n.). The aim of the borrowing is clear, namely to provide a scene of lively physical action as a contrast to the purely verbal argumentation of the preceding scenes, with the clear implication that this sort of variation was necessary to hold the attention of the Roman audience

(Introd. §32). But it is difficult to stitch in a scene from another play without leaving tell-tale signs or creating awkwardnesses, and several such signs have been detected here:

(i) the abduction scene (or the tail-end of it) is now being enacted on stage some time after it has already been reported;

(ii) the pimp is nowhere named in the dialogue (he presumably had a different name in Diphilus);

(iii) the slave Parmeno does not reappear in *Adelphoe* (he also presumably belongs to Diphilus' play);

(iv) the character of Aeschinus as displayed here does not quite square with his characterisation in the rest of the play (again it may have fitted his characterisation in Diphilus);

(v) the assertion of Aeschinus that the girl is free born constitutes a 'false foreshadowing' for Terence's play (194 n.), though it may have been a valid one in Diphilus'.

Of these points, the first is clearly a genuine awkwardness, which Terence was evidently prepared to accept for the sake of the liveliness of the scene; the second is minor (it is actually more effective for the scornful Aeschinus to address Sannio as 'you pimp' than to do so by name); and the other three will be discussed in due course.

[4] Aeschinus belongs to the type *adulescens* ('young man'), which is one of the major stock characters of Greek and Roman comedy (Introd. §1). More precisely, he belongs (or so it seems) to the sub-type who fall in love with young slave girls whom they hope to purchase. Most *adulescentes* are fairly weak characters who depend on the help of friends or slaves; here, by contrast, Aeschinus is brash and effective, even unpleasantly so, brushing aside Sannio's protests with violence and threats ('a second thrashing' 159, 'whipped within an inch of your life' 182). It remains to be seen whether this characterisation will be maintained in the rest of the play, but for the moment Aeschinus is scarcely a good advertisement for Micio's educational theory. The name 'Aeschinus', which is a very common Greek name (in the form 'Aeschines') but does not occur elsewhere in surviving comedy, suggests a person with a sense of shame.

[5] The pimp (Lat. *leno*) is another stock character of comedy (Introd. 11§). In general the pimp is the villain of the piece, and the natural sympathy of the audience will always lie with the *adulescens* against the *leno*. Here Sannio is allowed to argue at some length that he is scarcely getting a fair deal ('a poor innocent man' 155, 'as honest a man...' 161 n., 'a disgrace' 166 n., 'monstrous' 173 n., 'right' 179 n., 'fair' 187 n., 'injustice' 198, 'swindle' 205) and that this is the usual fate of pimps when faced with impecunious young men ('when you follow my profession...insults from these young men' 206-7). But there is a clear tension between Sannio's own stance of injured innocence and the fact that he is after all a pimp with all the pimp's undesirable qualities (188-9 n.); the audience will not shed too many tears for him. It is interesting to compare Terence's portrayal of

Dorio in *Phormio* (*Phorm.* 485ff n. 4).

[6] Parmeno and Bacchis are both mute characters, and neither appears again in the play. Parmeno is a typical *lorarius* ('whip-man' or 'thug-slave': *Eun.* 772 n.). Parmeno characters in other plays usually have a more extended role (on the name see *Eun.* 46ff n. 5), but whether this was so of Parmeno in Diphilus' play cannot be determined. 'Bacchis' ('worshipper of Bacchus', 'reveller') is a common name for a *meretrix* both in real life and in comedy; it occurs also in Terence's *Heauton* and *Hecyra*.

[7] This scene is in recitative, with changes of metre creating a three-fold division. Mixed metres are used for the opening, ia^8 from the point where Parmeno takes up his position guarding Sannio (from 'Now watch' 170), and tr^7 for Sannio's closing monologue. On the various metres and their effect see Introd. §28.

155 Help, help: This is addressed to imaginary bystanders, not direct to the audience; Terence (unlike Plautus) avoids blatant violation of the 'dramatic illusion' (Introd. §21).

161 slave-dealer: i.e. 'pimp' (Lat. *leno*).

346   **as honest a man:** Lit. 'of outstanding honour' (Lat. *fides*: Introd. §16). Sannio in this scene uses the ethical terminology of the upper classes against Aeschinus, in much the same way as Phormio does against Demipho in *Phormio* (*Phorm.* 894ff n. 4).

163 I shan't give that for it: i.e. I shall regard it as worthless. The text implies a stage-direction, correctly interpreted by the Penguin's 'snapping fingers'.

166 a disgrace: Sannio again appeals to ethical principles (Lat. *indignum*: Introd. §16).

173 It's monstrous: Lat. *indignum* again (166 n.).

175 Are you king here...?: Phormio similarly accuses Demipho of acting like a 'sole ruler' (*Phorm.* 404 n.).

347   **179 The girl's mine; I paid cash for her...:** The logic of Sannio's argument is undeniable, and Aeschinus can answer it only with a threat of more violence. The pimp Dorio uses a similar argument in *Phormio* (*Phorm.* 511 n.).

183 You brute: The pimp is traditionally the *recipient* of abuse of this sort (Lat. *inpurus*: *Phorm.* 83 n); here he occupies the moral high ground himself.

Is this where all free men are supposed to be equal? This looks like an allusion to the prized 'equality before the law' of Athenian citizens, and as such will be derived from the Greek original (i.e. Diphilus).

184 finished making a scene: The Latin is more colourful, lit. 'ceased your Bacchic revelries', implying that Sannio is being delirious or irrational.

187 a fair deal: Lat. *aequom* (64 n.).

188-9 a pimp, the bane of youth, a plague and a liar:
Sannio here tries a new tactic: he abandons his self-righteous stance
and admits to the morality of the traditional pimp, while still
maintaining that Aeschinus is not treating him fairly.

191 two thousand drachmas: The price paid by young men
in comedy to buy out their girls ranges from two thousand drachmas
to four thousand (*Phorm.* 557 n.). But we cannot assume that
Aeschinus' girl is right at the bottom end of the scale, since the pimp's
profit is in this case not being added.

193 Will you use force? / No / Good: On the surface
Sannio seems to mean 'Will you beat me until I agree to sell at your
price?', in which case Aeschinus in his blustering mood might well
have answered 'Yes'. But there may be an allusion to a Roman law
which made sales under duress illegal, so that Sannio is setting a trap
for Aeschinus into which he refuses to fall; in this case Sannio's
response ('I was afraid you would') is ironic.

194 The girl is free-born...to set her free: There is a
certain confusion here. If the girl is free-born, there is no need for
the formal 'laying on of hands' (970 n.) to set her free; and there
would be no need to purchase her from the pimp, who could not
legally sell a free person. Since Aeschinus is offering to pay two
thousand drachmas, the obvious conclusion is that the alleged free
status of the girl is a mere bluff intended to frighten the pimp into
accepting Aeschinus' offer. There is then no explicit foreshadowing
that the girl will turn out to be free (and that Aeschinus will marry
her), though the idea might nonetheless cross the minds of an audience
familiar with the conventions of comedy (151 n.).

p.348   **196 you pimp:** With this final blast, Aeschinus storms off into
Micio's house in mid-line (81 n.), leaving Sannio to complete the line
of verse and reflect on the situation.

196-208 Gods above...like this: Sannio remains on stage to
deliver a 'link' monologue (Introd. §22); this one of only three link
monologues in the play.

198-200 That fellow has dragged me...: Sannio's account
of the abduction is almost as graphic as Demea's: it omits the breaking
down of the door and the beating up of the household (81ff n. 4).

on my wretched back Donatus implies that this line is based
on Menander, which is our evidence for supposing that the Diphilus
borrowing is now ended (above, n. 3).

201 Supposing it's a fair offer..: This remark must be
heavily ironic.

204 moonshine: Another echo of Dorio (*Phorm.* 492-4 n.).

II. ii: SYRUS, SANNIO (209-53, pp. 348-50)

[1] The slave Syrus emerges from Micio's house, promising to
persuade Sannio to accept Aeschinus' offer. Syrus reveals that he

knows that Sannio is about to depart for Cyprus on urgent business, and Sannio, faced with the suggestion that he cut his losses and settle for half of the price of the girl, is more than ready to accept the original offer. At this point Aeschinus' brother Ctesipho approaches.

[2] The scene continues the development of the previous scene to the point where it is clear that Aeschinus will be able to keep the girl; and the introduction of Syrus as the abettor of Aeschines' schemes adds a new (but not unexpected) dimension to this side of the plot. At the same time the appearance of Ctesipho at the end of the scene, with the cryptic reference to his girl-friend, foreshadows a second love affair and thus a dual plot in tbe Terentian manner (81ff n. 3). The focus has now moved from the old men and their educational principles to the schemes and love affairs of the young.

[3] Syrus is immediately characterised as the 'tricky slave' (Lat. *servus callidus*: Introd. §7). His particular role here is to discomfit the adversary of his young master, and he fulfils this with aplomb: he begins by promising that Sannio will be glad to accept Aeschinus' offer and by the end of the scene he has carried out this promise. Syrus is very much in calm control of the situation; there is no sign here of the exuberance and the occasional desperation which characterise the tricky slaves of Plautus or of the bumbling incompetence exhibited by some of his counterparts in Terence. His language is colourful, with a number of effective metaphors (220 n., 228 n., 239 n., 242 n.), but not vulgar or inelegant. So, at first sight, he does not quite correspond to the stock type of the tricky slave; it will be interesting to see how his character develops. The name 'Syrus', like many slave names (*Phorm.* 35ff n. 5), denotes ethnic origin (lit. 'the Syrian'); it is a common slave name both in real life and in comedy, occurring again in Terence's *Heauton* and in three of Menander's surviving plays.

[4] Sannio's characterisation continues from that of the previous scene. He again proclaims that he is getting a raw deal, giving further graphic accounts of his physical injuries (211-15 n., 244-5 n.) and duly protesting against Aeschinus' lack of ethical principles (237 n., 244 n.). But he is clearly no match for Syrus, and in the end he has to accept Aeschinus' offer whether he likes it or not.

[5] The scene is again divided metrically, beginning in animated recitative (ia^8) and changing to spoken verse (ia^6) at the point where the more serious negotiation begins (from 'That stung him' 228).

209 All right, sir: By a common convention of comedy, Syrus' opening words are spoken 'over the shoulder' to someone inside the house (Introd. §20), in this case evidently Aeschinus. It should be noted that the Latin (*tace*: lit. 'be quiet') is much more impatient in tone than the translation 'All right, sir' implies.

210 What's this I hear, Sannio?: Syrus addresses Sannio by name (cf. 220, 240), in contrast to the scornful 'you pimp' of Aeschinus in the previous scene (184, 196). As Donatus points out, Syrus is adopting a deliberately conciliatory approach (*Phorm.* 1048 n.).

211-15 Scrap?...punch me on the jaw: Sannio gives a second graphic account of his injuries (cf. 198-200 n.).

p.349   **219 get your cash back - and with interest:** i.e. Aeschinus would continue to be a profitable customer; exactly the same argument is used by Phaedria to the pimp Dorio (*Phorm.* 493 n.).

220 set your traps: An image from fowling (*Eun.* 247 n.).

221 I'm not sharp enough: Sannio poses as the simple businessman, who prefers ready cash to promises.

224 I'm told you are off to Cyprus: It is not explained how Syrus obtained this crucial piece of information. Sannio reacts to it with an involuntary cry of dismay (Lat. *hem*), which Syrus ignores. Cyprus, advantageously situated in the eastern Mediterranean, was always an important trading centre in the ancient world. Donatus (on 230) suggests that, as an island sacred to Aphrodite (Venus), it may have been a particularly suitable market for pimps and their wares.

228 That stung him: For the metaphor see *Phorm.* 954 n.

228-35 Curse him...later on: This is an unusually lengthy aside. The most convincing staging would be for Syrus to walk triumphantly away from Sannio after delivering his bombshell about Cyprus, and to return for the kill after a pause, during which the pimp tried desperately to work out his best plan.

232 take it up again: Lit. 'I will be taking up a case which has already been decided', i.e. 'wasting my time' (cf. *Phorm.* 419 n.).

233 gone stale: Lit. 'gone cold': the metaphor seems to be original to Terence (cf. *Eun.* 268 n.).

237 right: Lit. 'worthy' (Lat. *dignum*: Introd. §16).

p.350   **239 he's wavering:** Lat. *labescere* (*Eun.* 178 n.).

242 scrape up: On the metaphor see *Phorm.* 40 n.

244 Has your master no shame? Sannio appeals to the concept of *pudor* (57 n.).

244-5 Thanks to him...with his blows: Sannio indulges in another graphic account of the physical injuries inflicted on him by Aeschines; this is the first mention of his teeth and skull.

250-1 my friendship...I'll be grateful: Sannio tries desperately to set up a 'friendship' (Lat. *amicitia*) involving mutual benefits (72 n.).

251-2 I'll do my best: The Penguin stage direction looks dubious; there is no hint of a bribe in the text.

252-3 here comes Ctesipho...smiles about his mistress: This is something of a puzzle for the audience. The name Ctesipho has not previously occurred in the play, and, though his mask and costume will indicate clearly enough that he is an *adulescens*, the audience may not immediately identify him with Aeschinus' brother, who has been described by Demea as 'thrifty, sober, living in the country' (95, p. 343). 'Ctesipho' is not a common name in real life, and it does not occur elsewhere in comedy.

mistress: Lit.' girl-friend' (Lat. *amica*).

II. iii-iv: CTESIPHO, SANNIO, SYRUS, AESCHINUS (254-87, pp. 350-2)

[1] Ctesipho enters in raptures over the help he has received from Aeschinus, who rebukes him for having kept his troubles to himself. Aeschinus goes off to the forum with Sannio to pay him his money; Syrus follows, after telling Ctesipho to join his girl inside and prepare for a celebration.

[2] This pair of scenes (which are here taken together for the sake of convenience) confirm that Ctesipho is Aeschinus' brother, and by the end of them the audience will have grasped the surprising information that Aeschinus has stolen the girl not for himself but for Ctesipho. This means that several judgements made in the previous three scenes have to be revised. Aeschinus is not after all resuming his habits of '[going] the round of the whores' (149, p. 345), but is un-selfishly helping his brother; since Aeschinus is not after all deceiving his father, Micio's system of education does appear to be working; and, since Ctesipho is not as sober and virtuous as his father fondly imagines (94-5, p. 343), Demea's system is seen to be failing. So at this stage of the play the educational debate is clearly favouring Micio. At the same time a further link has been forged between the two halves of the double plot, in that one of the young men is involving himself in the love affair of the other (cf. *Phorm.* 231ff n. 2).

[3] This is a rather disjointed pair of scenes with a number of awkwardnesses of staging. Sannio is required to stand around ignored during the Ctesipho-Syrus and Aeschinus-Ctesipho conversations, and the second scene needs four speaking actors contrary to the Greek custom (Introd. §24). It is tempting to see these features as resulting from Terence's stitching into the play of the Diphilus scene, which has involved bringing Sannio on stage at an earlier point than in Menander's version, and interweaving Aeschinus-Ctesipho and Aeschinus-Sannio conversations which were origianlly separate (266 n.). Moreover, there is no parallel in surviving Menander for the withholding of crucial information from the audience for as long as this (Introd. §33), and so we have to reckon with the possibility that Menander's play had a divine prologue (perhaps postponed until after the opening scene) in which the audience were told the truth about Ctesipho's girl. The expository section of Menander's *Adelphoi* can be plausibly re-constructed on the following lines:

(i) Micio and Demea scenes (as in Ter. I. i and I. ii);

(ii) Divine prologue containing (among other things) the truth about the abduction of the girl;

(iii) Entry of Aeschinus and Ctesipho with the girl, and Aeschinus-Ctesipho conversation (as in Ter. II. iv), after which they all go into Micio's house;

(iv) Entry of Sannio in pursuit, uttering a monologue of complaint (as at the end of Ter. II. i);

(v) Syrus-Sannio scene (as in Ter. II. ii), with the appearance of Syrus motivated by *Ctesipho*'s fearfulness (hence Syrus' impatience: 209 n.);

(vi) Aeschinus-Sannio-Syrus scene, ending with their departure to the forum to pay the money (as in Ter. II. iv).

In general, of course, we have to allow for adaptations of the dialogue by Terence to suit his own scenario: in the above reconstruction the Ctesipho-Syrus dialogue of II. iii is his own invention.

[4] As suggested above (n. 2), our estimate of the character of Aeschinus now has to be revised and for the better; we are now perhaps seeing the Aeschinus of Menander's play rather than the young man of Diphilus'. Ctesipho clearly belongs to the 'helpless' type of *adulescens* (Introd. §1), whose reaction to the problems of a love affair is to fly the country (275 n.) and who needs the assistance of both brother and slave; his one redeeming feature is his generous acknowledgement of Aeschinus' help ('how can I find words to praise you?' 256, 'The splendid fellow!' 261, 'no one could do more' 264). One effect of the scene is thus to bring one of Terence's favourite themes into prominence, namely the duty of loyally helping one's friends (Introd. §15; cf. *Phorm.* 485ff n. 3).

[5] The recitative continues (with excited ia⁸ in both scenes).

254-9 Any man's welcome...in every virtue: Ctesipho's monologue is the first of six examples in the play of one of Terence's favourite scene openings, the 'overheard entrance monologue' (Introd. §19). Here the convention is realistically treated in that (i) Ctesipho's monologue is a self-absorbed soliloquy, so that it is reasonable for him not to see Sannio or Syrus, (ii) there are no asides, and (iii) the transition to the following dialogue is achieved without any of the usual formulae (Introd. §30). The direction of Ctesipho's entry is hard to determine. He has heard about the abduction but it is not clear in Terence's version that he played any part in it, so that he could as easily approach from the town (right) as from the direction of Sannio's house (left: 155ff n. 2).

254-6 Any man's welcome...the very man you want: Lit. 'it is a joy to accept a kindness (*beneficium*)...especially when the man who does the kindness is one for whom it is right and proper (*aequom*)'. The translation rather disguises the ethical concepts .

p.351 **263 Who's that at the door?:** Lit. 'the door creaked' (Introd. §20).

265 Where's that dirty liar: Lit. 'that committer of sacrilege' (Lat. *sacrilegus*: *Eun.* 419 n.).

That's me he wants: Sannio acknowledges the description (cf. 188-9 n.).

266 good, I was looking for you: This is a typical 'response formula' (81 n.). It is striking that Aeschinus addresses it to Ctesipho (who has not uttered a word), though in the previous line he was calling for the pimp; Sannio continues to be ignored for another ten lines.

271 you idiot: Lat. *inepte* (*Eun.* 311 n.).

274 Not ashamed but stupid: Aeschinus sees Ctesipho's unwillingess to disclose his love as folly rather than true *pudor*.

275 nearly drive you out of the country: Donatus reveals that Ctesipho's Menandrian equivalent had contemplated suicide, not just flight (cf. *Phorm.* 551-2 n.): Terence has toned down his threat, presumably in the interests of realism.

277 I'm going to town to settle up: Since the money is Micio's, Aeschinus will need to find Micio, who has in fact gone to town to find Aeschinus (154, p. 345).

352   **281 that horrible man:** Lat. *inpurus* (183 n.).

283 reach my father's ears: Lit. 'leak out to my father'; for the metaphor see *Eun.* 105 n.

286 come home with the fish: Fish was something of a luxury both at Athens and in Terence's Rome; the implication is that the solution of Ctesipho's problem calls for a special celebration.

287 we must celebrate today: As Ctesipho goes indoors, the stage is left empty. This is where the renaissance editors put the end of Terence's second act, and it would be a good place for an act-division in the Greek original, though there are grounds for thinking that it was the end of the first act in Menander (154 n.).

III. i-ii: SOSTRATA, CANTHARA, GETA
(288-354, pp. 352-5)

[1] The old lady Sostrata emerges from the next-door house talking to her nurse Canthara: it emerges that Sostrata's daughter is about to give birth, and that Aeschinus is the father of her child. Their slave Geta arrives with news that Aeschinus has deserted the girl in favour of one stolen from a pimp. Sostrata refuses to hush up the situation, and sends Geta to fetch her relative Hegio, while Canthara goes for the midwife.

[2] This pair of scenes (which are again taken together for convenience) presents the audience with another startling piece of new information. They had no way of foreseeing that Aeschinus is in love with a poor citizen girl and has made her pregnant; and, as with the revelation of Ctesipho's love affair in the previous scene, they have to piece together the new information as the scene progresses. Terence is thus exploiting the element of surprise in this play to an even greater

extent than in *Phormio* (*Phorm.* 567ff n. 2). The result is that the audience are compelled once again to revise their judgement on Aeschinus' behaviour and on the success of Micio's educational system. It seems highly unlikely that Menander treated his Greek audience in the same way; this is a further reason for supposing that Terence has omitted a divine prologue from Menander's version, which will have revealed the truth about Aeschinus as well as about Ctesipho (254ff n. 3). On the other hand, now that the Roman audience has been told the truth, there is as much scope for irony in Terence as there was in Menander. And there is plenty of room for suspense on both sides of the double plot, as we wait to see how the respective fathers come to find about about their sons and how they react.

[3] We are now in a much better position to appreciate the character of Aeschinus. He is guilty of raping the girl next door, and he is also guilty of failing to tell his father of his predicament or of his desire to marry the girl. On the other hand it is clear that Sostrata and Canthara think very highly of him ('he never lets a day pass' 293-4, 'such a nice young man...' 297) and that it is his sworn intention to marry the mother of his child. So, in spite of Micio's theories and in spite of his own high-handedness with Sannio, Aeschinus is turning out to be not very different from the typical weak but decent young man of comedy (333 n.).

[4] Of the three new characters in this scene, Geta is clearly the 'loyal slave' type (Introd. §7), indignant on his mistress's behalf and anxious to help. But his indignation is expressed in exaggerated terms (312 n.); he has in fact misinterpreted the situation (Aeschinus is not actually in love with the girl from the pimp); and in the end his advice on the question of keeping the birth secret is overruled by his mistress (337-42 n.). So, at first sight, he does not resemble his namesake in *Phormio*, who has at least some of the qualities of the 'tricky slave', so much as loyal but dull slaves like Daos in Menander's *Dyskolos*, who, though unswervingly faithful to his master Gorgias, actually achieves nothing on his behalf.

[5] Sostrata belongs to the general type of the 'married woman' (Lat. *matrona*: Introd. §5), but differs from Terence's other married women in being a widow, so that the interest is not in her relations with her husband but in her concern for her daughter. Sostrata's situation is thus unusual in Greek and Roman comedy, the nearest parallel being that of Myrrhine in Menander's fragmentary *Georgos*, another widow with worries over her unmarried daughter's child. Terence portrays Sostrata with much sympathy, emphasising her lack of friends, her distress, her concern for her daughter, and her refusal to take the easy course (291-2 n., 294 n., 337-42 n., 351 n.). The name 'Sostrata' (which is the name of married women also in *Heaut.* and *Hec.*) should mean 'saviour of the host'; whatever the precise significance of this, it is clearly a name which implies respect.

[6] Canthara is the typical 'nurse' (Lat. *nutrix*) with a typically small part (Introd. §14). She differs from Terence's other nurses in that her role is to support her mistress rather than to act as a recognition agent, but she is not characterised in any detail (337 n.). The name 'Canthara', which is rare both in real life and in comedy, suggests a fondness for wine, in keeping with a common (but here irrelevant) characterisation of old women in comedy as drunken.

[7] The scene is in recitative, with a change in the middle to reflect the variation of tone. A mixture of tr^7 and ia^8 is used for the farcically exaggerated running slave sequence, and continuous ia^8 for the near pathos of the discussion of Sostrata's predicament (from 'Oh no, no' 330).

287 Please, nurse...: By a common convention Sostrata and Canthara come on stage in mid-conversation (Introd. §20). In naturalistic terms the whole conversation would have taken place indoors, but it is brought out on stage for the sake of the audience.

289 My poor dear: Canthara is referring to the daughter.

291-2 Alas, I'm friendless...: This speech underlines the pathos of Sostrata's situation; it establishes that she is a widow with only one slave and a nurse to support her.

.353 **294 my sole comfort in my woes:** Lit. 'my sole remedy' (Lat. *remedium*); it is not clear how strongly the medical origin of this metaphor would have been felt (cf. *Eun.* 439 n.).

296 once the damage was done: The Latin (*vitium offerre*) is rather more blunt, with the clear implication 'once the girl had been raped'. Premarital intercourse by young lovers in comedy is always described as rape, which was regarded as much less dishonourable for the girl than allowing herself to be seduced.

299-329 Here's a state...saw it with my own eyes: This is a 'running slave' monologue, a particular form of the overheard entrance monologue, and should be compared with the two examples in *Phormio* (*Phorm.* 179-96 n., 841-53 n.). It has many of the stock ingredients of the running slave routine, including exaggerated exclamations on the significance of the news (312 n.), failure to see that the master (in this case mistress) is on stage, puzzled asides by the master to a friend ('why is Geta running about?' 305, 'What *is* he saying?' 308-9), abusive rejection by the slave of the master's approach ('Don't bother me' 321), formulaic recognition (320-2 n.), and breathless delivery of the news ('Get your breath back' 324) amidst anxious questioning. The total effect of the routine is comic: here the potential pathos of the situation is relieved by the fact that the audience (by the end of the speech at least) knows that Geta's report of the situation is misjudged. Geta presumably arrives from the direction of Sannio's house (left), since he claims to have seen the abduction of the girl with his own eyes (329).

302 Beset on all sides: The image is military.

306 Honour: Lat. *fides* (161 n.).

308 vilely seduced: Lit. 'unworthily raped'. The Latin words are *indignum* (166 n.) and *vitium offerre* (296 n.).

312 vent my rage: Lit. 'spue out...' (Lat. *evomere*). The violence and vividness of Geta's threats throughout this whole speech are notable. The audience is presumably meant to smile at his exaggerations while applauding his loyalty.

315 that Syrus who put him up to this: This could be a mere inference on Geta's part, since it is not clear how he would have gained the information.

316 grab him by the waist...: The description seems to be based on the throws of wrestling.

p.354 **320 Now I'd best hurry:** This is an 'action formula' (lit. 'do I delay?') commonly used to herald overdue action (Introd. §29; cf. *Eun.* 265 n.); Terence is implicitly admitting that Geta's monologue has been far too long for the urgency of the situation.

320-2 Let's call him...I was looking for you: The phrases are again formulaic (cf. *Phorm.* 195-6, p. 235). There follows a sequence of twenty-five changes of speaker, which occupies only ten lines of Latin text (320-9).

333 he would put the baby in its grandfather's arms: We might well criticise Aeschinus for not approaching his father for permission to marry well before the baby was born. But Sostrata implies no such criticism here (she is lamenting that he appears to be breaking his promise), and Aeschinus is no worse than the average *adulescens* of comedy: in a similar situation Moschion (in Men. *Sam.*) cannot bring himself to approach his father even after the baby is born, and neither he nor Lyconides (in Plaut. *Aul.*) have the courage to approach the girl's father before the birth. If the audience have time to reflect, they may now see the significance of Aeschinus' reported hint to Micio (150-1, p. 345) that he was now intending to marry; this will have been a fumbling attempt to broach the subject of Sostrata's daughter with his father.

p.355 **337 the sort of news to spread around?:** Like Euclio's old servant Staphyla at Plaut. *Aul.* 74-6 Canthara instinctively takes the view that extramarital pregnancies are best kept secret.

337-42 No I don't...best keep it quiet: Geta produces pragmatic arguments to support Canthara's view, based on a concern for the reputation of mother and daughter and for the daughter's future happiness. But Sostrata takes a more principled attitude.

341 won't help: Lit. 'is not expedient' (*Phorm.* 449-51 n.).

346 reputation: Lit. 'virginity'. It is an interesting commentary on social and moral values in ancient Greece and Rome that the dowry is the first consideration.

347 the ring he sent her: The reference is apparently to the engagement ring given by the man to the woman on the occasion of her betrothal as a pledge that he would honour his side of the contract (cf. Juvenal *Satires* 6. 27, Pliny *Natural History* 33. 12). But in this case there has been no formal betrothal, and we would have to imagine a ring given informally by Aeschinus which Sostrata might be able to use in court as evidence of a pledge on his part. On the other hand the MSS preserve an alternative reading 'the ring which he *lost*', which would refer instead to an identification device common in comedy, whereby a ring lost by one of the partners during a rape serves to establish who this partner was (e.g. Men. *Epitr.* 450-7; Ter. *Hec.* 572-4, p. 316). But Terence has kept the rape out of focus in *Adelphoi*, and we have heard nothing about the circumstances.

349 nothing unworthy of her or me: Sostrata is referring to the possible accusation that, because of her poverty, she had put her daughter to work as a prostitute. Despite her poverty Sostrata has a concern for 'worthy' behaviour (Lat. *indignum*).

351 her relative Hegio: Donatus informs us that in Menander the Hegio character was in fact Sostrata's brother: Terence has made this small change to heighten Sostrata's lack of support.

354 run and fetch the midwife: There is a puzzling discrepancy with the opening of the scene where Sostrata had declared that she had 'no one to send for the midwife' (292). There is no obvious explanation. One possible hypothesis is that Terence has himself added Canthara to the play but without properly integrating her part; in the original, Sostrata would have had only Geta to send.

There are no explicit stage directions in the Latin text, but the Penguin edition rightly sends Geta and Canthara off-stage on their different errands and Sostrata back into her house. We may perhaps imagine balanced exits, with Geta departing left (in the direction of the country) to fetch Hegio and Canthara right (towards the forum) to get the midwife. The stage is now left momentarily empty.

III. iii: DEMEA, SYRUS (355-446, pp. 356-9)

[1] Demea returns from the town (140 n.), having heard that Ctesipho took part in the abduction, and is followed by Syrus, who is bringing fish for the celebration (286 n.). Syrus pretends to share Demea's indignation at Micio's lenience to Aeschinus; he then tells him the false story that Ctesipho, after reprimanding his brother, is now back on the farm. Demea consoles himself with the thought that at least he is himself bringing up Ctesipho properly, and is about to return to the farm himself, when he sees Hegio approaching.

[2] This scene switches the focus from the Micio-Aeschinus side of the dual plot to the Demea-Ctesipho side. But it does not develop this side very far, in spite of its length: Demea's discovery of the truth about Ctesipho is averted rather than advanced by Syrus' lying assurances. So its main points are the humour of the deception and the

further characterisation of the two men.

[3] Demea is characterised here as angry and gullible, which are stock characteristics of the *senex durus* (Introd. §3). His anger is conveyed in a number of forceful expressions ('I'm finished' 355 n., 'dissolute' 360 n., 'the brute' 363 n., 'Ye gods' 366, 'I shall explode' 369, 'It's a scandal' 379 n., 'Heavens above' 381, 'Damn it' 383); and his gullibility is underlined by his smug assumption that he knows what is going on ('Of course not. I should have got wind of it' 396-7). The portrayal of Demea is not completely unsympathetic, compared with that of some of Plautus' stern fathers (e.g. Theopropides in *Most.*), but the total effect of the scene must be to make us take him, and his educational principles, less seriously.

[4] Syrus is portrayed, as in his previous scenes (209ff n. 3), as an elegant version of the tricky slave. His technique for fooling Demea is not to take an antagonistic position (like some comic slaves) but to ingratiate himself, which he does (i) by echoing Demea's criticisms of Micio's household ('I don't like it either, sir, I often protest' 379-80, 'it's his father's foolish weakness' 390-1), (ii) by flattery ('you can look to the future' 387-8, 'You're all wisdom, from top to toe' 394), and (iii) by playing on Demea's pride in Ctesipho's upbringing ('*you* wouldn't have let your son carry on like this' 395-6, cf. 417-19 n.). Having thus won Demea's confidence, he is able to tell him blatant lies ('He's been up at the farm' 401, 'I went along with him myself' 402, 'he's had a row...with his brother' 404) without raising any suspicion; and after all this he gets away with an absurd parody of Demea's educational practice (419-31 n.). His language, which is always elegant, is spiced with proverbial expressions ('seeing what's under your nose' 386-7 n., 'Like father, like son' 399, 'You have to take men as they are' 431).

[5] The scene is in spoken verse (ia⁶), which is usual metre for scenes of rapid dialogue and deception (Introd. §28).

355-64 I'm finished...what I want: This is the first example since the opening scene of an entrance monologue delivered on an empty stage (Introd. §22). There are five 'straight' entrance monologues in *Adelphoe*, which is a larger number than usual in Terence (cf. 141-54 n.).

355 I'm finished: Demea's first word establishes his mood. This particular exclamation (Lat. *disperii*) is a forceful one which occurs only three times in the whole of Terence.

Ctesipho...was with Aeschinus...in this abduction: It looks as if Demea is misinformed; this does not quite square with Terence's account (pp. 350-1).

360 dissolute: Demea uses the strong word *inpurus* (183 n.) usually reserved for pimps and the like, to describe Aeschinus, his own flesh and blood.

361 Now here comes Syrus: Demea terminates his own

monologue with a common introduction formula (78 n.).

362 gang: Lit. 'flock', a common metaphor for a group of humans, usually derogatory in tone

363 the brute: Lit. 'the hangman' (Lat. *carnufex*: *Eun.* 668-70 n.), a common term of abuse, usually (as here) applied to slaves.

364-72 Well, we told...the job well done: Though the Penguin translator labels Syrus' opening line as an aside, this is better regarded as an overheard entrance monologue by Syrus, with asides by Demea. It is not clear that Syrus is *pretending* not to see Demea; if he is, this is a example of a 'faked' monologue (*Eun.* 943 n.).

368 thanked me for the advice...: This confirms Syrus' part in the abduction plan (315 n.).

370 something to spend: The Latin specifies the amount, half a mina or fifty drachmas. This is a generous sum: for comparison Men. *Epitr.* 136-41 suggests that a girl could be hired from a pimp for twelve drachmas a day, and that a starving man could be fed for three days on one drachma.

376-81 Gut all those fish...properly soaked: Syrus is evidently something of a culinary expert. Dromo and Stephanio are other slaves in Micio's household.

p.357 **379 It's a scandal:** Lat. *flagitium* (101 n.).

385 leave home...and serve overseas: As Ctesipho nearly did (275 n.); the audience will appreciate the irony.

386-7 what's under your nose: Lit. '...under your feet'.

388 that girl: Lit. 'that music-girl', 'that lute-player'. Demea uses the Greek word *psaltria* rather than the usual Latin equivalent *fidicina* (*Eun.* 457 n., *Phorm.* 109 n.). Girls who worked for pimps were often musical entertainers as well as purveyors of sexual favours (*Phorm.* 82 n.). Demea is of course being scornful: respectable women at Rome did not play musical instruments.

392 sick and tired: Lit. 'ashamed and irked'. The allusion to *pudor* is calculated to appeal to Demea (cf. 84 n.).

397 got wind of it: Terence uses a coarser form of a common metaphor (*Phorm.* 474 n.), as if to characterise Demea.

401 I'll pack this one off: Lit. 'drive off': Donatus suggests that this is a metaphor from driving cattle. Note the aside in conversation (83 n.).

403 hanging around: Lit. 'sticking' (Lat. *haerere*), with connotations of being stuck in a mire.

p.358 **408 disgrace:** Lat. *flagitium* (379 n.): Syrus again appeals to Demea's sense of moral outrage.

411 *[shrugs his shoulders]*: In the Latin Syrus has the exclamations *hui* and *phy*, both expressing feigned admiration.

413-14 spare no pains...let slip...sound training: In the Latin there are some verbal echoes of Micio's description of how he has brought Aeschinus up (50-4, pp. 341-2). If the audience notice, they may be amused.

415 look at other men's lives as in a mirror: The idea of parents training their children to observe examples of virtue and vice goes back to Plato (*Protagoras* 325c-d) and becomes a commonplace (cf. Horace *Satires* 1. 4. 105-6). It is here combined with the image of the mirror, which is also derived from Greek philosophy and appears at Plaut. *Epid.* 382-6 in a similar (but not identical) application. We cannot say whether it was Menander or Terence who put the two together.

417-19 Naturally...Perfect: Syrus' develops his flattery of Demea into a pattern of rapid repartee.

419-31 Excuse me, sir...men as they are: Syrus' parody of Demea's educational practice (412-16) is enhanced by several verbal echoes, notably 'train', 'spare no pains', 'look... like a mirror'.

p.359 **432 Only that you all had more sense:** This is an example of a standard 'leave-taking formula' ('Anything else...?') being taken literally (Introd. §30). Demea finally perceives that Syrus has been mocking him.

435-46 Off to the country...have a word with him: As Syrus goes indoors to see to the fish, Demea is left on stage to deliver what at first looks like an exit monologue. But it turns into a link monologue as he sees Hegio approaching (cf. 196-208 n.).

437 As for the other one, Micio can see to him: Demea repeats his angry dismissal of Aeschinus at 133-4 (p. 344), but we may suspect that his concern for his son is deeper than this (81ff n. 4).

438-9 Now who can I see coming? ...Hegio I do believe: Demea once again terminates his own monologue with an introduction formula (361 n.). The fact that Demea catches sight of Hegio after himself beginning to leave for the country (left) suggest that Hegio's home should be situated in this direction and supports the idea that Geta left by the country exit to fetch Hegio in the first place (354 n.).

comrade: Lit. 'fellow tribesman'. Both at Athens and at Rome the citizen body was divided into tribes. But in both cases the tribes were too large for everybody to know each other; it is possible that in Menander the word was 'fellow demesman', the deme being a much smaller unit roughly equivalent to a parish, and that Terence has not been able to find an exact Latin equivalent.

442 a man of worth and honour of the good old sort: Lit. 'a man of old-fashioned virtue and faith' (Lat. *fides*: 161 n.). It will be interesting to see whether Hegio will take the same view of Aeschinus' behaviour as Demea himself.

III. iv-v: HEGIO, DEMEA, GETA (447-516, pp. 359-62)

[1] Geta returns with Hegio, who is shocked at the news of Aeschinus' behaviour and promises to stand by Sostrata and her

family. He informs Demea of Aeschinus' seduction of Pamphila and his desertion of her for a music-girl, and, as Pamphila's birth cries are heard off stage, demands that Demea and his family take the proper action. Demea goes off to find Micio; Hegio goes in briefly to reassure Sostrata, and follows Demea into town.

[2] This scene restores the focus to the Micio-Aeschinus side of the plot, and brings Micio's discovery of the truth about Aeschinus' behaviour one stage nearer. It also ensures that Demea will continue to be involved with Aeschinus, thus maintaining this link between the two halves of the plot (cf. 254ff n. 2).

[3] This is essentially a serious scene, in contrast to the humour of the preceding Syrus-Demea scene, though the seriousness is undercut by the inherent dramatic irony: the audience is well aware that all three characters are misjudging the gravity of the situation. Hegio's attitudes are interesting, granted Demea's fulsome praise of his old-fashioned standards (442 n.). His attitude to the rape is in fact strikingly moderate (469-71 n.); it is the fact that Aeschinus has (apparently) deserted the girl that calls down his indignation. Hegio is very much a believer in doing one's duty; he himself stands by his old friend's widow and would rather lay down his life than fail her (498); correspondingly, he expects Demea to ensure that his family does what is right and proper. The scene abounds in allusions to Terence's favourite ethical concepts (Introd. §16), most of them in Hegio's mouth, notably *indignum* ('monstrous' 447), *liberalitas* ('ungentle-manly' 449), *aequom* ('right' 454, 503, 'proper' 505), *pudor* ('ashamed' 485), *fides* 'honour' (489), *decet* ('the proper course' 491, 'your duty' 506), *oportet* ('you must' 504), *officium* ('duty' 514). To modern taste Hegio's moralising seems a little pompous, but we can scarcely doubt that Terence intends to endorse Hegio's view.

[4] The other two characters are both overshadowed by Hegio. There is an interesting change in the presentation of Demea, who is here neither angry nor gullible, but rather genuinely ashamed at what has happened (485): it is only at the end of the scene that his righteous indignation against Micio reasserts itself (507-10 n.). Geta is warmly commended by Hegio ('an honest man...the prop and mainstay of the whole household' 480-2), and his loyalty is further underlined by his offer to give evidence under torture (483 n.).

[5] The spoken verse (ia^6) continues.

447-61 Good heavens...The same to you, Demea: The scene opens with an overheard entrance dialogue, accompanied by an aside and terminated formulaically (460-1 n.). The technique is very similar to that of the overheard entrance monologue (254-9 n.).

451 that girl: Lat. *psaltria* (388 n.). Demea is again mis-judging the situation; Hegio has indeed heard about the *psaltria* but his indignation is caused by Aeschinus' apparent desertion of Pamphila, something as yet unknown to Demea.

p.360 **456 protector:** Hegio is the 'patron' (Lat. *patronus*) of the widow Sostrata and her daughter in much the same way as Phormio is of the orphan Phanium (*Phorm.* 307 n.). But it is interesting to note that, in the Greek original, if Hegio was Sostrata's brother (351 n.), he would have been bound in Athenian law as the nearest male relative to marry Pamphila or to find her another husband (*Phorm.* 125 n.).

457 with his dying words: This strengthens the obligation placed on Hegio. At *Andr.* 284-98 (p. 51) the dying Chrysis similarly entrusts her orphan daughter to the young man Pamphilus.

459 when duty calls me: The Latin here is *pietas*, a Roman concept which embraces loyalty to one's family, friends, country, and gods; it is the first of these loyalties which is in question here. Unlike the other ethical terms used in this scene, *pietas* is not a common word in Terence, though the quality it describes is closely related to his general concept of humanity and concern for others (107 n.).

460-1 I'll meet him..The same to you: The whole sequence is formulaic (Introd. §29-30), but, as often, Terence uses the formulae to some point, in this case for characterisation. Demea addresses Hegio with an elaborate version of the greetings formula ('with all my heart': cf. *Eun.* 270-1 n.), as if to temper Hegio's indignation; Hegio responds with the impatient 'I was looking for you' (81 n.) before returning the greeting in a much abbreviated form (Lat. *salve*).

467 seduced: Lit 'raped' (296 n.).

469-71 This could have been borne...human nature: This is a significant attitude, coming as it does from a man of old-fashioned morality. The act of rape is seen as understandable, granted the ardour of youth, the effect of wine, and the opportunity provided by darkness; but (as Hegio makes abundantly clear) it is the young man's duty to stand by the girl he has wronged and marry her (Introd. §2). On the phrase 'human nature' in this context see *Eun.* 880-1 n.

471-4 When he realized...hushed up: This complements Sostrata's account of Aeschinus' behaviour after the rape (331-4, pp. 354-5): Aeschinus emerges with some credit.

girl: Lit. 'maiden' (Lat. *virgo*), which is the standard term for the young citizen girls of comedy, even though (having been raped) they are not technically virgins (cf. *Eun.* 440 n., *Phorm.* 201 n.).

p.361 **483 Put me on the rack:** This is an allusion to the torturing of slaves for evidence (*Phorm.* 292-3 n.).

486-7 Ah the pain! Juno Lucina...!: Juno Lucina was the Roman goddess of childbirth. It is a convention of Greek and Roman comedy that, where the young girl who has been raped gives birth during the play, the birth is announced by her off-stage cries (e.g. Plaut. *Aul.* 691-2). Terence here, for once, plays the convention straight; at *Andr.* 473-6 (p. 61) he makes the old man Simo query the cries as a deliberate deception, and at *Hec.* 318 (p. 305) he has the mother hushing the girl's cries from within in an attempt to keep the birth secret.

496 the hardships of poverty: This dispels any illusion that Hegio comes from a comfortable middle-class background.

499 I'll find my brother: Hegio has been addressing Demea with the plural form of 'you', with the implication that this is a matter for the whole family. The Penguin stage direction 'at a loss' may not be quite accurate: Aeschinus' behaviour is strictly speaking Micio's business, so that Demea has no option but to refer it to his brother.

501-4 The more easy...honest men: The clear implication of the plural 'you people' (501) is that Hegio is still relatively poor (496 n.) and that he regards both Demea and Micio as relatively rich. This rather contradicts the impression given in Micio's opening speech, where Demea was described as thrifty and hardworking (45-6, p. 342) and where poverty might have suggested itself as a reason for the adoption of his older son (47 n.). At any rate, Terence uses the contrast to take up the theme of rich-poor relationships, and to point the moral that wealth and status carry with them the obligation to behave properly towards the less fortunate (Introd. §15).

362 **507-10 I warned him...the whole story:** As Hegio goes in to reassure Sostrata, Demea is left to utter a brief exit monologue (141-54 n.), in which he finally gives vent to some self-righteous indignation against Micio. He then exits (right) to find Micio, who, when we last heard of him (364-72, p. 356), was still in town.

510 pour out: Lit. 'spue out' (Lat. *evomere*: 312 n.).

511-16 Bear up...steps to take: The act closes with a perfunctory scene (III. v), in which Hegio returns after only a brief word with Sostrata and delivers an entrance-and-exit monologue (*Eun.* 628 n.) before following Demea into town (right). There is an obvious compression of time here; the purpose of this arrangement is presumably to separate Hegio's departure from Demea's so that they shall not both find Micio at once. There would have been an act-break in the Greek original at this point (the end of the second act) in order to cover the journey into town of the two characters (Introd. §23).

IV. i: CTESIPHO, SYRUS (517-39, pp. 362-3)

[1] Ctesipho emerges from Micio's house with Syrus, worried that Demea will soon be back in town looking for him. Syrus undertakes to deal with the situation, and has to send Ctesipho hastily back inside as Demea unexpectedly approaches.

[2] We now return to the Demea-Ctesipho side of the plot, as Terence continues to interweave the two halves. The scene makes use of both dramatic irony and suspense: unlike Syrus and Ctesipho, the audience know that Demea is not in fact back at the farm, and they are expecting him to reappear at any moment.

[3] The scene does something to fill out the character of Ctesipho, whom we have not seen since his brief earlier scenes (254ff n. 4). He

is basically a weak character, with his previous exhilaration now replaced by anxiety; he relies on Syrus to counter Demea's questions ('Can't you think of anything? / Nothing at all' 528), and panics at Demea's sudden reappearance ('Oh Syrus, what are we to do? 538). But he is naive rather than vicious: he would like Demea kept away by tiredness rather than anything worse (519 n.), he cannot see himself deceiving his father with an outright lie ('But I wasn't. I can't say that' 530), and he is well aware of his own failings ('*My* virtues?' 536). Syrus exudes the confidence of the tricky slave ('I'll...have him as quiet as a lamb' 534, 'I can have the old man crying...for joy' 536-7), and his language has a colourful mixture of repartee (521 n., 532 n.), hyperbole (535 n.), imagery (534 n.), and proverbs (537 n).

[4] The scene is in recitative, mixed metres at first and then ia^8 (from 'he'll...ask me where I've been' 527). The change from spoken verse reflects the change in tone, with Ctesipho's agitation and the imminent danger of Demea's return: it is significant for Ctesipho's characterisation that all of his scenes in the play are in recitative.

519 so long as he doesn't kill himself: By contrast, the young man at Plaut. *Most.* 233 wishes his father dead.

521 or something even better / Agreed: Donatus suggests that Syrus might be referring to Demea's death, but he may only be thinking of a somewhat longer period of incapacitation.

523 one thing I don't like about our farm - it's too near: Ctesipho manages something approaching a witticism. It is the standard situation of Roman comedy that the families who appear on stage have a farm no great distance away from the city (*Eun.* 633 n.).

p.363　**529 Haven't you a dependant...companion...friend?:** Lit. 'client...friend...guest-friend'. It is important to note that the 'you' is plural', and that the references are to the network of relationships of the family rather than to the personal acquaintances of the young man. It follows that Demea's family is not only not poor (501-4 n.) but not lacking in connections either, and that what Ctesipho is invited to pretend to is some dutiful pursuit of the family's obligations.

Yes I have: Better 'Yes we have'.

532 if only people made a habit...: This is another piece of witty repartee by Syrus.

534 seethe: Lit. 'boil' (Lat. *fervere*: cf. 152 n.). This is the first in a bag of mixed metaphors by Syrus: in the space of four lines Demea is described as boiling like a pot, quiet as a lamb, crying like a child, and dangerous as a wolf (537 n.).

535 sing your praise to heaven: Lit. 'make you a god in his eyes'. This hyperbole is not uncommon in comedy. In this context 'god' means 'of 'superhuman virtue', in others it means 'of superhuman benevolence' (*Phorm.* 345 n.) or 'of superhuman happiness'.

537 Talk of the devil: Lit. 'the wolf in the fable', another proverbial phrase (cf. 'quiet as a lamb' 534). Donatus offers two explanations: the first associates the saying with the sudden silence which falls on people if they see a wolf, the second with tales told by nursemaids to frighten children. But it is clear from other ancient commentators and from the usage of writers like Cicero (*Letters to Atticus* 13. 33a. 1) that the proverb does function very much like our 'talk of the devil', i.e. it refers to the sudden appearance of the very person who is being discussed, often with the added implication that the speakers had better discontinue their discussion.

IV. ii: DEMEA, CTESIPHO, SYRUS (540-91, pp. 363-6)

[1] Demea returns fom the town (right), having failed to find Micio and having discovered from one of his farm-hands that Ctesipho is not on the farm. Syrus finally pushes Ctesipho back into the house, and tells Demea that he himself has been beaten by Ctesipho as a punishment for his part in the abduction of the music-girl. Syrus then sends Demea off on a wild-goose chase for Micio, whom he claims to be at a carpenter's shop on the edge of the town, and goes indoors himself to sample the food and drink.

[2] This scene is parallel to the previous Syrus-Demea scene (355-434, pp. 356-9), and it is worth comparing the two. Once again Demea's discovery of the truth about Ctesipho is averted by Syrus' talent for deception, and the plot is not advanced; the interest of the scene lies in the characterisation and the humour of the deception.

[3] Syrus uses two of the same techniques as in the previous scene; he invents stories about Ctesipho to appeal to Demea's paternal pride (559 n.), and he has no compunction about telling outright lies (571-85 n.). His language continues to be colourful, with a combination of metaphor (556 n.), exclamation ('Why the hell...?' 557) and abuse (587 n.). Demea is, as before, both angry and gullible; his anger is emphasised by his abuse ('that scoundrel Syrus' 553) and his threat of violence (571 n.), and his gullibility by his absurd claim that he 'was the first to guess' the truth (546-7). At the same time he is not completely stupid; he twice catches Syrus out and forces him to improvise (560-1 n., 578 n.). In Ctesipho's case, it is again his anxiety which is to the fore ('Then I'm done for' 543, 'For heaven's sake don't let him in' 550, 'I just can't trust you' 551); instead of trusting to Syrus and hiding in the house, he risks betraying himself by prolonging the conversation.

[4] In contrast to the previous Syrus-Demea scene (and indeed to most scenes of trickery in comedy) this one is in recitative (tr^7). This presumably reflects the heightened emotional level as Demea becomes more and more exasperated.

540-56 Just my luck...What can he want?: This is technically an overheard entrance monologue, accompanied by asides and terminated formulaically (254-9 n.). But the convention is varied here by the fact that there are two eavesdroppers, one of whom is desperate not to be seen, which changes the character of the asides.

541 one of the farm hands: The Latin makes it clear that the reference is to a hired labourer. If Demea can afford to hire free labourers in addition to his slaves, he is not as poor as we might have supposed (cf. 529 n.).

p.364   **542 I don't know what to do:** Presumably Demea cannot decide whether to pursue Micio or Ctesipho.

543 [*putting his head out*]: Ctesipho's precise movements are not certain. Syrus told him to go inside at the end of the previous scene ('Quick, go in' 538). But it is not clear that he had time to enter the house and close the door; we might equally envisage him as lingering at the door and uttering his remarks to Syrus from that position. The fact that Demea does not see either Syrus or Ctesipho, both of whom are clearly near Micio's door, might suggest the placing of Micio's house on the further side of the stage from Demea's approach, i.e. on the left.

Syrus...Bear up: These six utterances occupy only one line of Latin verse: Terence's dialogue can be very rapid (*Eun.* 697 n.).

552 find a room: The Latin (*cella*) rather suggests a store-room. Ctesipho finally enters the comparative safety of the house.

553 There's...Syrus: Demea finally sees Syrus, and terminates his monologue with a 'recognition formula' (Introd. §30). But before he can initiate a conversation, Syrus launches into a 'faked' monologue of his own (cf. 364-72 n.).

556 whining: Lat. *gannire* (*Phorm.* 1030 n.).

p.365   **558 girl:** Lat. *psaltria* (388 n.).

559 he's split my lip: Syrus points to the alleged wound, of which there would of course been no sign visible to Demea or to the audience; we should almost certainly imagine the traditional slave mask with its rounded open mouth (on masks see *Phorm.* 210-11 n.). The physical aggression which Syrus invents for Ctesipho here matches the verbal aggression which he ascribed to him in the previous scene (403-10, p. 358).

560-1 I thought you said...: The reference is to Syrus' claim at 402 (p. 357); Syrus has to cover hastily.

562-3 ashamed...: Syrus appeals to the concept of *pudor*.

an old man...I held him in my arms: This makes explicit what we might have assumed, that Syrus is an old long-serving slave of the family. What is not explained is how he comes to be in Micio's household now rather than in Demea's.

563 *so high*: This is an implied stage direction (cf. 163 n.); Syrus indicates Ctesipho's height with a gesture.

564 you're your father's son: Theopropides at Plaut. *Most.* 639 reacts with similar pride to his slave's invented tales about his son's behaviour.

568 you're at the bottom of all this: Lit. 'you are the head [i.e. source] of...'. Like Geta (315 n.) Demea readily assumes that Syrus was the master-mind behind the abduction (cf. 368 n.).

569 Now, is my brother at home?: These words mark the transition from Demea's first concern (Ctesipho) to his second (Micio) (cf. 542 n.).

570 I'm certainly not telling you: Syrus is using one of Phormio's techniques for dealing with the *senex iratus*, viz. to fuel his anger by deliberate provocation (*Phorm.* 348ff n. 3).

571 I'll knock your head off: Lit. 'your brain-matter will be diminished', a colourful threat. Demea is rising to the bait; he can be imagined brandishing the traditional stick of the comic *senex*.

571-85 Well, there's a man...with oak legs: Syrus misleads Demea about Micio's whereabouts as he had misled him in the previous scene about Ctesipho's (400-3, p. 357). There is no parallel in Greek and Roman comedy for this lengthy series of misdirections.

366   **576 chapel:** Perhaps better 'shrine'.

alley: Lat. *angiportum* (cf. *Eun.* 845-6 n., *Phorm.* 891 n.). Here the word clearly refers to a side alley off the main route; it is glossed by Donatus as 'a narrow and curving street'.

578 That alley hasn't *got* a way through: Demea again catches Syrus out.

581 Cratinus: On the name see *Phorm.* 448 n.

583 pond: Donatus explains that it was customary to have a *lacus* (the Latin word covers 'pond', 'reservoir, 'trough') at the gate of a city for the use of baggage animals and also to help exstinguish fires lit by enemies.

585 for sitting in the sun...with oak legs: Syrus hastily improvises some details to make the story more convincing.

586 I'll be off: Lit. 'do I delay?' (320 n.).

587-91 That's right...a day like this: Syrus closes the scene with a brief exit monologue, the third in the play (141-54 n.).

587 old dry bones: Lit. 'you funeral feast', with reference to the offerings made to the spirits of the dead at funerals. This is a novel term of abuse and a colourful way of implying that Demea has (as it were) one foot in the grave. The nearest parallel in comedy is at Plaut. *Pseud.* 412, where a slave calls his master an 'old sepulchre'.

588 lunch is spoiling: The reference to the midday meal (Lat. *prandium*) is a reminder of the time-frame: the play begins sometime after dawn (26 n.) and the various activities so far have taken up most of the morning.

589-91 time for myself...have a sip of the wine: This is the traditional behaviour of the tricky slave after carrying out a successful deception (*Phorm.* 832 n.).

IV. iii: MICIO, HEGIO (592-609, p. 367)

[1] Hegio returns from the forum (right) with Micio, who has promised to do his duty and put things right. Micio agrees to explain the situation to Sostrata in person, and they go into Sostrata's house.

[2] We now return to the Micio-Aeschinus side of the plot. Micio has been off stage since the end of the first act (154, p. 345), and with his return we can expect a chain of events leading to a second Micio-Demea confrontation. Meanwhile Terence continues to divulge more of the truth to the various characters. Micio now knows all the facts about Aeschinus and Ctesipho, as does Hegio; Sostrata and Pamphila are about to be informed; Demea will, as usual, be the last to find out.

[3] The main interest of the scene is Micio's handling of the discovery that Aeschinus has got Pamphila pregnant. The news has been conveyed off stage by Hegio, so that we do not see Micio's instant reaction; what we do see is entirely to Micio's credit, namely his ready acceptance of his duty to rectify the situation. Hegio, who had previously been threatening to 'take steps' if Micio failed to respond appropriately (516, p. 362), is now full of civility, as befits a gentle-man of the old-fashioned kind; he has nothing but praise for Micio's reaction ('That's good of you' 601 n.).

[4] Donatus comments that 'the scene is full of old men's moralising'. The appropriate ethical vocabulary is duly deployed, as in the previous Hegio scene, notably *peccatum* ('offence' 593 n.), *officium* ('duty' 593, 603), *aequom* ('right' 601). There is also some emphasis on doing a kindness (*beneficium*: 601 n.) and on the proper treatment of the poor by the rich (605-8 n.). Terence may be mildly satirising the exaggerated civility of the dialogue, but there can be little doubt that he endorses the ethical ideals (cf. 447ff n. 3).

[5] The choice of metre is interesting in relation to this last point. If there was to be a change of metre to mark the change of tone from the preceding Syrus-Demea scene, we might have expected a return from recitative (tr^7) to spoken verse (ia^6). But Terence actually changes to ia^8, normally one of the more animated recitative metres, as if to highlight the artificiality of the dialogue.

592 I really can't see ...: Hegio and Micio enter in conversation. Terence leaves it unexplained how Hegio has succeeded in finding Micio when Demea, who had left in the same direction on the same errand at almost the same time, had failed to do so (511-16 n.).

593 offence: Lat. *peccatum* (*Phorm.* 958 n.). The audience is left to infer that Micio is referring to Aeschinus' rape of Pamphila; with his usual economy Terence has refrained from repeating details with which the spectators are already familiar. They also have to deduce that by 'put[ting] things right' Micio must mean ensuring that Aeschinus marries Pamphila.

599-600 all you've said to me...: Terence again refrains from spelling out the details. Micio himself had learned the truth about the music-girl from Syrus (364-5, p. 356).

601 That's good of you: The Latin here and at 604 ('It really is good of you') is *bene facis* (*Eun.* 186 n.).

602-3 She's wearing herself out: The reference is presumably to Sostrata, though Donatus takes the 'she' to mean Pamphila.

605-8 People who are not so lucky...take it better: Hegio tactfully explains why he is so keen for Micio to speak to Sostrata in person. In doing so he repeats a recurring idea of comedy, namely that the poor entertain a prickly suspicion of the rich and have to be treated with tact (Introd. §15; cf. Men. *Dysk.* 295-8). The ancient anthologist Stobaeus preserves a quotation from Menander to the effect that 'the poor man...imagines that everyone is looking down on him', which may well come from the corresponding point of Menander's *Adelphoi*.

609 Come in: As Micio and Hegio go in to see Sostrata, the stage is empty for the second time in less than twenty lines.

IV. iv: AESCHINUS (610-35, pp. 367-8)

[1] Aeschinus returns from the town (right) in distraction; he has met Canthara on her way to fetch the midwife and discovered that he is believed to have deserted Pamphila. He resolves to explain the situation to Sostrata, and knocks at her door.

[2] The various developments of the plot are being dovetailed together with some skill. We now see that Terence's aim in sending Demea off to the other end of the town was to postpone the expected Micio-Demea confrontation and make way instead for a scene between Micio and Aeschinus and an exploration of the father-son relationship. The return of Aeschinus, who has been off-stage since the end of the second act (280, p. 352), has been carefully timed to coincide with the point where Micio is making peace with Sostrata on his behalf.

[3] The scene confirms the characterisation of Aeschinus as the weak but basically decent *adulescens* of comedy (288ff n. 3). He is typically at a loss what to do (610-14 n.), and, having finally steeled himself to knock at Sostrata's door, he panics again as soon as the door is opened ('I'll stay over here' 635). But his unwillingness to betray his brother to save his own situation ('this mustn't get abroad at all costs' 625-6) is a clear point in his favour, as is his recognition that he is at fault in not having approached his father long before (629 n.).

[4] This is one of three set-piece monologues in the play (Geta's running slave monologue at 299ff is rather different), and it is interesting to compare it with the other two (Micio's at 26ff and Demea's at 855ff). Aeschinus' combines all all three of the potential functions of the monologue (reflection, narrative, deliberation), and is to that extent a more realistic soliloquy (Introd. §22).

[5] Aeschinus' monologue also stands out from the all other monologues in the play in that it starts off as a song; its first eight lines are in lyric metres, after which it modulates into different kinds of recitative (ia^8 from 'when I caught sight of her' 617, and tr^7 from 'Now what can I do?' 625). Songs are very rare in Terence, though relatively common in Plautus (Introd. §27-8), and the intention here must be to highlight Aeschinus' emotional stress. It is notable that Terence revives in his last play a technique otherwise used only in his first: his other songs are both in *Andria*, one by the midwife Lesbia (481-4, p. 62) and the other by the love-crossed young man Charinus (625-38, p. 69).

610-14 This is sheer torture...out of this confusion: Aeschius opens with a very vivid statement of the traditional indecision of the comic *adulescens*.

p.368 **616 girl:** Lat. *psaltria* (388 n.).

617 the old woman: i.e. Canthara. Canthara was sent to fetch the midwife at 354 (p. 355), but the baby has now been born (486, p. 361) and we have not seen her return. The awkwardness of Canthara's role in Terence has led to the speculation that she played no part in Menander's version (354 n.). In that case it was presumably Geta who found Aeschinus in Menander's play and confronted him with the family's suspicions, and there may be a lingering hint of this in Terence at 484 (p. 361), where Geta says 'the boy won't deny it; bring him face to face with me'.

619 Pamphila: Not only does Pamphila never appear on stage in the play, but this is the only place where she is actually named (appropriately enough by her lover Aeschinus), being generally referred to as 'the girl' (Lat. *virgo*: 471-4 n.). Her counterparts in other plays fare slightly better (*Eun.* 440 n., *Phorm.* 201 n.).

621 promises: Lat. *fides* (cf. 306 n.).

624 gossip: Garrulousness is a stock characteristic of old women in comedy.

625 Now what can I do?: This is a common question of the indecisive *adulescens* (*Eun.* 46 n., *Phorm.* 534 n.).

629 This at least was all my doing: Perhaps better 'But this whole situation is all my fault' (Lat. *culpa*).

630 however I'd managed it: i.e. however badly I had behaved.

Pamphila: The Latin simply says 'her' (619 n.).

631 Now's the time, Aeschinus: On the self-address see *Phorm.* 317 n.

632 go to the women and clear myself: Aeschinus does not say how: he is still presumably hoping to keep Ctesipho's affair secret.

633 without a shudder: This is scarcely a shudder of fear, since Aeschinus has been a regular and welcome visitor to Sostrata's house (293-8, pp. 352-3). Donatus interprets it as the lover's shiver of anticipation on approaching his beloved, comparing Phaedria's reaction to the sight of Thais at *Eun.* 83-4 (p. 168). If Donatus is right, Terence is subtly reminding us of the genuineness of Aeschinus' love.

635 I'll stay over here: This is in fact the standard 'eavesdropping formula' 'I will stand aside here' (Introd. §29). Here there is a typical variation on Terence's part, which gives a new twist to the convention: Aeschinus stands aside because he is apprehensive, whereas the usual eavesdropper is merely curious.

IV. v: MICIO, AESCHINUS (635-712, pp. 368-72)

[1] Micio emerges from Sostrata's house, and teases Aeschinus with the story that Pamphila has to marry her nearest relative, who is about to take her to Miletus. Micio then reveals that he knows the truth about Pamphila, rebuking Aeschinus for his behaviour and then giving him permission to marry. Aeschinus is overjoyed, and, after Micio has gone in to make preparations for the marriage, expresses his appreciation of Micio as a father.

[2] The scene brings a happy solution to one of the love affairs (Aeschinus-Pamphila) and, apparently, a verdict on one of the father-son relationships (Micio-Aeschinus); this leaves for the rest of the play the solution of the other love affair (Ctesipho-*psaltria*), a verdict on the other father-son relationship (Demea-Ctesipho), and, above all, a resolution of the clash between Micio and Demea. It is in fact the common pattern of Terence's dual plots that the first love affair to be solved is the one that can end in a marriage (cf. Chaerea's in *Eun.*, Antipho's in *Phorm.*); there is no easy solution to an affair with a *meretrix*, and this is the one which is left to the end.

[3] To the modern mind Micio's treatment of Aeschinus is a model of how a liberal but responsible father should behave. He rebukes Aeschinus at some length for being 'heedless' (684) and 'thoughtless' (695), for seducing a girl he 'never should have touched' (686), and for doing nothing 'while nine months went by' (691). He does not mince his words ('your first fault [was] quite bad enough' 687, 'the greatest wrong you could do' 692 n.), but he softens the lecture by declaring his love and understanding ('I understand, for I love you...' 680) and by allowing that it is 'human' even for honest men to err (687 n.). Some commentators have accused Micio of cruelty in teasing Aeschinus to the point where he is reduced to tears (679), but this is surely no more than Aeschinus deserves.

[4] As for Aeschinus, granted that he has behaved badly (and that Micio's methods do not therefore produce perfect results), he too comes out of the scene with credit. His blush when he is discovered outside Sostrata's door is evidence of his basic decency ('He's blushing: all's well' 643), and his agonised asides as he listens to Micio's tale ('No - I can't bear it' 652, 'Oh my head reels' 655) and

his spirited defence of the 'unhappy man who first loved' the girl (666) confirm the strength of his own love, as indeed does the incredulous joy with which he receives the news that he can marry ('I'm so desperately anxious for this to be true...' 698). And his confession of guilt and shame (683-4) and his resolve to 'deserve [Micio's] love in future' (681) and 'never...to do anything he doesn't like' (711) seem to imply exactly the relationship at which Micio was aiming in his opening monologue (48-58, pp. 341-2).

[5] But is Terence holding this up as the ideal father-son relationship? As many have pointed out, Aeschinus' enthusiastic comparison of Micio's generosity at the end to that of a brother or a friend (707-11) may have raised, particularly in Roman minds, the thought that fathers should after all behave like fathers, i.e. should exercise the discipline that brothers and friends are not called upon to exercise (52 n.). There is no doubt that Aeschinus' language is extravagant (709 n.) and that he sees Micio as indulgent and obliging (708 n., 710 n.). Granted that even the Roman audience would not have wanted Micio to play the stern father at this point (i.e. to disown Aeschinus or forbid the marriage), they might still have been blaming him for allowing the situation to develop in the first place.

[6] The scene is very complex metrically, including both spoken verse and different kinds of recitative, all reflecting changes of tone. The pattern is: (i) tr^7 for Micio's entrance (635-7), continued from the previous scene; (ii) ia^6 for Micio's invented tale (from 'What can he want?' 638), the usual metre for narrative; (iii) tr^7 from the point where Micio relents (from 'Why are you crying?' 679); and (iv) ia^7 for Aeschinus' closing monologue (707-12) as the emotional level reaches its highest.

635 Do as I say, Sostrata: Micio emerges talking over his shoulder to Sostrata (209 n.). It is an abrupt entrance, staring in mid-line (81 n.); no wonder Aeschinus is startled.

636 our arrangements: Evidently for the wedding between Aeschinus and Pamphila.

p.369   **643 He's blushing...:** This is another aside in conversation (83 n.). The audience has, of course, to imagine the blush, whether the actor is masked or not, so that the line has no bearing on the question of whether Roman actors in Terence's day wore masks (559 n.). The anthologist Stobaeus preserves a quotation from Menander 'Anyone who blushes seems to me to be honorable', which he ascribes to a different Menander play (fr. 301); scholars have reasonably wondered whether it is in fact the corresponding line of his *Adelphoi*.

646 witness: Lat. *advocatus* (*Eun.* 340 n). Micio implies that the supposed friend is still inside with Sostrata.

647 in a poor way: Lit. 'poor little women'. Micio uses the scornful 'diminutive' form as part of his teasing of Aeschinus, who will infer that Micio is unlikely to agree to his marrying Pamphila.

649 they have not been here long: This is news to the audience, who have had no reason to assume that Sostrata and her family are new neighbours of Micio's (cf. *Eun.* 359 n.).

652 That's the law: See *Phorm.* 125-6 n.

654 to Miletus: Miletus was a Greek city on the south-west coast of what is now Turkey. The girl's alleged 'relative' must be an Athenian citizen now living overseas but still liable to Athenian law.

.370   **660 that's right:** Lat. *iustum* (lit. 'just'). Aeschinus' plea on behalf of the 'other man' is heavily based on the ethics of what is right and proper for a gentleman, involving the words *inliberalis* ('dishonorable' 664), *indignum* ('a sin and a scandal' 669) and *aequom* ('you could have' 675).

666 first loved her: Lat. *consuescere*, which almost implies 'seduced' (*Phorm.* 873 n.); this is a different word from the following 'still loves' (Lat. *amare*).

670-1 How do you make that out...?: As Donatus points out, Micio is implicitly rebuking Aeschinus for not taking proper steps to secure the girl in marriage.

promised...gave her away: Athenian law required the bride's father or guardian to betroth her formally and transfer her to her new family.

Who witnessed it?: Better 'Who gave his authority?', i.e. on the bridegroom's side (*Phorm.* 232 n.).

672 was meant for another: i.e. as an orphan she was due to marry her next-of-kin. The Latin could also mean 'was alien to him', i.e. belonged to a family with which he had no connections (cf. *Phorm.* 721 n.).

.371   **682-3 guilty and ashamed:** The allusion to *pudor* ('shame') recalls Micio's principle of restraining children by a sense of honour rather than by fear (57 n.).

684 honourable: Lat. *liberalis* (57 n.). In the context there may be an echo of Aristotle's doctrine that 'gentlemen' do not need to be disciplined by threats of punishment (74-5 n.).

686 seduced: Better 'raped' (296 n.).

687 no more than human: Micio echoes the view of the old-fashioned Hegio (469-71 n.); he can scarcely be accused of being irresponsibly lenient.

690 ashamed to confess: Note that, though *pudor* is a virtue, it does not always lead to the right course of action. Ctesipho was similarly inhibited by *pudor* from confessing his love affair (274 n.).

691 nine months: The Latin actually says 'ten', i.e. it refers to lunar months.

692 This was the greatest wrong you could do: The translator is rather improving Micio's sermon here; the Latin simply says 'you betrayed...'. It is interesting that in Micio's ethics Aeschinus has betrayed himself as well as the girl and her child.

693 and go on dreaming: Lit. 'while you slept', a proverbial phrase.

696 Cheer up: The change of tone is sudden. We can imagine the Aeschinus actor showing increasing signs of contrition, so that Micio, having made his point, relents.

you shall marry her: Micio declares his consent to the marriage without a word of complaint at the poverty of the girl and her lack of a dowry; in this he can be contrasted with most fathers of comedy (*Phorm.* 120 n.).

p.372   **701 love you more than my own eyes:** This is another proverbial phrase.

702 What, more than - her?: Micio shows a delightful sense of humour in this and his following remarks.

704-5 Father, you go...better than I: This suggestion combines a proper show of humility with a touch of humour of Aeschinus' own. At the same time Terence wants to remove Micio from the stage so that Aeschinus can express his gratitude in a soliloquy.

707-12 What do you think...my own wedding: This is another exit monologue, the fourth in the play.

708 couldn't do more for me: The Latin phrase has connotations of indulgence rather than mere helpfulness.

709 cherish in one's heart: Lit. 'hold in one's bosom', as of a mother holding a baby.

710 kind: i.e. obliging.

712 I must hurry indoors: Lit. 'do I delay?' (320 n.). The stage is again empty stage (609 n.), and we can imagine an act-break here in the Greek original (the end of the third act); one would have been needed before Demea could return from the town (511-16 n.).

IV. vi-vii: DEMEA, MICIO (713-62, pp. 372-5)

[1] Demea returns (right) from his fruitless search for Micio at the far end of the town. Micio reacts with calm amusement to Demea's 'news' of further wicked deeds on Aeschinus' part; he explains that he has arranged for Aeschinus to marry the girl without a dowry, and the music-girl is to be kept as well. Micio goes into Sostrata's house to invite the women across, leaving Demea expostulating in anger.

[2] This pair of scenes (here taken together for convenience) do not advance the plot: the truth about Ctesipho and the music-girl is yet again concealed from Demea, this time by Micio. We can scarcely have the final showdown between Micio and Demea until this truth is known. But this is the first Micio-Demea clash since the opening scenes, and there is therefore considerable interest in its outcome.

[3] Micio clearly emerges as the victor. He remains calm while Demea loses his temper; he knows all the facts while Demea continues to be deceived. Micio is moreover given a plausible defence of his

attitude and behaviour: he does not like what has happened but is doing the best he can to mend the situation (739 n.). Some have found Micio's teasing of Demea cruel; in Micio's defence it can be said that he has tried other methods of dealing with Demea unsuccessfully (143-7, p. 345), and that to tell Demea the truth about the music-girl would have meant betraying Ctesipho's secret, which he is understandably reluctant to do. Demea's anger is underlined by a whole series of oaths and exclamations (*oho* 726 n., 'Good god!' 731 n., 'Heavens above' 746, 'God help me!' 749, 'Ye gods!' 757). He is in no mood to listen to Micio's arguments, and does not really counter them; as often with the *senex iratus*, he shows almost as much concern for the financial aspects of the situation as for the moral ('without a dowry' 728-9 n., 'two thousand drachmas on that music-girl' 742-3, 'without a penny' 759 n., 'too much money' 760). There is an effective contrast in language between the two old men: Micio speaks in simple unemotive phrases, whereas Demea peppers his responses with expletives; Demea also uses the more vivid imagery (715 n., 761-2 n.).

[4] The scene is in spoken verse (ia⁶).

713-18 I've walked...till he comes back: This is a brief example of an entrance monologue on an empty stage (355-64 n.).

715 trailed: Lit. 'crawled' (Lat. *perreptare*), a word applicable to reptiles and plants as well as to humans and here suggesting the slow and weary progress of Demea in his search. The word occurs twice in Plautus in similar contexts *(Amph.* 1011, *Rud.* 223).

719 I'll go across: Micio enters talking over his shoulder (209 n.), presumably to Aeschinus.

we are all ready now: Micio went in to make preparations for the wedding only thirteen lines ago (at 706), which is an unrealistically short period of time. The preparations would have been covered by the act-break in the Greek original (712 n.).

720 Here he is. I've been looking for you: It is a sign of Demea's anger that he neither offers nor expects any greeting (81 n.).

721 wicked deeds: Lat. *flagitia* (101 n.).

723 appalling: Lit. 'capital', i.e. for which the penalty is death. This is not literally true: Demea is talking of Aeschinus' rape of Pamphila, and rape was not a capital offence (cf. *Eun.* 957 n.).

723-9 Yes I have...Evidently: Micio offers a whole series of infuriatingly calm responses to Demea's angry complaints.

725 honest girl: Lit. 'citizen girl' (Lat. *virgo*: 471-4 n.).

726 You *know*?: In the Latin this is preceded by the angry exclamation *oho*.

728-9: The girl has nothing...married without a dowry: This objection to the marriage is a reflection on Demea's character (696 n.). In any case, since Aeschinus is now legally Micio's son, the financial aspects of the marriage are Micio's concern, not Demea's.

731 Good God!: In the Latin Demea invokes Jupiter here, as also at 757, whereas at 746 and 749 he simply refers to 'the gods'.

732 the proper thing: Lat. *oportet* (447ff n. 3).

734 only human to *pretend* you have: This seems a very shallow notion of the concept of humanity, and Micio's version ('that is what seems to me only human' 736) is obviously superior. But it would be unfair to Demea to suggest that he is advocating pretence as a way of life or even the keeping up of appearances (cf. *Phorm.* 713ff n. 3); he is exasperated by Micio's nonchalance, and may be simply saying that it would be better for all concerned if Micio could bring himself to show proper moral indignation.

p.374   **the girl:** Lat. *virgo* (725 n.).

739 Life is like a game of dice: This is a traditional image, already found (e.g.) in Sophocles, Plato, and the Greek comic poet Alexis. As the following sentence shows, Micio is not referring to games of mere chance, but to those where the skill lies in moving one's pieces according to the fall of the dice (the Greeks and Romans both had a form of backgammmon or draughts). He is thus expressing a perfectly sensible philosophical position, which acknowledges the power of fortune (*Eun.* 1046 n.) but does not surrender to it.

741 make the best: Lit. 'correct'.

742 two thousand drachmas: 191 n.

745-53 No; I have no intention...if we want one: This is another series of infuriatingly calm responses by Micio (cf. 723-9).

747 mistress...wife: Lat. *meretrix...materfamilias*. Demea chooses his vocabulary to highlight the contrast: *materfamilias* is the dignified term for the mistress of the household.

750-3 partner your own singing...three of you dancing: Demea's moral indignation is directed against (i) old men singing with courtesans, (ii) young brides associating with courtesans, (iii) old men dancing with young girls. The scene as envisaged may have been more shocking to the Greek mind than the Penguin footnote (p. 375) allows.

752 hand-in-hand: Lit. 'holding the rope'. This is something of a puzzle. We read in Livy (27. 37. 14) of a choir of maidens taking hold of a rope as they process towards the temple of Juno while singing a hymn, but the dance envisaged for Micio and his two partners is evidently much more salacious.

753 With you to make a fourth: Micio is being deliberately provocative (cf. 570 n.).

p.375   **754 sense of shame:** This is yet another allusion to *pudor*.

755 behave properly: Lit. 'as it befits you' (Lat. *decet*: 108 n.). Demea and Micio are trading ethical terms.

757-62 Ye gods...beyond saving: This is the third and last link monologue in the play (196-208 n.).

759 Without a penny: Lit. 'without a dowry'.

girl: Lat. *psaltria* (388 n.).

761-2 Salvation...beyond saving: The paradox 'even Salvation couldn't save' is a recurrent one in comedy (cf. Plaut. *Capt.* 529, *Most.* 351). For the Romans Salvation (Lat. *Salus*) was not merely a personification but a goddess; she had a temple at Rome and appears frequently on coins.

V. i-ii: SYRUS, DEMEA, DROMO (763-86, pp. 375-6)

[1] Syrus emerges from Micio's house rather drunk, and is reprimanded by the disgusted Demea. Dromo calls from the house to tell Syrus that Ctesipho wants him. Demea picks up the name Ctesipho, and storms in despite Syrus' resistance. Syrus decides to lie low.

[2] This is a crucial scene in that it leads to Demea's long awaited discovery of the truth about Ctesipho. It is scarcely reasonable to complain that Terence uses an inorganic character Dromo to bring about the recognition. Dromo is only the messenger; and the blame actually falls on Ctesipho, who, having nearly betrayed himself before by his anxiety (540ff n. 3) now actually does so, which creates a neat structural link. The plot is now moving towards its dénouement.

[3] The scene is one of few in the play to offer visual humour of a slapstick kind, both in Syrus' drunken behaviour and in his attempt to restrain Demea by physical force. But in neither case is the slapstick carried very far. Syrus' drunkenness is on a par with that of Chremes at *Eun.* 727-738 (pp. 198-9); i.e. it is mildly amusing rather than uproariously funny. And Syrus' attempt to restrain Demea is tamer than the old men's attempt to restrain Phormio at *Phorm.* 982-9 (pp. 276-7) and even than the physical scuffles over Sannio and the music-girl earlier in *Adelphoe* (167-75, p. 346).

[4] This is the third (and shortest) of the Syrus-Demea confrontations, and this time Demea comes out on top. Demea's anger is still very close to the surface, but he is no longer deceived by Syrus' inventions ('It's someone else...' 779), and in the end Syrus cannot prevent him from entering Micio's house. The language of the scene reflects the characters. Syrus is drunk and therefore uninhibited, indulging in puns ('*inside*' 765,' *'firm'* 771), personification (769 n.), and various other impressive or ironic turns of phrase (764 n., 766 n., 783 n.); Demea, being angry, does not mince his words, adding abuse and threats ('Scoundrel' 768, 774 n., 'brute' 777 n., 'rascal' 781 n., 'knock your brains out' 782 n.) to his usual moral expostulation (773 n.).

[5] The spoken verse (ia⁶) continues.

763 Syrus my lad: Syrus addresses himself with the affectionate diminutive form 'Syriscus'; the self-address is this time humorous (cf. 631 n.).

764 done your duty handsome-ly: This is ironic: Syrus means 'eaten and drunk' (cf. 590-1, p. 366). The hyphen is intended to suggest the faltering speech of the inebriated, though there is nothing parallel in the Latin.

765 [*Hiccups*] That's better: This is another example of imaginative interpretation by the translator: the Latin has simply the colloquial *age* ('get away with you').

766 stretch my legs: Syrus uses a rare compound verb meaning 'take a leisurely stroll'.

767-8 Why, here's our old man! How do?: Syrus concludes his overheard entrance monologue with a recognition formula and a greeting, which Demea typically ignores (720 n.).

769 Father Wisdom: This is a playful personification on Syrus' part, recalling his previous description of Demea as 'all wisdom, from top to toe' (394, p. 357).

772 What have *I* done?: Syrus desperately adopts a pose of injured innocence.

p.376 **773 dreadful wrongdoing:** Lat. *peccatum* (*Phorm.* 958 n.). Donatus comments that Demea's heavy moralising is rather ludicrous when addressed to a drunken slave.

774 wretch: This is the same Latin word translated 'Scoundrel' at 768.

776 Hey, Syrus, Ctesipho wants you: This is Dromo's only line in the play, though he was addressed by Syrus off-stage at 376 (p. 356). Terence leaves us to imagine Ctesipho's motivation for sending Dromo: either with typical anxiety he wants Syrus to reassure him that Demea is not around, or perhaps he fears that Syrus may give the game away in his drunken state. In the latter case Syrus, who has hitherto been the artful protector of Ctesipho's secret, would be finally responsible for its betrayal, a good ironic twist.

777 brute: Lit. 'hangman' (Lat. *carnufex*: 363 n.).

780-2 Let me go...knock your brains out: These are clear stage-directional phrases: Syrus grabs hold of Demea, who raises his stick and threatens to strike him. on the head.

781 you rascal: Lat. *mastigia* (lit. 'you whip-dog'). This a Greek-derived slang word found in both Aristophanes and Menander, which is common in Plautus but not otherwise found in Terence. The Latin equivalent is *verbero* (*Phorm.* 684 n.).

782 knock your brains out: Lit. 'scatter your brains' (cf. 571 n.).

782-6 He's gone...That's the idea: Syrus utters a brief exit monologue before departing for a quiet sleep.

783 visitor: Lit. 'fellow-reveller', an ironic description.

785-6 find a quiet corner: We might have expected Syrus to steer clear of Micio's house, as the Penguin stage direction suggests, but in fact he must go into it here, as he emerges from it when we next see him (882, p. 380).

V. iii: MICIO, DEMEA (787-854, pp. 376-9)

[1] Micio emerges fom Sostrata's house, and is confronted by an angry Demea, who demands to know why Micio has broken their agreement and involved himself with Ctesipho. Micio suggests that, on the financial side, no harm has been done: Demea can continue to scrape and save to provide both sons with an inheritance, and any money that Micio spends on them can be regarded as a windfall. And as for the moral question, both sons are basically of good character, and can be brought back to the right path any day. Demea, though not convinced, agrees to put on a cheerful face for the wedding; but he is going to remove Ctesipho to the country at dawn and set his girl-friend to work on the farm.

[2] The third Micio-Demea confrontation follows hard on the heels of the second (713-62, pp. 372-5), in which Micio was able to use his superior knowledge about Ctesipho to tease Demea. But now both know the truth about both sons, and the third confrontation is in fact more comparable to the first (81-154, pp. 342-5), when neither knew the truth about either. In fact, the first and third confrontations follow a very similar pattern: Demea complains bitterly; Micio presents reasoned arguments for his point of view; Demea is not convinced but offers no counter arguments; Demea relents to the extent of conceding an immediate point; Demea's anger rises again but is finally restrained. There was no resolution of the conflict in the first confrontation, and there is still no resolution in the third, so that the issue remains alive right to the end of the play.

[3] The interpretation of this scene is very important for the interpretation of the play. In the first confrontation Micio was allowed to present the more convincing case, though the portrayal of Demea was not totally unsympathetic and there would have been those in the Roman audience who sympathised with his moral stance (81ff nn. 4-6). Here Micio is rather less convincing, and Demea is allowed to score a point: we need to assess carefully (i) the point about each concerning himself with one son (796-805 n.) and (ii) the validity of Micio's educational arguments (820-30 n.).

[4] The language of the scene reflects the characterisation. Demea begins with exaggerated expostulations (789-90 n.), calms down to dispute questions of fairness and right (801 n.), replies to Micio's arguments with a sneer ('Witty, aren't you' 805), then an objection (820 n.), then a warning (836-7 n.), and finally develops a colourful picture of what he will do to the music-girl on the farm (848 n.). Micio begins with a metaphor (792 n.), resorts to a proverb (804 n.), has two speeches of patient argument (807-19, 820-35), and finishes with a series of witty remarks at Demea's expense (841 n.).

[5] The spoken verse (ia^6) continues; this is in fact the metre of all three of the Micio-Demea confrontations.

787 Everything's ready: Micio emerges, as before (635 n.), talking over his shoulder to Sostrata.

788 Whoever is that hammering on my door: Lit. 'Who has struck my door?' This is virtually the same phrase as used by Micio of Aeschinus knocking at Sostrata's door at 637 (p. 368), and the natural assumption would be that it refers to someone knocking at the door from the outside. But in this case the noise is being made by Demea as he *exits* from Micio's house. There is no easy explanation of the use of the verb 'strike' in this and similar cases (there are Greek examples at Men. *Dysk.* 188, *Sam.* 300-1). Granted that doors opened inwards, an emerging character, especially one in a temper or a hurry, might bang or rattle them in the act of opening them; see Introd. §20.

789-90 Good God...Neptune's ocean!: As Donatus points out, Demea's anger reaches its climax in the third of the three confrontations, because this time it is his own son Ctesipho's morals which are concerned. The exclamations have a tragic ring and are meant to sound exaggerated; contrast the more realistic behaviour of the angry father at Men. *Sam.* 325-7, who, having exclaimed 'O citadel of Cecrops' land, O vault of heaven on high!', pulls himself up with the question 'What's all this shouting, Demeas? What's all this shouting, you fool?'

p.377 **792 battle:** Lit. 'quarrel'. The image is not military, but legal, since the primary reference of the Latin word (*lites*) is to lawsuits.

go to the rescue: To Ctesipho's rescue, presumably.

795 I *am* controlled, I *am* calm: Donatus is sceptical: he suggests that we consider not the words but the way in which they are spoken. It would very easy for an actor to make the delivery bely the words (by shouting them), but an examination of Demea's following utterances suggests that he does succeed in suppressing his anger, at least for the moment.

796-805 Let's face facts...that sort of talk?: On the obvious interpretation, Demea here, for the first time in the play, scores a point over Micio in argument. Micio had suggested that they each concern themselves with one son (129-32, p. 344): he has broken this agreement by helping Ctesipho over the music-girl, and his only reply now is to quote a somewhat irrelevant proverb. As Donatus puts it, 'Micio, seeing that he has a poor case, treats the whole thing in a facetious and obsequious manner'. If this is the right interpretation (and it probably is), Terence is signalling a change in the balance between Micio and Demea in Demea's favour. But there are points which could be made on Micio's side (803 n., 804 n.), and these need to be considered: whether they were in fact made in Menander's version we have no means of telling..

800 mistress: Demea now uses the word *amica* (lit. 'girlfriend': 252-3 n.) here rather than the more derogatory *psaltria* or *meretrix.*

801 a right to expect fair play: Demea combines the idea of a justice (Lat. *ius*) with that of fairness (Lat. *aequom*).

803 you're not being fair: Lat. *aequom* again. Donatus comments that Micio appeals to fairness because he has no case in justice. In fact Micio leaves unsaid two points that he might have made on his own behalf (and it could be claimed that he is tactfully avoiding an argument by passing over these points):

(i) that Demea had not kept his side of the agreement: Demea *has* been 'worrying about' Aeschinus ever since he met Hegio and heard the news about Pamphila (447-516, pp. 359-62); and

(ii) that he himself, in paying for the *psaltria*, was only acting on his principle of trying to make the best of the situation (739-41, p. 374): was he to refuse to pay for the girl and thus leave Aeschinus guilty of abduction, or was he to return the girl to the pimp and risk Ctesipho fleeing the country as threatened?

804 friends have everything in common: This is an old Greek proverb, which Donatus and others ascribe to the Pythagorean school of philosophy. It is quoted also twice by Plato (*Laws* 739c, *Phaedrus* 279c) and by Aristotle (*Ethics* 8. 9. 1). The ancient commentator on the second Plato passage tells us that the proverb occurs in Menander's *Adelphoi*, which means that Terence is closely following Menander at this point. In the context Micio can only mean 'just as friends have everything in common, so you and I share both sons', and this does go directly against the previous agreement. What is left unsaid here is 'and so we shouldn't have made this agreement in the first place', and this would fit very well with Terence's basic philosophy that friends should concern themselves with each other's problems (Introd. §15).

807-19 First of all...deal of trouble: Micio's argument that Demea can continue to build up a legacy for both his sons regardless of any money that Micio chooses to spend on them is perfectly sound, though it does not answer the moral objection that the sons are being corrupted by the money Micio is spending. There is an interesting difference between Roman and Athenian law here. There would be no problem for the Roman audience in the idea of Demea leaving a legacy to both Aeschinus and Ctesipho, since a Roman could bequeath his money as he wished. But Athenian law compelled a father to bequeath his property to his sons, and, since Aeschinus was now legally Micio's son, Demea's property would have come to Ctesipho and Micio's to Aeschinus. So it seems that Menander must have arranged this argument differently: this is one way in which Terence is 'Romanising' Demea's character.

809-12 you were supporting both your sons...: This passage does a little to clarify the circumstances in which Demea decided to give Aeschinus to Micio to adopt (47 n.).

814 merit: Lit 'glory' (Lat. *gloria*). Micio is implying that

Demea's plan to leave a legacy for both sons is a matter of pride and even of public appearances (cf. 734 n.).

p.378   **820 I'm not talking about money. It's their morals:** In fact Demea *has* been talking about money as well as morals (713ff n. 3). Some have seen it as a sign of the weakness of Micio's case that he chooses to argue the financial side first; but this is justifed by the concerns that Demea has himself expressed.

820-30 Wait. I know...well enough: This speech should be read in conjunction with the theory of education which Micio outlines in the opening scene (50-77, pp. 341-2). It amplifies what he says there in one important respect, picking up a point at which he has already hinted in his scene with Aeschinus (684 n.). His educational method is not after all suitable for everyone, but only for those who are essentially 'generous' in character (828 n.), among whom he includes Aeschinus and Ctesipho. Micio is here in fact following the teaching of Aristotle, who makes a distinction in his *Ethics* between the education of 'the liberal' and that of 'the many' (74-5 n.). We might conclude that, with this refinement, Micio's theory of education is likely to have commended itself to the audience of the Greek original; on the other hand, those in the Roman audience who preferred a stricter approach based on the exercise of *patria potestas* (52 n.) may not have been any more convinced than before.

828 open and generous: The two English words represent the one Latin word *liber* (which is here equivalent to *liberalis* in the sense of 'liberal' or 'gentlemanly': Introd. §15).. It is often pointed out that, though Aeschinus has done something to redeem himself in the play, Ctesipho has given no signs of an 'open and generous' character or indeed of the qualities just listed (good sense, intelligence, deference). This being so, Micio is either (i) getting things wrong, or (ii) falsifying the truth in order to justify his treatment of Ctesipho (and either of these will diminish our respect for Micio and his theories) or (iii) being tactful about Ctesipho for Demea's sake or (iv) representing the truth about Ctesipho which the rest of the play fails to bring out. As frequently in this play, it is hard to know which of the alternative interpretations Terence intended.

830-5 You may say...well enough: Micio returns to the financial aspect, and has again come under criticism for doing so (820 n.), as if this was a concession that his arguments on the moral side were inadequate. But he *has* put his moral arguments very clearly; and, if he returns to the financial side, it may be that this is the side in which he feels he can more easily overcome Demea's worries.

831 my dear Demea: Lit. 'our Demea'; Donatus describes this form of address as ingratiating.

833 the besetting fault of old age: Concern for money is a traditional fault of the old: see e.g. Cicero *On Old Age* 65-6.

835 Time will develop: Lit. '...will sharpen'.

836-7 these fine-sounding arguments...may destroy us:
Demea is not convinced, and, though Micio dismisses Demea's objections very easily ('No, no, impossible'), some of the Roman audience may have shared Demea's reservations.

840 I suppose I'll have to. But tomorrow morning...:
Demea agrees to swallow his objections and put on a cheerful face for the wedding. But nothing has changed in his attitide to Ctesipho: he is to be removed from the temptations of the city, and his *psaltria* is to earn her keep by slaving away on the farm. There is no question of Ctesipho being allowed to grant the girl her freedom, as some Plautine *adulescentes* do (*Epid.* 509, *Most.* 1139).

841 *Before* dawn, I dare say...: Having won his immediate point, Micio permits himself a series of witticisms, as he did at the end of his scene with Aeschinus (702 n.). But Demea is scarcely in a mood to appreciate them ('All right, laugh at me' 852).

844 tying him down: It is typical of Terence that the metaphor is conveyed by a single phrase (one word in the Latin); Plautus manages to extend a similar image for seventeen lines (*Men.* 79-95).

p.379 **848 gleaning:** Lit. 'collecting stubble'. The whole description is amusingly colourful, as Demea warms to the prospect.

853 I've done: The scene ends very much as the first confrontation did (cf. 'I've done' 137, p. 345), with Demea becoming angry again but finally restraining himself.

854 Come in then...: This is a stage-directional phrase, and the natural interpretation is that Demea accompanies Micio into Micio's house for the wedding festivities, leaving the stage empty. And this would be the place where Menander's fourth act ended.

V. iv: DEMEA (855-81, pp. 379-80)

[1] Demea explains in a soliloquy that men learn from experience. He is now abandoning his former hard way of life, since it is clear that a life of affability and tolerance is much better. Micio has lived such a life and won praise and affection from everyone; Demea himself has toiled and slaved to make money for his sons, and has received no reward for his trouble. So now he will try being generous and agreeable himself, since he wants to be loved and appreciated; and, if his money runs out, he is not concerned, since he does not have long to live.

[2] There is a problem of staging here, in that Demea reappears immediately after entering Micio's house. In the Greek original there will have been an intervening choral ode (854 n.), but in the Latin text the play continues without a break. The Penguin stage direction should be regarded as an imaginative hint to a modern producer rather than as having any validity for the Roman stage. There seem to be two possibilities for the latter, (i) that there was a pause, covered by a musical interlude in the form of flute-music and (ii) that Demea

did not after all follow Micio inside but turned back at the door. Of these the latter seems more likely: there is only one example of a musical interlude in the whole of Roman comedy and this is clearly signalled in the text ('Meanwhile the flute-player will entertain you': Plaut. *Pseud.* 573).

[3] This monologue represents a startling development in the characterisation of Demea, who has not shown any previous sign of revising his convictions. It is important to analyse what exactly Demea says (he has learned from experience 855-8; he is abandoning his previous hard life 859-60; he is going to try being generous and affable 877-80; he is not going to concern himself with the expense 881), and what motive he gives (he wants to be loved and appreciated by his sons 879). It is also important what he says about Micio (he wins praise and affection from everyone 865, he enjoys the benefits of fatherhood without lifting a finger 871, and he has made the sons his own for next to nothing 875-6). On the surface Micio is simply being used as an example of the effectiveness of affability as a principle; we might infer a certain jealousy on Demea's part and even a desire to outdo Micio, but it *would* only be an inference. The audience will expect, as the logical consequence of the speech, that Demea is going to speak and act generously to Aeschinus and Ctesipho and try to win back their affection.

[4] There is a parallel to Demea's speech in the 'conversion speech' of the misanthrope Knemon at Men. *Dysk.* 708-47, and it may be helpful to bear this in mind as a guide to interpreting Menander's intentions in *Adelphoi*, if not Terence's. Knemon similarly claims to have learned from experience and to have revised his basic principle of life, namely the belief that he could be completely self-sufficient. But, in his case (unlike Demea's), there is an obvious catalyst for the change of heart, in that he has just been rescued from drowning in a well by his stepson. And it is notable that, though he modifies his misanthropic behaviour to the extent of adopting the stepson and consenting to his daughter's marriage, he does not really change his misanthropic character; he has to be dragged into the wedding celebrations against his will.

[5] The language of Demea's speech is rhetorical, as is to be expected when a character is arguing a philosophical position. Among the rhetorical aspects are the frequent antitheses (between past and present 855-60, between Demea and Micio 863-76), doublets of synonyms ('affability and forbearance' 861, 'generous and agreeable' 880), exaggerations (871 n., 874 n.), rhetorical questions ('And why?' 860), and a variety of metaphors (855 n., 860 n., 880 n.).

[6] The scene is in recitative (tr^7, which is also the metre of Knemon's speech in *Dysk.*), with the obvious effect of highlighting the speech above the spoken verse of the surrounding scenes.

855 A plan...worked out: Lit. 'an account...drawn up', an metaphor which suits Demea's characteristic concern for money.

860 my course is almost run: This image is derived from the running-track, and is not a Roman image, since athletics was not a Roman institution. Where it is found in comedy (cf. Plaut. *Merc.* 547, *Stich.* 81), it may be taken over direct from the Greek original.

863-4 He has always led a life of leisure...: This passage echoes Micio's own description of his way of life at 42-4 (p. 341).

865 lived for himself and spent on himself: Micio has, of course, spent money on Aeschinus and Ctesipho, but this is spending on himself in that he has thereby gained their praise and affection. In the context Demea is commending Micio's approach and is going to imitate it; but the audience may well wonder whether he actually approves it..

866 I'm the country bumpkin...: Demea implies that he is the typical countryman with the typical countryman's qualities: the description again echoes Micio's description in the opening scene (44-6, p. 341). The Byzantine scholar Photius records a very similar line 'But I the country labourer, scowling, unpleasant, mean', which he ascribes to Menander without naming the play: it is a fair conjecture that the line comes in fact from Menander's *Adelphoi* at precisely this point.

.380 **871 They don't like me:** The Latin bluntly says 'Hatred'. Demea is exaggerating throughout to emphasise the contrast between himself and Micio.

874 counting the days for me to die: This is another exaggeration, recalling Micio's ironic suggestion at 109 (p. 343); Ctesipho positively refrains from wishing his father dead (519 n.).

878 take up his challenge: i.e. to emulate Micio's whole way of life. Micio has not explicitly challenged Demea to do this, but it is hard to find any other convincing interpretation.

880 take the lead: The metaphor is theatrical (*Eun.* 354 n.).

881 I'm old enough for it to last *my* time: Demea is here thinking only of himself; he has thus abandoned his lifelong plan to build up a legacy for his two sons (813-14, p. 377).

V. v-vii: SYRUS, DEMEA, GETA, AESCHINUS
(882-923, pp. 380-2)

[1] Syrus comes out to find Demea on Micio's instructions: Demea greets him affably and promises to do him a favour. Geta emerges from Sostrata's house to tell Micio that they are ready for the wedding: Demea commends him on his loyalty, and similarly promises to do him a favour. Aeschinus comes out impatient at the delays to the wedding: Demea wins him over by telling him to break down the garden wall and bring the whole of Sostrata's household across.

[2] There are three short scenes here, of which the last (i.e. the Aechinus scene) requires four actors. The simplest supposition for the third scene of the Greek original is that it did not involve both slaves; either (or even both) could have disappeared after his own scene.

[3] Demea puts his new policy of being generous and agreeable into immediate practice and congratulates himself on the results ('That's three things already...' 884-5, 'my affability improves with practice' 896-7, 'Bravo, now I'm splendid' 911). His expressed aim is to win the favour of his sons, and by the end of the third scene he has won Aeschinus over. His affability to Syrus and Geta can be regarded as a legitimate preliminary and useful practice; there is also a hint that he may be able to exploit the goodwill of the two slaves to further his main purpose (898 n.). So far there is nothing incompatible with what Demea announced in his monologue (855ff n. 3), but the new motive of revenge over Micio begins to obtrude (912-13 n., 914-15 n.), and it is becoming clear that Demea is changing his behaviour rather than his nature (885 n., 896-7 n., 911 n.).

[4] It is ironic that the first recipient of Demea's new affability is Syrus, who, after the way he has deceived his master, could least expect to be treated civilly; Demea's last words to him were a threat to knock his brains out (782, p. 376). But Terence handles this realistically by making Syrus duly surprised (887-8 n.). Geta also, who has had few dealings with Demea in the past, is suitably puzzled and grateful ('It's kind of you to think so' 897, 'Heaven bless you, sir' 917-18). But the winning over of Aeschinus is rather less convincing (901 n., 911 n.).

[5] The scene is in ia^6 (spoken verse).

882 Please, sir: It is worth noting that there is nothing in the Latin corresponding to the eight 'sir's which the Penguin translation gives to the slaves in these three scenes (cf. *Eun.* 50-6 n.). Syrus simply says 'Demea' here.

883 Syrus, my man: Lit. 'our Syrus'. Demea is here being doubly ingratiating, in (i) addressing an inferior by his name (*Phorm.* 1048 n.) and (ii) using the form of greeting with 'our', which is usually reserved for the greeting of old men (831 n.).

good evening: In the Latin this is the common simple greeting *salve* ('hullo': *Eun.* 304 n.). The translation 'good evening' reflects the fact that evening was the traditional time for weddings; the play has thus spanned the day from dawn to dusk (588 n.).

how are you? how are things going?: These are standard 'greetings formulae' (Introd. §30) but not usually addressed to slaves.

885 which aren't like me: Lit. 'contrary to my nature', which is a clear hint that Demea is not changing his nature but learning to behave in a way contrary to it.

886 you have your finer points: Lit. 'you show yourself not illiberal' (Lat. *inliberalis*), i.e. your behaviour would not be unworthy of a free man. Syrus may even see a hint that Demea may persuade Micio to give him his freedom.

887-8 But I mean it: This response shows that Syrus' 'Thank you' was spoken incredulously. It is doubtful whether Syrus goes back into the house after this line as in the Penguin stage direction, since there is no exit line here and no indication that Syrus returns with Aeschinus at the end of this scene. It seems preferable to suppose that Syrus simply stands aside while Demea practises his affability on Geta.

381 **889 I'm just going next door...:** The second scene opens with a brief over-the-shoulder remark.

890 Good evening, sir: Cf. 883 n. Geta in fact uses a slightly expanded greetings formula (Lat. *salvos sis*, lit. 'may you be well').

891 what's your name?: Demea is eager to address Geta by name, but has forgotten what it is. He had heard it from Hegio at 479 (p. 361) together with an account of Geta's loyalty to Sostrata and her family. Demea makes up for his lapse of memory by using the name twice in his next speech, though it occurs only once in the translation.

895-6 I should be glad to do you a good turn: Demea repeats exactly the same phrase as he had used to Syrus (886-7), as if, being a recent convert to affability, his vocabulary is limited.

896-7 my affability improves with practice: Again Demea is changing his behaviour rather than his nature.

898 winning over the masses: Lit. 'making the plebs my own'. Demea speaks like a Roman statesman building up political support by befriending the plebs. There is a hint that he hopes to use the goodwill of Syrus and Geta against Micio.

899-900 They're killing me...: The third scene opens with a brief overheard entrance monologue: Terence is deliberately varying his scene-opening patterns (cf. 889 n.).

901 father: Aeschinus addresses Demea as 'my father', which is more affectionate than a simple 'father', even before Demea has given any sign of his new affability. The play has given no previous hint of Aeschinus' feelings for Demea.

902 Father...in heart and nature: Contrast Micio's claim to be Aeschinus' moral father at 126 (p. 344).

903 more than his own eyes: Demea is making a strong bid for Aeschinus' affection (cf. 701 n.).

903-4 why don't you bring your wife home?: Demea sets about winning Aeschinus over by practical advice rather than mere affability or promises.

905 flute-player...marriage hymn: At both Athens and Rome, the bride was conveyed to the bridegroom's house by a torch-lit procession, accompanied by the singing of the marriage hymn.

908 garden wall: The clear implication is that a single wall separates the gardens of Micio and Sostrata. This is another piece of evidence against the idea of an *angiportum* running back from the stage at right angles between the stage houses (*Phorm.* 891 n.).

910 bring the whole lot of them...over to us: The 'whole lot' will consist of Sostrata, Pamphila, Canthara, Geta, and the baby.

911 you're splendid: Lit. 'most charming'. It is ironic, and rather sudden, that Aeschinus applies to Demea the epithet (Lat. *lepidus*) usually reserved for the lenient father or the helpful old bachelor. At *Andr.* 948 (p. 87) Pamphilus applies the word *lepidus* to his father Simo, another *senex durus*, but with rather more cause.

p.382   **Bravo, now I'm splendid:** Donatus makes the interesting comment 'It is clear that Demea is assenting for the sake of the experiment, not because he does it from the heart'

911-15 Bravo...on the spot: This is the longest of the four asides in conversation in which Demea comments on the success of his new policy (cf. 884-5, 896-7, 898), and thus the least realistic, especially as there are three bystanders who do not hear it.

912-13 all these people...no end of expense: Demea is exaggerating, whether he is thinking of the expenses of the wedding (cf. *Phorm.* 666 n.) or of the permanent maintenance of the family. More significantly, the motive of repaying Micio in is own coin becomes explicit, and a new idea begins to appear, that Demea can become popular at Micio's expense.

914-15 Tell that Croesus to pay out: As the footnote explains, 'Croesus' (the wealthy Lydian monarch) is the translator's substitution for the 'Babylonian' of the Latin; Micio is of course meant. By 'two thousand' Demea must be referring to what Micio paid for the music-girl (cf. 742, p. 374); the thought is 'let Micio continue with that sort of expenditure on the sons; I am the one who is winning their favour'.

921-2 She's not well yet: Demea shows some sympathy for the bride, as another bid for Aeschinus' favour.

922 father: Aeschinus uses 'my father' again, this time with rather more cause (901 n.).

V. viii: MICIO, DEMEA, AESCHINUS (924-58, pp. 382-5)

[1] Micio comes out of his house, demanding to know whether Demea has in fact ordered the demolition of the wall. Demea explains that it is part of his plan to unite the two families, and with Aeschinus' help he persuades Micio, much against his will, to marry Sostrata and give a plot of land to Hegio.

[2] In this fourth confrontation between Micio and Demea, Demea has the upper hand throughout. Micio feebly agrees to marry Sostrata, which he regards as 'foreign to [his] whole way of life' (944) just because Demea and Aeschinus ask him to. He agrees to give the plot of land to Hegio, though he clearly does not want to, because Demea is able to quote back at him his own maxim (953-4 n.). The moral seems to be that Micio's much vaunted leniency towards

Aeschinus is in fact a sign of a general weakness of character whereby he cannot resist giving in to the demands of others.

[3] The ostensible relationship of all this to Demea's 'conversion speech' (855-81) is that Demea is seeking Aeschinus' love and affection by being generous and agreeable to the family of Aeschinus' bride. But the motive of revenge upon Micio has almost become the dominant motive (958 n.), and the idea of becoming popular at Micio's expense, which was not even suggested in the conversion speech (912-13 n.), has supplanted Demea's plan to use his own funds for this purpose. These developments are worrying if we are looking for a dénouement of the play which preserves probability of plot and consistency of character. The Demea of the first 850 lines, with the single exception of the point he scores in the third confrontation (796-805 n.), showed no signs of the imagination or wit which enable him to dominate Micio here. Micio, for his part, has not before been lost for words or unable to maintain control of the situation. As for Aeschinus, the developments of the first four acts left him singing the praises of Micio as the ideal father (707-11, p. 372); even supposing that the objective of uniting the two families is dear to Aeschinus' heart, it is surprising to find him now teaming up with Demea against Micio.

[4] The most significant of all the comments by Donatus on the play is his comment on 938: 'In Menander the old man does not complain about the marriage; so Terence is inventing'. This can only mean that Menander treated Micio's character, and indeed the whole ethos of the scene, very differently. If in Menander Micio willingly agreed to the marriage, it is hardly likely that he objected to giving Hegio his plot of land. It follows that there was no 'victory' for Demea, no need for Aeschinus to take Demea's side, and no implication that Micio was a weak person persuaded against his better judgment. So it must be Terence's innovation to give Demea the upper hand in the ending of the play. His motives for doing so will be examined in the discussion of the final scene.

[5] The language of the scene is interesting in two respects:

(i) Demea now monopolises the ethical vocabulary which has been prominent in earlier scenes, notably *decet* ('duty' 928, 'ought' 948, 'must' 954), *aequom* ('proper' 933), and *oportet* ('must' 955);

(ii) as if to emphasise the reversal of roles, both Demea and Micio now use terms previously used by the other (934 n., 936 n., 937 n.).

[6] The scene begins in spoken verse (ia^6), but changes to recitative (ia^8) at the point where the conversation becomes more animated (i.e. from '*I* marry' 934, where Micio begins to object to the marriage). It then returns to spoken verse (ia^6) at the very end, where Micio agrees to give the land to Hegio (from 'Very well' 956).

924 My brother's orders?: Micio is presumably talking over his shoulder to Syrus, whom he has caught dismantling the wall.

928 I suppose I have to agree: The translation is a little more grudging than the Latin, which simply says 'I don't disagree'.

p.383 **931 past the age to have children:** There are two separate points here in favour of the marriage, (i) Sostrata cannot bear any more children to protect her, and (ii) Micio is in no danger of producing a son to share Aeschinus' inheritance.

932 no one to look after her: Demea is exaggerating, as often: Sostrata now has Aeschinus to support her, to say nothing of Hegio (cf. 492-8, p. 361).

934 *I* marry?...: The conversation becomes extremely rapid, at this point, with six different utterances in the one line of verse.

You're joking: Lit. 'you're absurd' (Lat. *ineptire*). Demea had used a similar phrase of Micio at 63 (p. 342: 'You've no sense').

as man to man: Lit. 'if you were a man', i.e. 'if you had true human qualities, you would persuade him'. Micio had used the same phrase to Demea at 107 (p. 343: 'if you had any humanity').

935 Father: Lit. 'my father'. Aeschinus applies this phrase, which he had previously used to Demea (901 n.), three times to Micio in this scene. Here and in his next speech it is a form of persuasion; at 956 it expresses gratitude.

936 You're crazy: Demea had applied this word (Lat. *delirare*) to Micio at 761 (p. 375: 'the old one off his head').

937 You're off your head: Lit. 'are you sane?'. Demea had asked Micio this question at 748 (p. 374: 'Are you really in your right mind?').

938 sixty-four: This is our first indication of Micio's age.

940 I've promised them: This is presumably an invention by Aeschinus to help persuade Micio. There has been no opporunity during the play for Aeschinus to make this promise.

p.384 **945 Well done!:** Lat. *bene facis* (*Eun.* 186 n.).

950 he'll make good use of it: Demea is proposing that Hegio should be given use of the property, not ownership. There is a similar arrangement at *Phorm.* 364-5 (p. 244), where Phanium's father allegedly 'had a bit of land to farm' from Phormio's father. This seems much less of an imposition on Micio than the marriage with Sostrata, but Micio's resistance to it is psychologically plausible; having been persuaded once against his will, he is not likely to accede graciously to subsequent requests.

953-4 the besetting fault...: Demea here quotes back Micio's maxim on old age from 833-4 (p. 378), just as at 796 (p. 377) he had quoted back Micio's proposed agreement about the sons.

p.385 **958 I've got his own knife at his throat:** This aside suggests that the desire to pay Micio back is now Demea's strongest motive. The phrase is a proverbial one, though there are no surviving instances before Terence.

V. ix: SYRUS, DEMEA, MICIO, AESCHINUS
(958-97, pp. 385-7)

[1] With Aeschinus' help, Demea persuades Micio to grant Syrus his freedom, together with his wife's, and a loan of money. Demea explains that he is doing all this to show Micio that his popularity was based simply on indulgence. He then offers the two sons correction and reproof and support in the right place, which Aeschinus willingly accepts, and announces that Ctesipho can keep the music-girl, though she must be his last.

[2] This final scene completes the victory of Demea and the discomfiture of Micio, who again feebly agrees to the demands of Demea and Aeschinus. The moral that Micio's lenience is in fact a culpable indulgence, implicit in the previous scene, is now made explicit. The future of Ctesipho's love affair is settled; and the play ends with a new philosophy of education, in which the father offers not indulgence but correction and reproof and support.

[3] So the various conflicts of the play are in the end resolved. But it has to be admitted that this is not where Demea's conversion speech was actually leading. There was nothing in that speech about Demea teaching Micio a lesson; and the implication was that Demea would indulge the sons, not that he would offer what is clearly going to be fairly stern guidance. In fact the Roman audience may have approved of the educational stance taken by Demea at the end, just as they may have enjoyed the discomfiture of Micio; but it is hard to see that Terence has arrived at either by a very coherent process. We can scarcely assume in retrospect that the conversion speech was a bluff, since by convention monologue speakers do not deceive the audience (even though Donatus expresses this view: 985-95 n.). And the alternative supposition is not much more satisfactory, that Demea did actually decide to court popularity by indulgence but then modified his tactics in practice to accord better with his real feelings.

[4] To this inconsistency between Demea's conversion speech and his subsequent actions has to be added the inconsistency already noted between the characterisation of Micio, Demea, and Aeschinus in the finale and their characterisation in the rest of the play (924ff n. 3). And there is a further inconsistency of tone between the realistic comedy of manners offered by the first four fifths of the play and the farcical nature of the finale (the reasons given for the manumission of Syrus and Phrygia are patently absurd: 964 n., 975 n.). We can only conclude that these inconsistencies did not worry Terence, or, to put it another way, that he had other more important considerations in mind.

[5] One clue to Terence's aims may lie in the comparison with his Greek original. There are two solid pieces of evidence for Terentian adaptation, (i) Donatus' statement that in Menander Micio does not

object to the marriage (924ff n. 4) and (ii) the presence of four speaking actors in the final scene. The most likely implication of the first is that in Menander Micio willingly agreed to all the various acts of generosity (and Demea did not therefore win any kind of victory), and of the second that either Aeschinus or Syrus played no part in Menander's final scene (which means that Menander's final scene may have been very different from Terence's). As for the general thrust of Menander's play, scholars have not been able to agree. According to some, in keeping with the Aristotelian belief that virtue is the mean between two extremes, Menander portrayed Micio as excessively indulgent and Demea as excessively strict, in which case the finale will have presented, not a victory for either, but a compromise. According to others, Menander portrayed Micio as essentially right (but not perfect) and Demea as essentially wrong (but not absurd), in which case the finale must have confirmed Micio's point of view, with Demea admitting the error of his ways. Terence's ending is nearer to the first of these two Menander scenarios than to the second. But in either case it seems that he has altered Menander's ending to give Demea a clear victory, and it is tempting to suppose that the various inconsistencies noted above are in some measure due to this alteration.

[6] It may be helpful to refer again to the end of Menander's *Dyskolos* (855ff n. 4). That play ends with Knemon, subsequent to his conversion speech, being mercilessly teased by a cook and a slave (880-931) and then dragged into the wedding celebrations against his will (932-64). So Menander was perfectly capable of ending a realistic comedy of manners on a farcical note and in particular with a 'ragging scene' parallel to the ragging of Micio. It follows that we cannot deny the possibility of this sort of ending for Menander's *Adelphoi*, and this would be sufficient explanation of the the change of tone in Terence's finale. But this approach does not solve all our problems. If we press the parallels with *Dyskolos*, it is the Demea character who ought to be ragged in *Adelphoi*, and, importantly, *Dyskolos* offers no parallel for the inconsistency of characterisation which we have noted in Terence.

[7] This brings us to two explanations of Terentian endings suggested in the Introduction (§34). One is the purely dramatic one: Terence may have actually preferred to end his plays with a surprise twist rather than with a neat but predictable solution, and in this case the volte-face of the finale certainly provides good arresting theatre. The other is didactic, i.e. the desire to make the audience think. Of all Roman comedies *Adelphoe* is the one most likely to have sent the spectators away not only amused but discussing the issues of the play. The theme of education is one which must have polarised the audience of the day, with the traditionalists, who saw Greek ideas as a threat to Roman morality, on the one side and the philhellenists, who welcomed Greek ideas as being more civilised and humane, on the other. For the

former, who would have been askance at the apparent approval of
Micio in the first four acts, Terence's ending will have provided both
food for thought and a conclusion which would satisfy their natural
instincts; for the latter, who would have enjoyed the initial supremacy
of Micio, it provided a reminder that there were two sides of the
question. For discussion see Arnott (1975) 54-5, Forehand 108-19,
Gratwick (edn) 16-64, Hunter 105-9, Martin (edn) 16-29, Sandbach
145-6.

[8] The play ends with recitative (tr[7]), which is the traditional
metre for the finale (*Eun.* 1049ff n. 7).

958 Your orders...: This is the third example in the play of a
scene beginning in mid-line (81 n., 635 n.). The abruptness of Syrus'
entry cuts short Demea's self-congratulation.

960 Syrus ought to receive his freedom: Demea continues
argue from ethical concepts (924ff n. 5). He uses the word *aequom*
three times in this scene (each time translated 'ought': 960, 968, 976),
and *officium* once ('duty' 980).

961 Oh, master: Lit. 'our Demea': Syrus is using the same
form of address as Demea had used to him (883 n.).

962 I've looked after both the young masters: If Syrus
was pedagogue to both boys, he must have begun as a slave in Demea's
household; he presumably transferred to Micio's household together
with Aeschinus (cf. 562-3 n.).

963 always given them the best advice: This claim is no
doubt intended to be regarded with some scepticism.

964 reliable shopping: The alternative translation 'shopping
on credit' may be preferable, since Demea is being frivolous, and the
other services for which he commends Syrus are of a dubious kind.

966 splendid: Lat. *lepidus* (911 n.).

968 a good effect on the others: i.e. the other servants will
be encouraged to emulate Syrus' example of good service. Demea still
has his tongue firmly in his cheek.

970 take your freedom: Slaves could be freed by a simple
declaration by their master before witnesses. At Rome this could be
done formally before a magistrate, in which case a rod was laid upon
the slave's head as part of the ceremony, or informally before friends,
with the master's hand being used instead of the rod. The Penguin
stage directions suggest the kind of by-play that might accompany this
process in comedy.

973 my wife, Phrygia: Strictly Phrygia is Syrus' concubine
rather than his wife (*Phorm.* 152 n.). The name 'Phrygia', like many
slave names, denotes racial orgin; the Phrygians lived in what is now
north-west Turkey.

386 **975 come forward as wet-nurse:** This is another frivolous
reason; by calling it 'serious', Demea underlines the farcical tone.

977 I'll pay you her value: This is the one piece of

generosity for which Demea actually pays (or promises to pay). As such, it does not fit the pattern of his behaviour in the final scenes. But it does ensure that Syrus' fulsome thanks (978) are directed to Demea, not to Micio, and thus fulfils the original intention of his conversion speech..

980 carry on with your duty: At Rome a freed slave became the 'freedman' of his former master, who was still under an obligation to support him.

983 you're a darling: Aeschinus not only uses the phrase 'my father' (935 n.) but the word *festivus* (lit. 'one who enters into the festive spirit', hence 'delightful', 'charming'), which.is an even more enthusiastic word than *lepidus* (911 n.). He is being very extravagant with his thanks.

985 What's the idea? Why this...generosity?: This line is in fact a quotation from the comic poet Caecilius; Terence evidently saw it as a good resonant line which suited his own context.

985-95 I'll tell you...at your service: Most scholars are unwilling to believe that this speech is based on any similar speech in Menander, on the grounds that neither the reproof to Micio (985-8) nor the offer of guidance to the sons (989-95) is compatible with Demea's stated intentions in his conversion speech. Donatus (on 992) says 'Terence makes it clear that Demea has pretended to change his character rather than actually changed it', but, as we have seen, this is not a very satisfactory solution (above, n. 3).

986 good nature and charm: The same phrase is used of Demea at *Eun.* 1048 (tr. 'kindness and good humour').

987 from a way of living which was sincere: Some have seen this phrase as providing the essential moral of the play; neither of the two fathers and neither of the two sons have really practised 'sincerity of life' in their dealings which each other. This is certainly an idea in which Terence (and presumably Menander) were interested; it is one which recurs in *Heauton* (esp. 151-7, pp. 106-7), and can easily be related to the whole concept of humanity.

994 advice or reproof: Perhaps better 'reproof or correction'; both words imply the checking or criticising of faults.

p.387 **997 Well done, Demea:** Lit. 'This correctly'. Some MSS give the line to Aeschinus, who will then be expressing approval of Demea's permission to Ctesipho to keep his girl. If it belongs to Micio, there is a problem of interpretation. Donatus takes him to mean 'I approve *this* though not the rest', which leaves Micio still resisting or resentful; but it is more likely to be a final acquiescence ('All right, you win').

Now give us your applause!: *Eun.* 1094 n.

Select Bibliography

COMMENTARIES AND TRANSLATIONS
Menander: Plays and Fragments, tr. N.P.Miller (Penguin 1987)
Plautus: The Pot of Gold and Other Plays, tr. E. F. Watling (Penguin 1965)
Plautus: The Rope and Other Plays, tr. E. F. Watling (Penguin 1965)
Terence: The Comedies, tr. B. Radice (Penguin, 2nd edn 1976)
Terence: Adelphoe, ed. R. H. Martin (Cambridge 1976)
Terence: The Brothers, ed. A. S. Gratwick (Warminster 1987)
Terence: Phormio, ed. R. H. Martin (London 1959)

DISCUSSIONS
Arnott W. G., *Menander, Plautus, Terence* (Oxford 1975)
Arnott W. G., 'Phormio Parasitus: A Study in Dramatic Characterisation', *Greece & Rome* 17 (1970) 32-57
Bain D., *Actors and Audience: a Study of Asides and Related Conventions in Greek Drama* (Oxford 1977)
Beare W., *The Roman Stage* (London, 3rd edn 1964)
Duckworth G. E., *The Nature of Roman Comedy* (Princeton 1952)
Forehand W. E., *Terence* (Boston 1985)
Goldberg S. M., *Understanding Terence* (Princeton 1986)
Gratwick A. S., 'Drama' in *The Cambridge History of Classical Literature II* (Cambridge 1982), 77-137
Hunter R. L., *The New Comedy of Greece and Rome* (Cambridge 1985)
Konstan D., 'Phormio' in *Roman Comedy* (Ithaca 1983)
Konstan D., 'Love in Terence's Eunuch: The Origins of Erotic Subjectivity', *American Journal of Philology* 107 (1986) 369-93
Ludwig W., 'The Originality of Terence and his Greek Models', *Greek Roman and Byzantine Studies* 9 (1968) 169-82
Norwood G., *Plautus and Terence* (New York 1931)
Norwood G., *The Art of Terence* (Oxford 1923)
Sandbach F. H., *The Comic Theatre of Greece and Rome* (London 1977)
Webster T. B. L., *An Introduction to Menander* (Manchester 1974)
Wright J., *Dancing in Chains: the Stylistic Unity of the Comoedia Palliata* (Rome 1974)